THE
COFFEE
DICTIONARY

   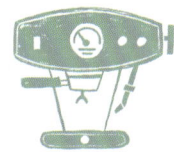 

An A–Z of coffee,
from growing & roasting
to brewing & tasting

MAXWELL COLONNA-DASHWOOD

ILLUSTRATED BY TOM JAY

MITCHELL BEAZLEY

For Lesley

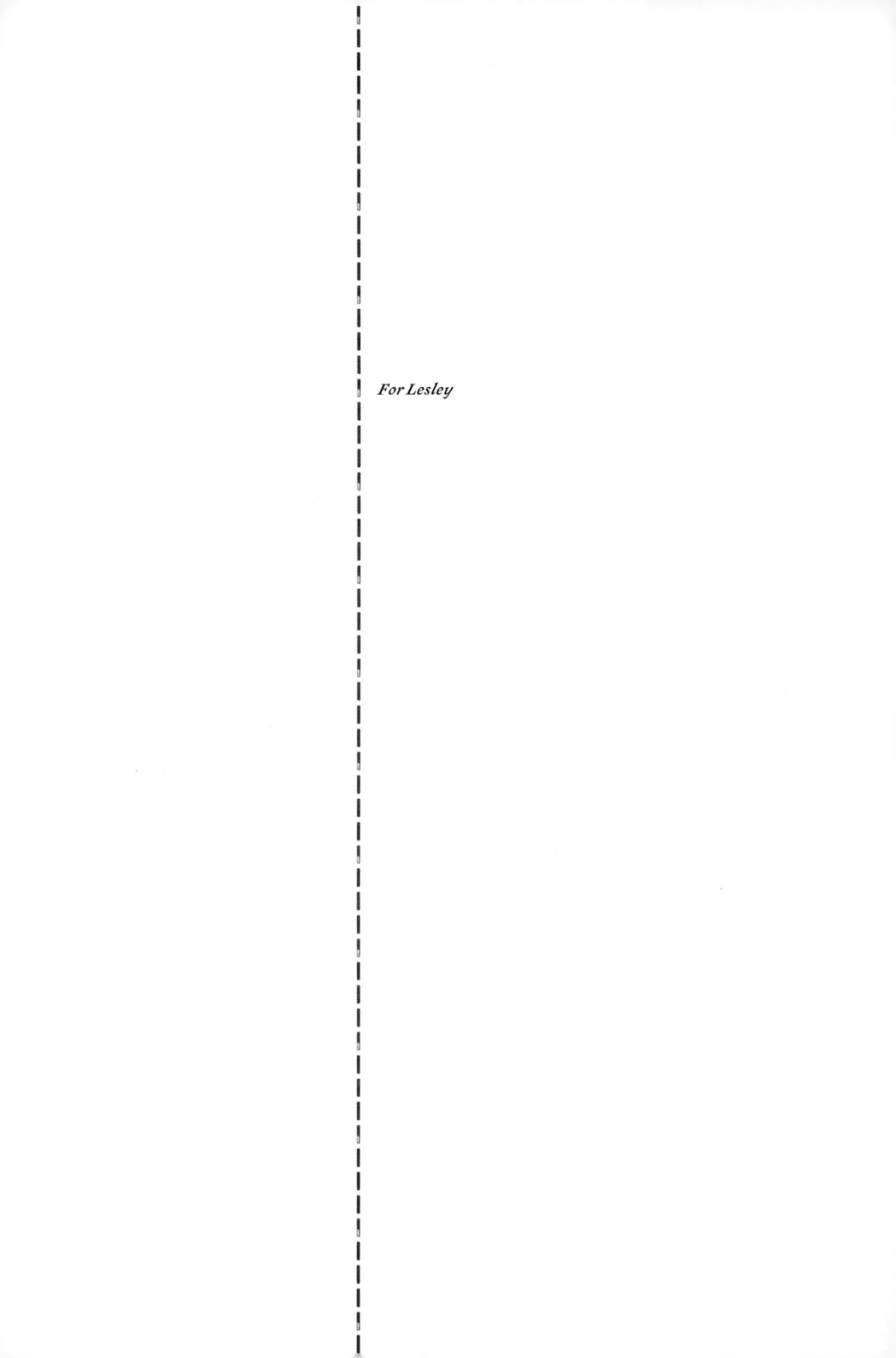

Contents

6   Introduction
13   A–Z
250   Index
254   Acknowledgements
256   About the Author

Introduction

It seems that there are two ways to fall in love with coffee. Either you start drinking coffee from an early age and develop a relationship with coffee over time, becoming more and more engrossed with its culinary and cultural potential; or, you can have almost no interest in coffee and then have an epiphany, a cup of coffee that changes everything. This is followed by disbelief and confusion coupled with excitement – and then you never look back.

The latter scenario applies to me. I had almost no interest in coffee. I drew portraits and painted things as my first real vocation. Like many an artist, I worked hospitality jobs on the side and over time, I realized my passion lies there. I met my wife and we thought we would do a bit of travelling. After six months in India, we ended up in Melbourne, Australia, with a work visa.

Unbeknown to us at the time, the city of Melbourne was home both to a vibrant café scene and to an equally impressive coffee culture. I got a job in a café in the city downtown and it wasn't long before I was discussing coffee with many of the regulars. It was they who brought the subject up, and, to be honest, I was a bit lost. Sure, I was finding it an interesting challenge to master this difficult "latte art" thing, but quite why coffee was a complex culinary phenomenon was not obvious to me. One of the regulars could see I was intrigued, though, and suggested that on my lunch break I pop up the road to a small café called Brother Baba Bhudan. I wandered up, and a lady with a coffee plant tattoo crawling up her leg asked me whether I would like to try the single-origin coffee. She said that it was from Kenya and had notes of strawberry and vanilla. I must be honest – I was sceptical. I had no idea what coffee coming from Kenya meant (why would it be different from any other coffee?) and the flavour notes, I thought, would be lost on me.

Then I stepped outside onto the pavement and tasted the espresso. There it was – the epiphany. I simply could not believe how incredible this little beverage was. It instantly changed how I saw coffee and its potential. Not only did I *get* the flavour notes, it was one of the most incredible things I had ever tasted. To say that I enjoyed it is a huge understatement. My mind started going crazy. Why have I only just found out that coffee could taste and be like this? Not just I but my wife, too, bubbled over with excitement and we knew immediately that we wanted to work in coffee. Next day, I changed jobs and began the ongoing and endless pursuit of chasing and understanding coffee. We used our time in Melbourne to visit roasters and cafés and take courses with barista champions, before finally heading home.

Back in the UK we started an events company, moved to a new town to open a shop, dived into the world of competitive coffee, collaborated with scientists and espresso machine manufacturers, and continued to learn and explore coffee. The coffee world really is a rabbit hole.

For me, coffee has proved to be endlessly fascinating, engaging, and rewarding. Coffee is many different things for different people. This amazing drink is full of flavour, intrigue, history, and countless stories. With this dictionary, I am excited to explore and discover coffee with you.

—*Maxwell Colonna-Dashwood*

SEE ALSO
Phosphoric acid *p176*

Acidity | TASTING

You may have heard acidity being described positively as "brightness" and negatively as "sourness". This is the thing about acidity: it is integral to a great cup of coffee, but it is also a broad term. There are good and bad acids where taste is concerned, and there are also compounds that from a scientific point of view are acidic, yet we wouldn't describe them as *tasting* acidic. Though there are many sources of acidity in coffee, it is only a mildly acidic beverage, with a pH of around 5, as compared to the pH 2 of wine. Coffees grown at a higher altitude often showcase more structured, complex, and positive acidity. Coffees without such acidity can be described as tasting flat and uninteresting. Brightness lifts a coffee in your mouth and gives it structure. A lot of perceived sweetness can also be derived from, or elevated by, acidity.

SEE ALSO
Brew ratio *p36*
Strength *p206*

Aeropress™ | BREWING

The name Aeropress™ is inspired by a high-tech frisbee called the Aerobie™, which was invented by the same man – Alan Adler. The Aerobie has set several world records for the furthest-thrown object; the Aeropress is instead designed to make the perfect brew. Alan is a self-taught inventor from the United States. The Aeropress houses

the ground coffee and the water inside a syringe-like brewing chamber. Manual pressure applied by the user forces the brewed coffee through a multi-holed lid that holds a custom-shaped filter paper. (Metal filter discs are also available.) The Aeropress allows you to be very versatile with brewing. You can opt for fine grinds and strong brews, as the pressure generated allows the grounds to be separated from the brew to a degree that a gravity-fed filter method could not manage. You can also brew lighter, more elegant brews. There is even a World Aeropress Championship, which, at the time of writing, attracts contestants from 51 countries.

Agitate | BREWING

To agitate is basically to fiddle with the brew in any way that mixes the water and the coffee grounds. By agitating, the brewer can allow the water to more easily access the coffee by mixing things up. This will increase extraction and can be very valuable in any brewing method where the coffee grounds might settle and stop mixing with the water, such as with a French press. Agitation can be achieved in a couple of ways: you can use a stirring stick of some kind or just give the brew a good old shake.

Agronomy | GROWING

From the Greek for "field law", agronomy is the science and study of the growing of crops and managing of land. An understanding of agronomy can transform the fortunes of a farm. Certain farms will have a dedicated onsite agronomist; others – with equal success – make periodic use of an independent agronomist to inform their practice. An understanding of

SEE ALSO
Extraction *p86*
French press *p101*

SEE ALSO
Terroir p214

agronomy will benefit how a coffee-growing plot is managed and maintained. Many coffee farms are now broken up into many smaller segments that are treated individually. Small changes in sunlight, climate, and soil can have a big impact on how coffee plants behave and on the quality of fruit they produce. Of course, weather and climate are out of a farmer's control, but adapting to make the most of changes is not – by tweaking irrigation or altering harvesting times to compensate.

Agtron scale | ROASTING

SEE ALSO
Maillard reaction *p145*

You may have heard people discussing the colour of a roast. When discussing colour we are really referring to light and dark, not to a more normal idea of colour – there are no orange or purple roasts! The Agtron scale is a reference point for how dark or light a coffee is. Agtron measuring devices are pricey. In essence, they measure how much light is bounced back off the roasted coffee bean: a darker roast will absorb more light and produce a lower reading, and a lighter roast a higher reading. (It may help to think about how a white T-shirt throws back sunlight, while a black one will absorb it.) There are many terms that have been attributed to the Agtron number such as "light city roast" or "French roast". The colour, though, is only one measurement of a roast, and a coffee can be roasted in many different ways to achieve the same colour.

Altitude | ORIGIN

SEE ALSO
Arabica *p18*
Species *p202*
Terroir *p214*

The general rule of thumb is the higher the better. But – and it is a big but – this is not a fixed rule. As with everything in coffee, it is a bit more complicated than it seems. The more prized

Arabica species is typically grown at altitudes higher than 1,000m (3,300ft) above sea level and can be grown all the way up to 2,500m (8,200ft) plus. The less desirable Robusta crops are grown between sea level and 1,000m (3,300ft). The idea is that at higher altitudes the climate is cooler and the cherry has a longer ripening period, developing a superior flavour. However, the plants do not like it too cold either, which is why coffee is grown in the Tropics. Cup quality is to do with many other aspects of provenance, such as soil, climate, and processing. It is true that no world-beating coffee is grown below 1,000m (3,300ft). It is also true that the world's most sought-after and prized coffees are not necessarily the very highest grown. Sometimes a cooler micro-climate at lower altitude can mimic a higher altitude and produce similar results.

Arabica | SPECIES

"100% Arabica" is a common billing adorning coffee packets everywhere, intended as a sign of quality. *Coffea arabica* is the name of the most widely grown coffee species in the world. (*C. robusta* is the other widely grown species, though a couple of others, such as *C. liberica*, show up here and there.) All of the world's highly graded coffees and essentially those that we would classify as "speciality" are of the Arabica species, or closely related to it. This is why you will see it noted on a packet as a major selling point. However, the species itself does not guarantee quality and there is far more commercial-grade Arabica than there is speciality. As Arabica is a given in the speciality market, you will more likely see the specific variety of Arabica noted on the packaging of speciality coffee companies. Arabica itself can be traced back to the Ethiopian

---

SEE ALSO
Cup of Excellence *p64*
Eugenioides *p83*
Species *p202*
Terroir *p214*

Highlands, where there is still the most genetic diversity of *C. arabica* varieties (subspecies). The range of flavour within this species is phenomenal as varying varieties combine with other elements of *terroir* to create distinct and varied flavour profiles. As you will see from the entry about the coffee-related species *C. eugenioides*, Arabica has its ancestry in Robusta, and crosses between the two species are commonly explored. There are Robusta–Arabica hybrids such as Catimor varieties that can produce high-quality results. The Lempira variety is a Catimor subvariety that is grown extensively in Honduras. I recently bought a Cup of Excellence lot of this variety that was exceptional, with complex acidity and tropical fruit notes.

SEE ALSO
Bean to cup *p24*
Espresso *p79*

Barista | BREWING; ESPRESSO

Directly translated from Italian, barista means "bar person". However, due to Italy's influence on world coffee culture, the term "barista" has come to refer solely to a professional coffee maker. Over recent decades the role of the barista has become more globally recognized and respected. This can be seen in many ways, as, for example, in barista competitions and barista-branded products on shelves, as well as in the increasingly specialized and specific function of the barista within cafés and restaurants. There is an increasing number of courses and qualifications surrounding the role, although most expertise is still learned through an on-the-job apprenticeship. The role of the barista has traditionally been a preparatory one – the making and serving of drinks. However, as coffee becomes more complex and customers more interested and discerning, the barista can take on a sommelier-like guise. With the increased automation in actual coffee preparation, there is a possibility that the role could one day become almost identical to that of a sommelier.

SEE ALSO
Crema *p63*

Basket | BREWING

Espresso is not defined by a certain size, shape, or consistency, but by its strength – it is a concentrated coffee. It is also fair to say that it needs to be brewed under pressure, which creates the crema. The size of the espresso depends on the size of the basket used. Group handles (the part of the espresso machine that is locked in and released for each shot) can fit a variety of basket sizes, typically ranging from 14g to 22g for double shots. The individual baskets are designed for a specific dose of coffee to be used. This will mean that there is enough room above the bed of coffee in the chamber for the water to pool before it passes through, and that the holes cut into the base of the basket will produce an appropriate resistance (more coffee will create more resistance and vice versa). It is therefore important to use the correct dose for each basket size, plus or minus a gram either side.

Bean to cup | BREWING

SEE ALSO
Capsules *p44*

Coffee brewing can range from fully automated to completely manual. There is a correlation in that higher-quality cups of coffee tend to be made more manually, though this is continuously being challenged. Often, automated machines are made with the goal of ease of use, potentially at the expense of cup quality, as they cannot be adapted to the specific needs of different coffees. At the same time, the coffee-making process is full of variables that technology advancements can help us address more rigorously. There is a huge range in sophistication and quality of bean-to-cup machines. The top machines on the market are quite remarkable and allow you to make excellent coffee. The key here, as with all automation in coffee making, is that the machine can still be programmed or driven by a person. It still requires the user to understand how to tweak the controls to adjust for different coffees.

Bicarbonate

See "Buffer".

Blending | ROASTING

The coffee blend is a ubiquitous thing. "Try our secret master blend/house blend, etc." is an opening gambit that every coffee drinker will have come across. There are a few reasons why roasters blend. One is to bring different flavour characteristics together; another is to save money and hide problems with a coffee or multiple coffees. Similarly, by blending, roasters can avoid the seasonal variations of coffee supply and instead offer a more continuous product. The problem with the term "blend" is that it does not really mean very much. In wine making, the term refers to a blend of different grapes usually from the same vineyard or village, but in coffee it more often refers to a blend of several coffees from different countries. Each coffee in that blend will already most likely be a blend of different types of coffee plant. Some coffee companies now eschew blends in order to highlight the characteristics of a coffee from a single source and focus on its story and origin. However, the term "single origin" technically just denotes coffee from only one country, so you could have a blend of lots of Brazilian coffees grown in farms across numerous regions and it would still be sold not as a blend but as a single origin. It is interesting to think about a big farm that covers a lot of land. A coffee could come from one farm but in essence be a blend of many plots. We have other terms that suggest more specificity, such as a single-variety lot, a micro lot, or even a nano lot. Blending has become less popular in speciality coffee – it is potentially

SEE ALSO
Origin *p166*
Variety *p228*

harder to roast a blend of different coffees and then be able to extract those coffees evenly. This is where the idea of "post blending" comes in. Here, the roaster will roast the coffees separately to find a roast that suits each bean and then blend them together afterwards. There are definitely conflicting views as to the benefits of blending and there will be different motivations as to why one might blend. It remains a very successful way to market and sell coffee, allowing a company to produce something unique to it and with a story customers can connect to.

Bloom | BREWING

The bloom is a term used to describe the rapid release of carbon dioxide (CO_2) that occurs when water hits ground coffee. It is that frothy, crust-like top you find on the top of a French press before you plunge down. The specific context in which we refer to this as a "bloom" rather than a "crust" is when brewing single-serve filter coffees. Often, the bloom will be singled out as a specific part of the pouring process. Brew recipes will indicate how much water to add at the beginning to "bloom" the coffee. This will be followed by a wait before the coffee is poured. The idea is that by expelling the carbon dioxide we can help the water access the flavour from the coffee and expel the potentially negative flavours of too much CO_2. There is probably some truth in this. There is an argument that the bloom time can affect flavour owing to the number of aromatics released, and the time the coffee is left to bubble away can be used to alter this. I am dubious as to the exact impact of varying "blooming" on coffee brewing, and see it more as an indication of how freshly roasted the beans are as opposed to the quality of the brewing.

SEE ALSO
V60 *p227*

SEE ALSO
Le Nez du Café® *p140*

Blossom | GROWING

Coffee trees are a flowering species. The plant is self-pollenating and therefore does not require insects to produce fruit. In most countries where coffee is grown there are distinct seasons and the flowering follows heavy rainfall. The flower is a beautiful, simple white blossom that is wonderfully aromatic and is often described as being very similar to jasmine. This flowering is followed by fruit bearing and the maturation of this fruit can take up to nine months, at which point the ripe cherries can be harvested, processed, and the precious beans released from inside. It is common to describe the coffee blossom aromatic as a flavour note in certain cups of coffee. This aroma is included in the Le Nez du Café® smelling box. It is a lovely aroma, a somewhat tricky one to familiarize oneself with, as in many coffee-consuming countries access to coffee blossom is almost non-existent.

SEE ALSO
Acidity *p13*
Flavour notes *p97*
Gustatory *p113*

Body | TASTING

Body is one of the slightly more elusive terms in the tasting repertoire, though I think that it needs to be considered alongside mouth feel. In essence, body can be described as how big and heavy the coffee feels in your mouth. The body of a coffee will usually be described on a spectrum of light to heavy, though it is interesting to consider that you could experience a light body with a sticky mouth feel or a big body with a juicy mouth feel. Tasting can be pretty hard going at first, as there is such a complexity of flavours happening at once. Focusing on some core aspects of the coffee, such as body and mouth feel, can be a great way to begin discussing and assessing coffee. Body and mouth feel have a certain degree of objectivity and so can be a little more shareable. Aromatics are extremely complex and pinpointing exactly whether you are tasting orange or mandarin is less tangible.

Bolivia | ORIGIN

SEE ALSO
Variety *p228*
World Barista Championship *p239*

With its staggering altitudes, some of the world's highest-grown coffee is found in Bolivia. The country has great coffee-growing conditions, yet production is small and diminishing. Production and transportation can be tricky due to the mountainous nature of the land, and cocoa can provide a more stable income. I used a coffee from Bolivia for my first World Barista Championship in 2012. Like the best coffees from this country, it was very sweet and clean and of the Caturra variety. This complex and ripe coffee from Finca Valentin in the Loayza region stands out as one of my all-time favourite espresso coffees.

Boston Tea Party | HISTORY

SEE ALSO
United States of America *p223*

In 1773 the North American colonies (as they were at the time) were becoming increasingly resistant to a taxation policy that was being decided upon by a British parliament as opposed to their own elected representatives. The importing of tea to the North American colonies was a particular bone of contention following the Tea Act of 1773. The resistance to the act culminated in the Boston Tea Party protests. On 16th December that year the tea-carrying ships of the East India Company were not allowed to unload their tea cargo. That evening, the ships were boarded by 30 to 130 men (accounts vary) and the chests of tea were symbolically thrown overboard. This event was a pivotal event in the

lead-up to the American Revolution (1765–83). Thereafter it was seen as unpatriotic to drink tea, and coffee became the hot beverage of choice. The United States has for many years now been the largest importer of coffee in the world and coffee is intrinsically linked to the culture of the country.

Bourbon | VARIETY

SEE ALSO
Terroir p214

There is no relation to the American whiskey beyond the name, which originates from the well-known dynasty of French kings. The Bourbon coffee variety was first grown on the island of Réunion, which was previously named the Île Bourbon after the French royal house. The Bourbon variety is well known in the world of speciality coffee for producing a distinct and sweet cup profile. The fact that Bourbon is so widely grown helps highlight how much other factors affect flavour. There is a wide range of cup profiles from around the world where Bourbon is grown. There is also a spread of Bourbon varieties and mutations over the years. Red, yellow, and orange are specific variations. A great tasting comparison is to pair the Bourbon coffees of Rwanda against Bourbon lots from El Salvador.

Brazil | ORIGIN

SEE ALSO
Producing p180

Brazil has for many years now grown and harvested more coffee than any other country in the world. The country produces a range of qualities across both the Arabica and Robusta species, mostly grown at lower altitudes. Brazil is known for round chocolaty and nutty flavour profiles with lower acidity, though there is a small variety of higher-grown, more acidic coffees produced as well. Brazil leads the world in the utilization of technology in growing, harvesting, and processing coffee. This is made possible by the flatter, lower-altitude farms, which permit the use of harvesting tractors. Coffee is grown in lines a lot like vineyards and the vehicles knock the cherries off the tree. This results in a mix of under- and overripe cherries. Complex sorting machinery is then required to separate the various qualities of cherry. During my visit to the Daterra farm in the Cerrado region, not only was I very well looked after but I was blown away by the technology the farm had and the ability of that technology to improve the quality of sorting and processing. The owners had a bespoke sorting system that separated the cherries by ripeness based on pressure and LED sorters that scanned thousands of beans per second. Brazil has also seen a continuing increase in the amount of coffee consumed internally.

Brew ratio | BREWING

SEE ALSO
Dose *p72*
Yield *p245*

A brew ratio refers to the ratio of coffee to water as part of a brew recipe. In many ways, it is easier to just explain the weight of ground coffee dose used and the weight of the yield (final beverage). All the same, the brew ratio can be useful in communicating and considering the beverage in its fundamental form. For example, one might say a 50 per cent brew ratio or a 1:2 ratio. Both mean that the beverage weighs twice that of the dose used. That means you could use a 15g dose for espresso or a 22g one but produce two shots with the same brew ratio by pouring 30g and 44g out respectively. Even though the second shot is bigger, it is actually the same style of shot – you just started with more coffee.

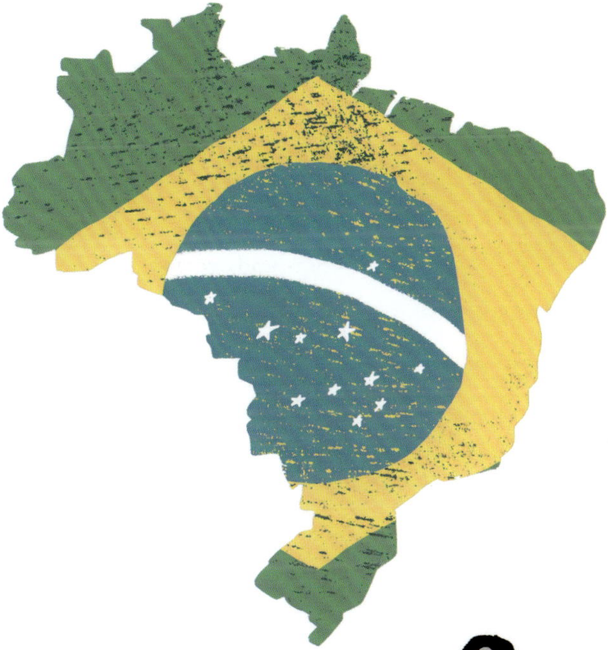
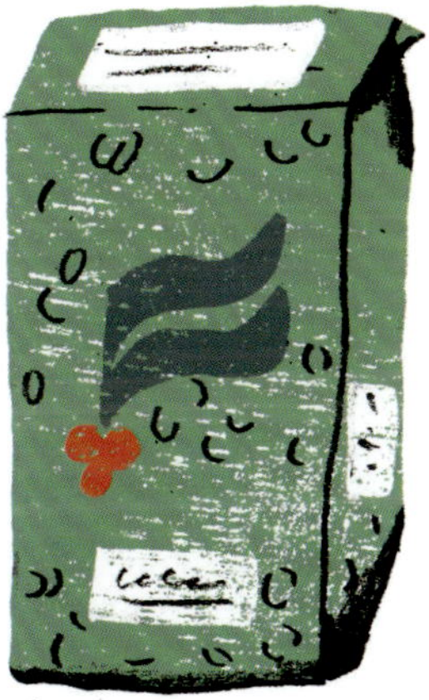
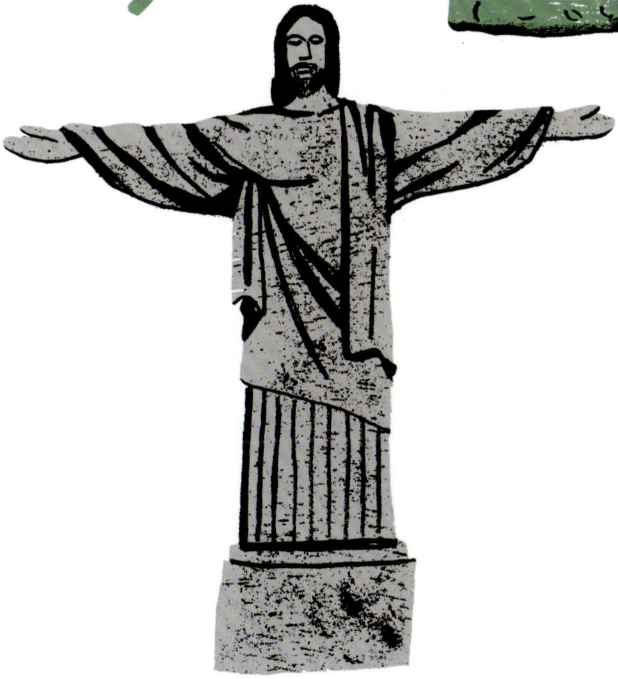

SEE ALSO
Refractometer *p189*
Ripe *p190*

Brix | GROWING

A degree Brix (1°Bx) represents 1g of sugar per 100g of aqueous solution. In effect, the Brix Scale is a measurement of how sugary a liquid is. Brix readings are used to assess the sugar in grapes for wine making as well as in a plethora of other vegetables and fruits. What does this have to do with coffee? Coffee farmers focusing on quality are looking outwards to utilize methods of assessing and improving quality. Brix readings are becoming more and more popular in assessing the ripeness of the coffee cherries based on the sugar content. A refractometer, much like that used to measure the strength of coffee, is used to assess Brix. Indeed, the only difference between the two is the interpretation of the reading.

SEE ALSO
Acidity *p13*
Water *p236*

Buffer | WATER

There is a lot to say on the topic of water. I chose to give "buffer" its own entry as I think it has the most dramatic impact on flavour. It can be slightly confusing to understand at first, mainly because it is a scientific process and because there are several terms for "buffering" in water chemistry. It can also be referred to as the "alkalinity" of the water or the "bicarbonate content". It is listed on most bottled waters and its job is to help maintain a stable pH. This "buffering" system is integral to life on planet Earth. The blood running through your body relies on the very same system to keep a steady pH. Coffee is an acidic beverage with a lower pH than the water you will have used to make it. Waters with high buffering ability will make the drink less acidic. This is a problem as we value good acidity in coffee. To see the startling effect of buffering, simply take the tiniest pinch of baking soda (a form of bicarbonate) and drop it into your cup of coffee. Taste and notice that it will have lost all of its acidity. The resulting cup will be bland and bitter.

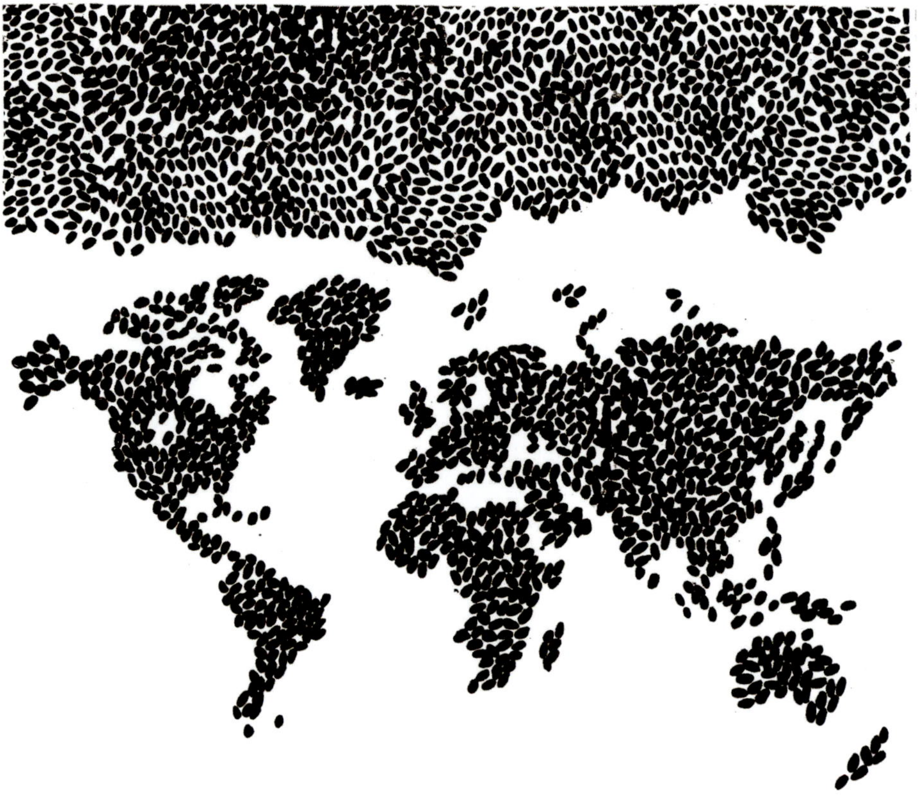

C

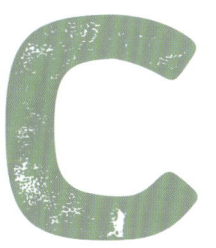

SEE ALSO
Fairtrade *p89*

C market | TRADING

The coffee futures market, or C market, is a global commodities market that operates in US dollars. Futures markets are based on contracts for a specific commodity to be delivered in the future (it is all in the name, really) and dictate the commodity price of a globally important product from day to day and year to year. The futures market has a huge impact on the livelihood of many working in the coffee industry, especially growers. A frost in Brazil can push the market price up due to worries that the world's largest producer will make less coffee – worries that quickly ripple around the globe. Coffee, like any commodity market, hits peaks and troughs. It is all good when the market is at a peak, but when the market is in a trough coffee is not even worth growing for many farmers. Speciality coffee prices mostly far exceed the C market prices, with a premium being paid for quality.

Cafetière

See "French press".

Caffeine | STIMULANT

Wine is culinarily complex and contains alcohol. Coffee is no different, except its drug

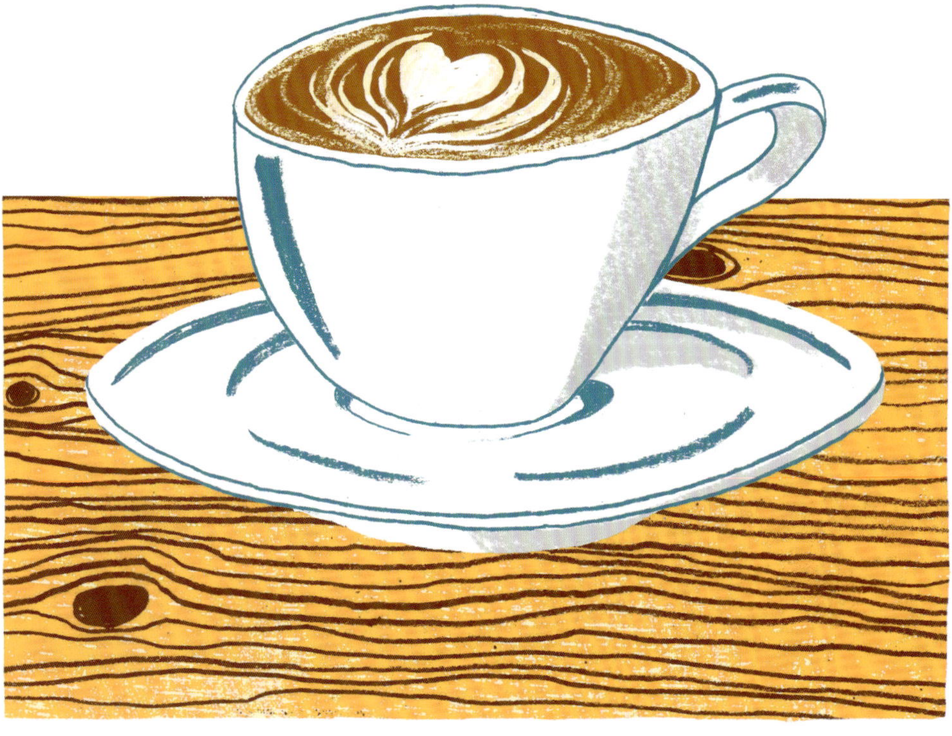

is caffeine. There is no doubt that, without the stimulating element of caffeine, coffee would not be the globally consumed drink it is today. Caffeine serves the same evolutionary purpose in the coffee plant as it does in many species: as an insecticide, it provides the plant with a natural defence mechanism. Caffeine content in a cup of coffee varies wildly. The origin of the coffee will have a huge impact, as does the species – Arabica typically has half the amount of caffeine Robusta has. Coffee grown at higher altitudes tends to have a lower caffeine content as it needs less defence. There are varieties of Arabica that are naturally low in caffeine and are seen as a potential solution to decaffeinating coffee, though the plants are likely to mutate and develop higher caffeine contents in different environments. What makes caffeine content slightly confusing for everyone buying coffee-based drinks in shops is that, without knowing the amount of coffee used to make the drink, it is very hard to predict how much caffeine is in the beverage. Cup size is misleading: a smaller cup could be made with more ground coffee and therefore have more caffeine than a larger cup made with less coffee. Strength is also misleading: an espresso may be very intense but probably does not have sufficient volume to contain as much caffeine as a large mug of filter coffee.

Cappuccino | DRINK TYPE

The cappuccino is an iconic drink, but what exactly is it? There is much debate about nearly all of the drinks on a typical coffee menu. What exactly should the ratio of a cappuccino be: how much espresso to how much milk? And how much foam and what type of foam? And how exactly

SEE ALSO
Flat white *p94*
Steaming *p205*
Strength *p206*

does it differ from other beverages on the menu? Strict definitions are hard to come by.
The cappuccino is possibly the most widely interpreted drink name out there. It is fair to say that a cappuccino is stronger than a latte (there is more coffee to milk) and has a decent amount of foam, though in a lot of commercial shops a cappuccino is just a latte with some chocolate sprinkles added on top. Beyond this, it is pretty tricky. Some claim that a perfect cappuccino is the hardest milk drink to master: dense milk foam that is also big on volume is nigh impossible to create. I have been told of the existence of the perfect cappuccino in which the foam does not separate, but this, I think, must be mythical – all foam separates to the top unless you drink it immediately. Saying that, for a while I did try really hard to make that legendary cappuccino. The origin of the cappuccino is not linked to a monk's hairstyle, as is often cited. Its origins are instead Viennese and refer to the brown robes of a Capucin monk, with the colour relating to the strength of the coffee-and-milk mix.

Capsules | BREWING

Nestlé invented capsule technology back in 1972, under the Nespresso™ banner. Since then, other systems from other companies have emerged and have been very successful. Capsule coffee consumption has continued to grow. The main benefit is the ability to control and oversee more of the coffee-brewing process. Capsules simply contain ground coffee, but the aluminium or plastic capsule coupled with inert gas flushing means that the freshness of the coffee is preserved for impressive lengths of time. Up until recently, the speciality coffee sphere has had little interest in capsules, and as such they

SEE ALSO
Bean to cup *p24*

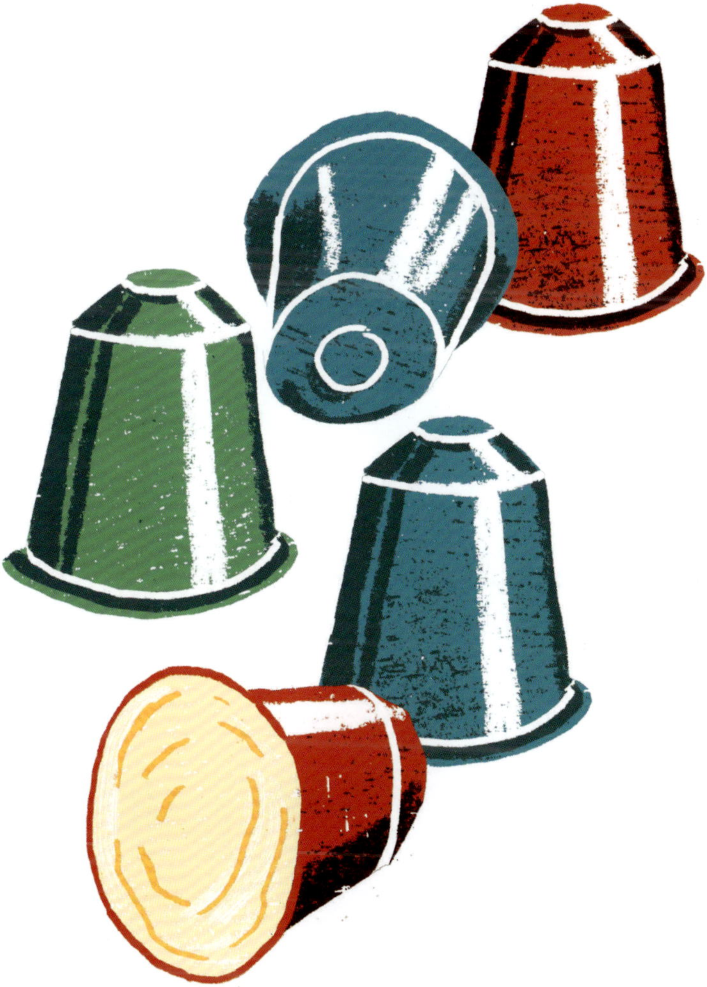

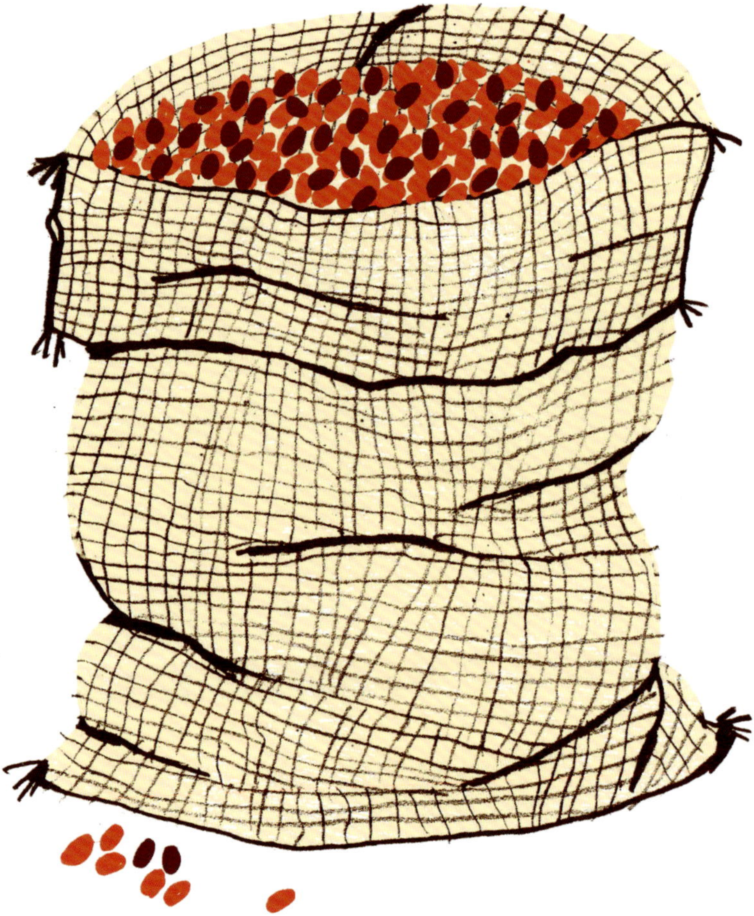

have been both non-artisanal and a vehicle for commercial flavour profiles. That said, the technology is capable of acting as a superb brewing system, and since certain Nespresso patents ended in 2012, speciality coffee roasters and companies have begun to enter the market.

Carbonic maceration | GROWING; PROCESSING

Carbonic maceration is a well-defined term in the world of wine. It was in 2015 at the World Barista Championship that the coffee community was introduced to the idea when the Serbian-born Australian Saša Šestić won the competition with a coffee that made use of the method. Lots of parallels can be drawn between coffee and wine: they are both complex, flavoursome drinks made from a singular ingredient in which the *terroir* greatly impacts the flavour. In wine, carbonic maceration uses the injection of carbon dioxide to ferment the grapes without breaking the skins, so the process happens inside each grape individually. When we process coffee we often utilize fermentation, but with coffee we are using the seed inside the fruit rather than the fruit itself. Šestić, together with his collaborator, the Colombian farmer Camilio Marisande, experimented with this technique to produce a coffee that had more aromatic complexity but a lower concentration of sharp-tasting acetic acid. They also put the beans through this process at much lower temperatures to avoid alcohol build-up. Exploration of coffee processing has never been more extensive and detailed, and boundaries are being pushed all the time. Even though we often categorize a coffee according to the process used, such as "washed" or "natural", specifics like the temperature of the cherries and the type of water all have an

SEE ALSO
Fermentation *p90*
Honey process *p118*
Natural process *p156*
Terroir *p214*
World Barista Championship *p239*

impact on the end flavour. If you get the chance, tasting coffees from a single farm but processed in two different ways can be illuminating: the differences are sometimes subtle but often astonishing.

Cartridge filter | WATER FILTRATION

More accurately described as an ion exchange cartridge, a cartridge filter is very commonly found in coffee shops, positioned under the counter. Much of the same technology also makes its way into the filtration water jugs you may use at home, like Brita®. Using a clever piece of chemistry, the cartridge features a "resin" that swaps ions in the water entering the cartridge for ions in the resin (hence the term "exchange"), thereby producing a different solution at the other end. There are different ways these resins can be configured. It is important to acknowledge here that the composition of the water going into the cartridge dictates what there is to swap around, so such systems do not create a specific kind of water. The filtered water's composition is unique to, and dependent on, the source water used. Nonetheless, you can predict what impact the cartridge will have on different types of water and often you have the ability to adapt the filter somewhat to suit. These systems will always be designed to lower your buffer.

Cascara | COFFEE BY-PRODUCT

Cascara is the name of the dried coffee cherry from which we take the coffee beans. The name is derived from the Spanish for "husk". Traditionally, cascara has been a by-product of coffee production that was little recognized

SEE ALSO
Buffer *p38*
Reverse osmosis *p190*

SEE ALSO
World Barista Championship *p239*

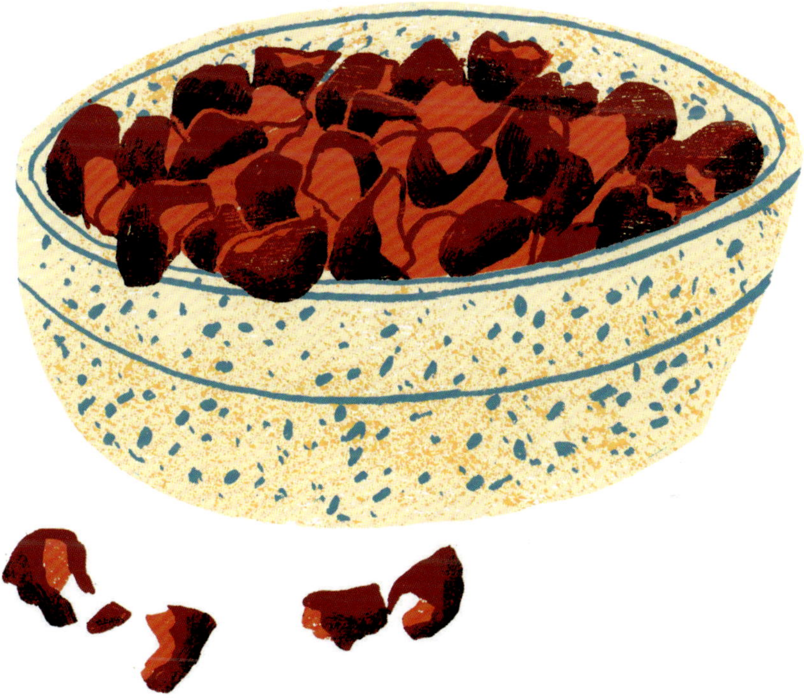

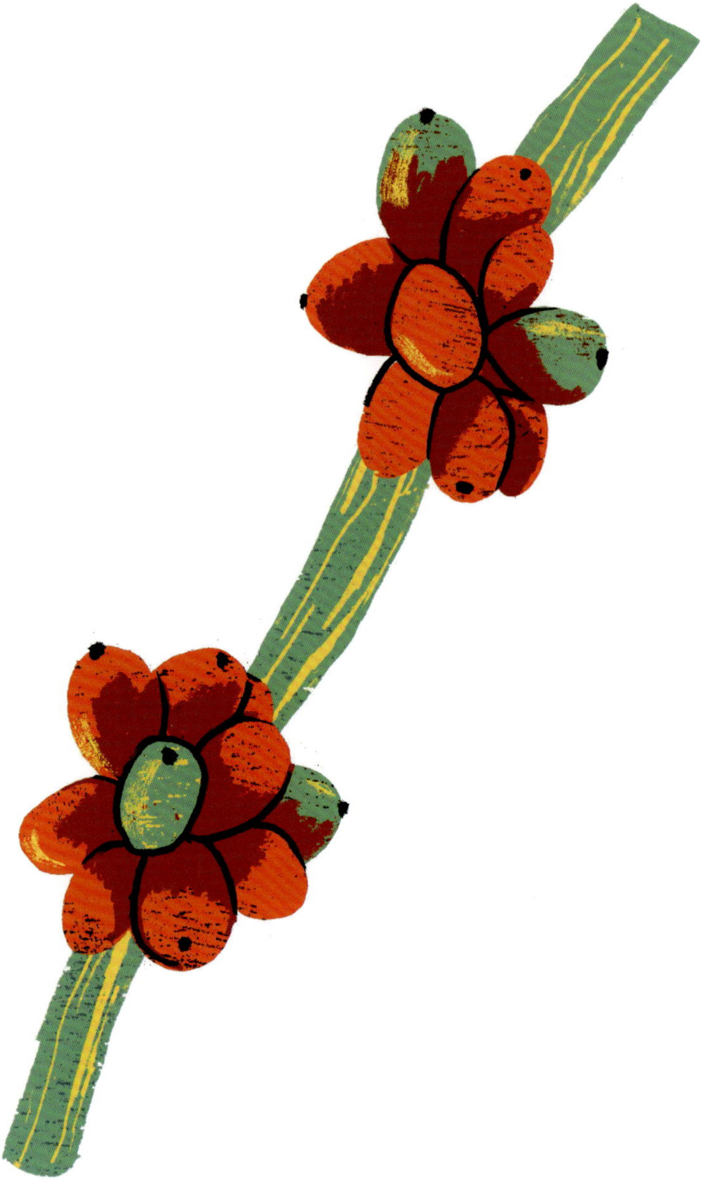

or used. In Bolivia, however, using slightly toasted cascara to make "cascara tea" is quite common, and is referred to as the "poor man's coffee". Recently, there has been a huge upsurge of interest in cascara. Cascara has made its way into many winning World Barista Championship routines for the signature drink round. It is, of course, a great narrative to mix the very same cherry the coffee was grown in with the coffee itself. Cascara is now used in a variety of ways, with many bottled cascara drinks beginning to turn up. My favourite use of cascara so far is a cold cascara infused with Earl Grey tea used as a palette cleanser before drinking espresso. I first had this in the Kaffeine coffee shop in London. Cascara can have varying flavour characteristics depending on the provenance of the coffee itself. An overarching flavour profile for cascara is that it displays notes of what it is – a dried fruit. It most often has notes of raisin, sherry, and botanicals.

Castillo | VARIETY

Castillo is a brilliant example of many aspects of coffee varieties/cultivars and their development. Many of the world's coffee varieties that are propagated today were influenced by the human touch at some point. The Holy Grail is to create cultivars that yield more coffee, are more disease resistant, and have a higher cup quality. This is difficult, as cup quality tends to be linked to lower yields and disease-resistant strains utilize Robusta stock, again decreasing cup quality. This is not always the case, however: the cultivars Kenya has become renowned for – the SL varieties – were cultivated during imperial rule for the very goal of achieving higher yields. In doing so, the growers stumbled

SEE ALSO
Kenya *p135*
Species *p202*

across incredible cup quality. Crippling crop disease is most problematic in the Americas, and Colombia has done a great job of exploring new cultivars that address this problem. The Castillo variety, like many cultivars, has met with much prejudice: its cup quality was expected to be a compromise and so the perception was that it could not compete with the lower-yielding and more disease-susceptible Caturra variety. The thing is, it is extremely difficult in coffee to isolate one variety and decisively label whether it is good or bad. For example, a variety may do extremely well in Kenya but not in El Salvador. The work of Michael Sheridan of the Coffee Lands Project has been instrumental in shifting perceptions on Castillo by challenging tasters' preferences on blind tastings between Castillo and Caturra. Essentially, Sheridan's work shows that expecting Castillo to produce high cup quality under the same growing conditions as Caturra was unfair and unproductive, and that the key was to figure out what growing conditions Castillo needs.

Channelling | BREWING

The term "channelling" refers to the way in which water passes though a bed of coffee. The term is most commonly found in the world of espresso. The idea is to get the water to pass evenly through all the ground coffee and pull flavour from every part. When the water fails to pass through evenly and instead creates either one main path or a number of pathways, we call this channelling. This is very problematic, as it means that the water takes too much flavour from the parts of the coffee it is passing through the most and not enough from elsewhere. There are a number of causes, including bad

SEE ALSO
Extraction *p86*
Grooming *p110*
Naked shot *p155*
Portafilter *p176*
Tamping *p213*

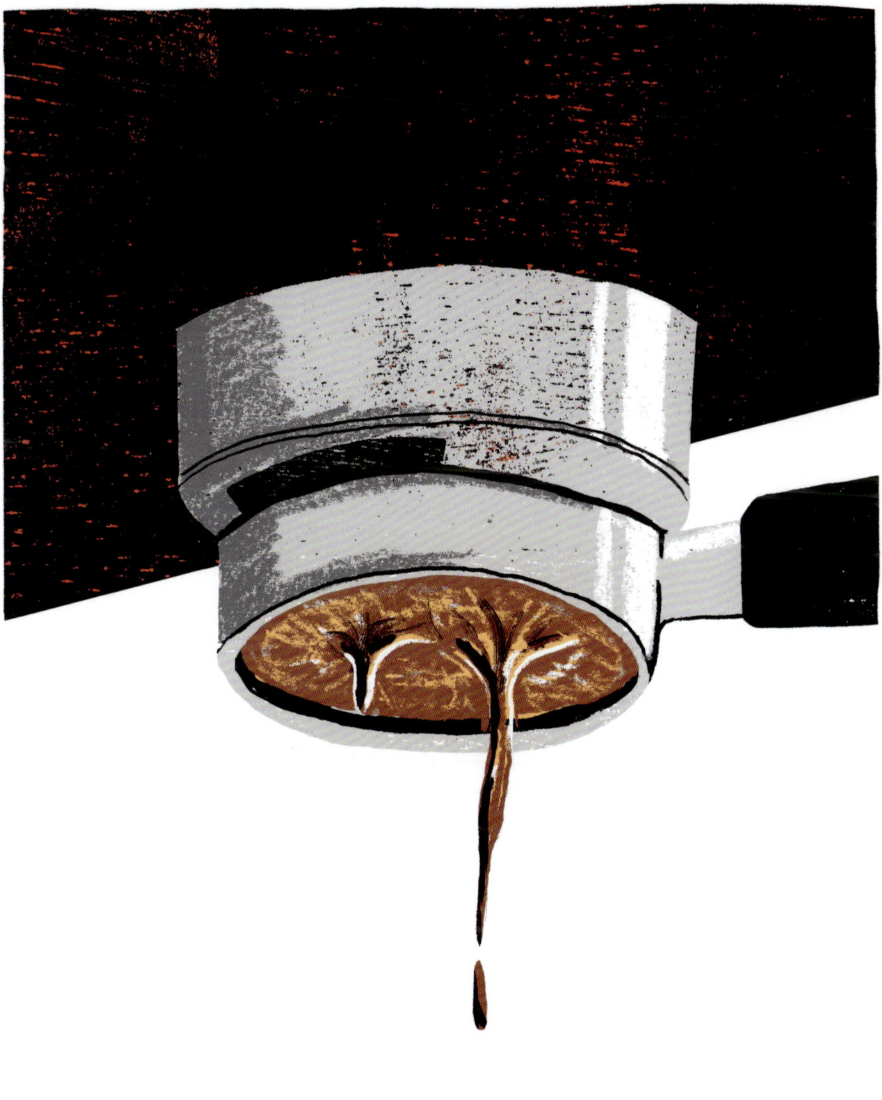

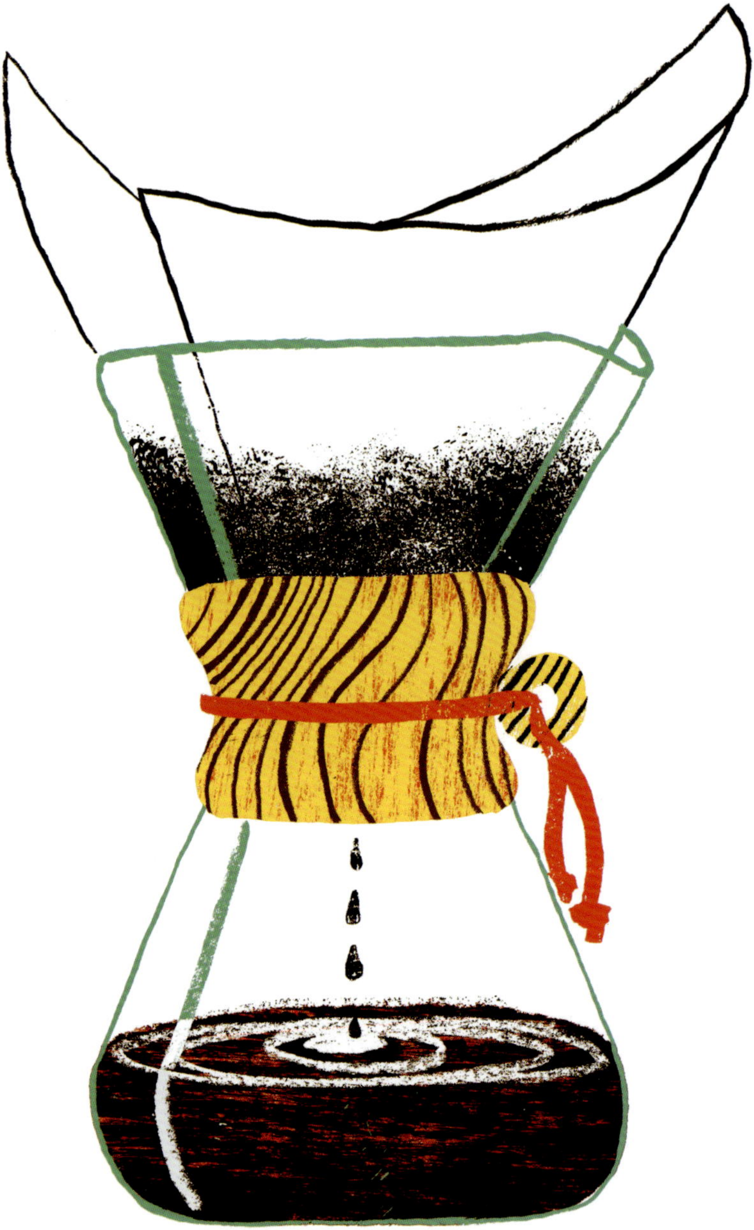

distribution in the basket, problems with tamping, and grinding inconsistencies. A naked (bottomless) portafilter will help show up when channelling occurs.

Chemex™ | BREWING

Invented in the early 1940s, the Chemex™ has become an iconic coffee brewer for both its aesthetic appeal and its brewing ability. A scattering of pop culture references shows the reach of the Chemex's appeal, my favourite being James Bond's use of the Chemex to brew his morning coffee in Ian Fleming's *From Russia with Love* (1957). Its beautiful glass and wood design may be a big part of its appeal, but it is the unique paper filters that have the biggest impact on the cups it produces. It is increasingly recognized that the paper filters used for different filter methods have a huge impact and arguably largely define which filter method we have a preference for. So-called "paper tastings" occur to decide which paper will impart the least negative flavours to the cup. The flavour of the paper is one thing and the ability of the paper to filter various elements of the coffee is another. The Chemex papers have a bonded, thicker gauge, leading to what we would call a very "clean" cup, with little sediment and most coffee oils removed. They also routinely do rather well in those paper tastings.

China | ORIGIN

The ultimate tea nation has started drinking more coffee, and it may be surprising to hear that a fair amount of coffee is now being grown in Yunnan Province. Coffee was introduced to China way back in the late 1880s, but it is only recently that both the growing and the consumption of coffee have picked up. The coffee grown in Yunnan has not until recently been of much interest to the speciality market, but crop quality is improving. Coffee-drinking habits are also taking a turn, with consumption increasing along with an interest in high-quality coffee experiences. The Tea & Coffee China Expo in Shanghai is one of the largest in the world. A visit to the show reveals the fervour and excitement around speciality coffee in China today.

Clean | TASTING

SEE ALSO
Defects *p67*
Natural process *p156*
Old Brown Java *p163*
Washed process *p235*

The term "clean coffee" often raises the question "As opposed to *dirty* coffee?" And the answer is "Well, yes." When growing coffee there is the potential for many problems to occur that impart unwanted flavours to the coffee. Many defect flavours often taste "dirty", such as the woody pungent notes in aged coffee. Well-processed coffee is often described as tasting clean. Natural-processed coffees are often contentious as they can lack the cleanness of washed coffee. However, these descriptors are not just a description of how well processed a coffee tastes. For example, a less high-quality-yielding variety grown at low altitude with a less than favourable environment could be extremely well picked and processed and still not produce a very clean cup.

Climate change | GROWING

SEE ALSO
Altitude *p16*
Arabica *p18*
Leaf rust *p140*
Sustainability *p211*

Climate change promises to have a huge impact on coffee growing, as indeed it will on many crops. The unique climates and temperatures required to grow outstanding Arabica occur above 1,000m (3,300 ft), but these sweet spots are moving ever upward, which means that there is

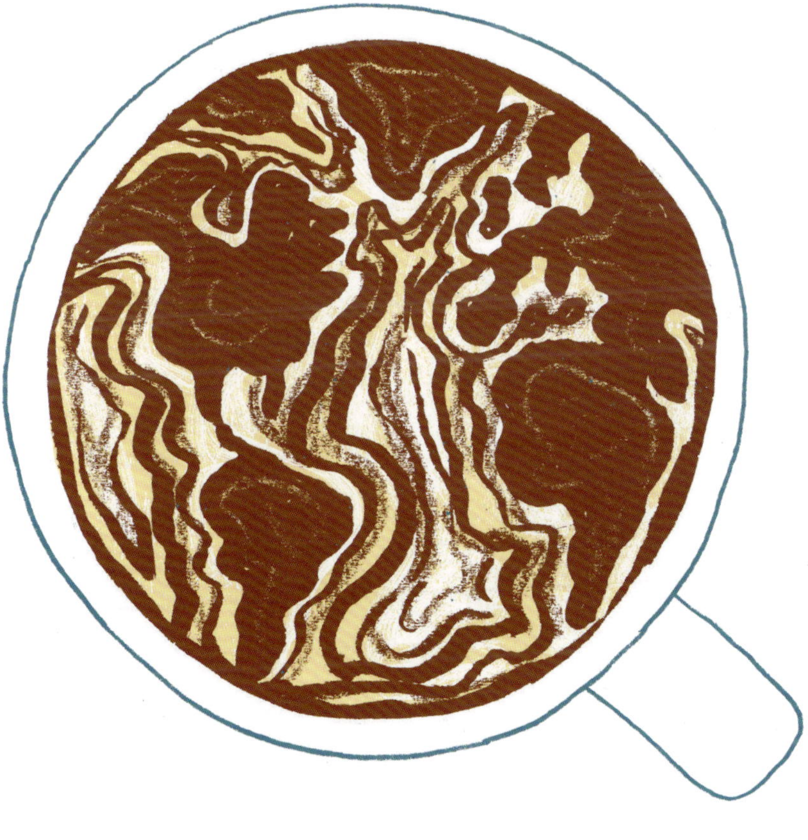

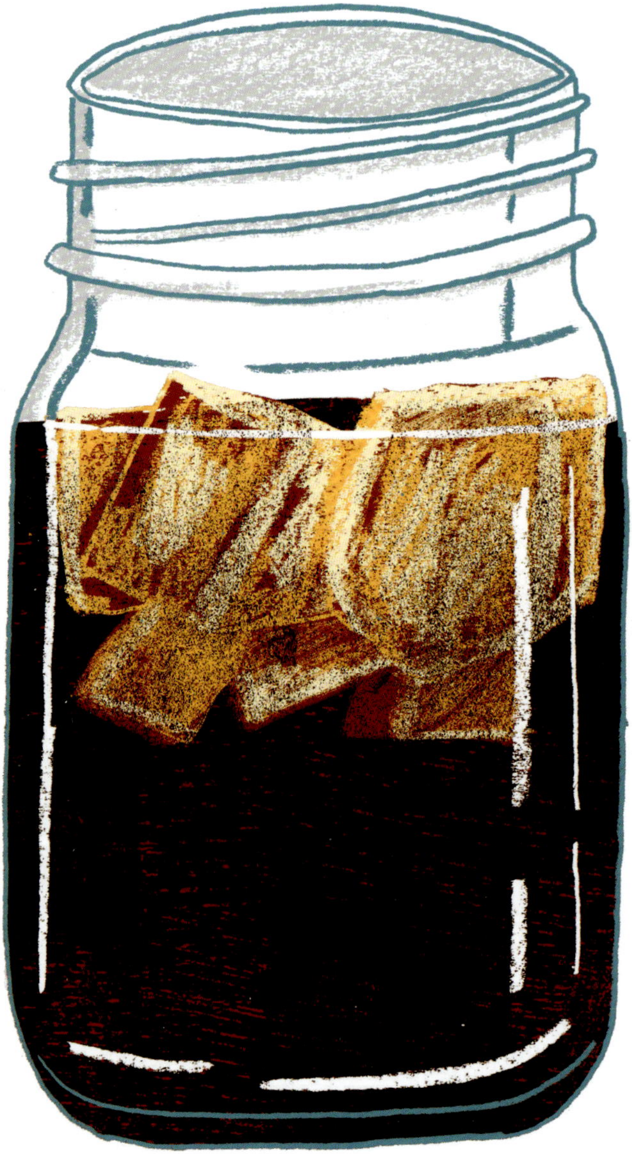

less potential space to harvest top-quality coffee. Increasing temperatures also mean that the spread of leaf rust gets all the easier and more problematic. Solutions include the potential exploration of varieties that produce a good cup profile at a lower altitude and are more resistant to rust. Mind you, this is not a new thing: it has always been valuable to try to achieve this, but maybe now there is more incentive to do so than before. The truth is that climate change will mean that cup profiles change and that growing excellent coffee will become more difficult.

CO_2

See "Bloom" and "Crema".

Coffee futures market

See "C market".

Cold brew | DRINK TYPE

The cold brew phenomenon is everywhere, from boutique coffee shops to multinational chains, and much like the flat white this relatively new drink format is here to stay. The principle is very simple: coffee gets brewed with cold water instead of hot. As the heat in water aids extraction, you need to compensate for this by dramatically increasing the brewing time, whether that is through a slow drip method or a slow steeping method. A cold brew is always going to take hours instead of minutes. Time, however, does not achieve the same things as heat, and the extraction is really quite different. The coffee has far less acidity and cold brews tend towards the chocolaty, malty, and often boozy end of the flavour spectrum. This has the bonus effect of

SEE ALSO
Extraction *p86*

making a lot of coffees smoother but the downside of not capturing the acidity and aromatics of characterful coffees. Nitro cold brew is also popping up on beer-like taps. Here, the addition of nitrogen gives a Guinness-like creaminess to the cold brew, complete with a beer-like head.

Colombia | ORIGIN

Colombia is one of the most diverse coffee-producing countries in terms of its quality flavour profiles. In departments such as Antioquia, chocolaty, full-bodied cups are found, while in Huila Department (the darling of the speciality market) one can find incredibly ripe, fruity, and juicy coffees whose flavour profiles are closely comparable to those of Kenyan coffees. Multiple microclimates also mean that Colombia can produce a lot of fresh crop coffee throughout most of the year, by using both main crops and smaller "fly" crops. As well as being one of the world's largest coffee-producing countries, Colombia has a highly developed and progressive coffee infrastructure. Bodies such as the non-profit Federación Nacional de Cafeteros de Colombia (National Federation of Coffee Growers of Colombia – Fedecafé, for short) and Cenicafé, a coffee research centre renowned for its development of more disease-resistant varieties such as Castillo, are good examples.

SEE ALSO
Castillo *p51*

Constantinople | HISTORY

It is said that the first ever coffee house opened its doors in Constantinople (modern-day Istanbul) in the mid-16th century, soon after the beverage itself was introduced to the Ottoman capital. Coffee-house culture, and in particular its ability to be a hotbed for public

SEE ALSO
Lloyd's of London *p142*
Third place *p217*

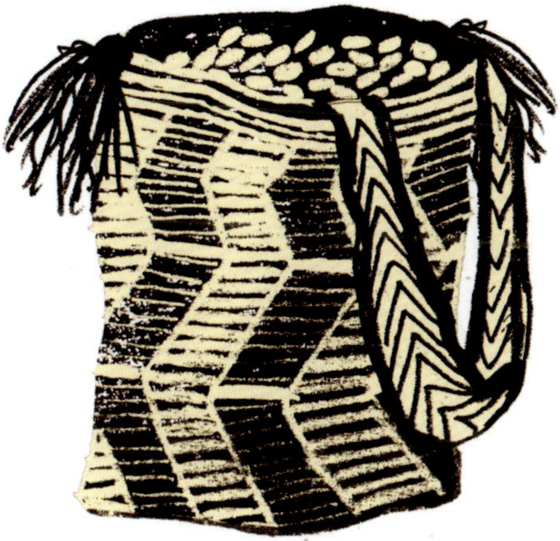
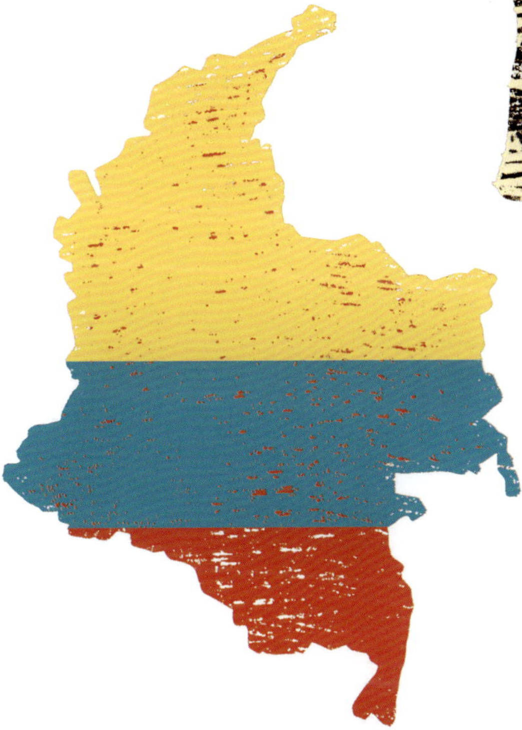
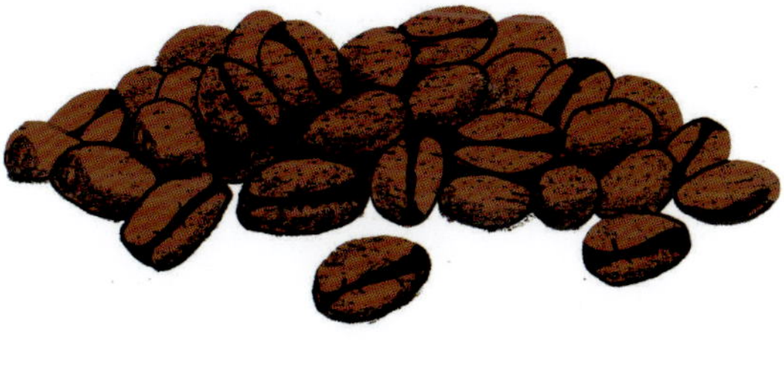

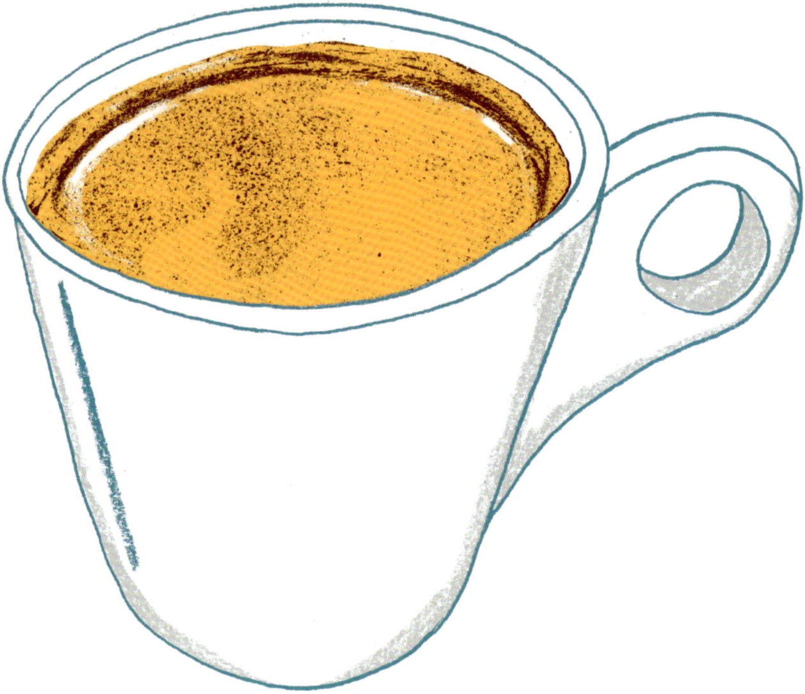

debate, business, and social mingling, can be traced back to this amazing city and its rich, complex culture. From Constantinople, the institution of the coffee shop spread throughout the Arabic world, Europe, and the world.

Costa Rica | ORIGIN

Costa Rica has long been known for the quality of its coffee. In recent times, the country has been very good at increasing traceability as individual farmers move towards having their own mills and processing their own lots. Many farmers have also focused on explorative processing – the phenomenon of honey-processing originated in this country. There are multiple growing regions in Costa Rica, with Tarrazú garnering much of the reputation for producing high-scoring coffees. There is a range of flavour profiles within Costa Rican coffee, though we most often see light, sweet, and aromatic examples with floral and berry notes and light nutty characteristics apparent.

SEE ALSO
Honey process *p118*

Crema | ESPRESSO

Beautiful crema. For a long, long time the appearance and quality of the crema – the thin layer of foam on top of a cup of espresso – was one of the defining characteristics with which the quality of an espresso was judged. Traditionally, the perfect crema is a deep, reddish hazelnut colour and will hold a teaspoon of sugar for several seconds. If you are really lucky it will have "tiger stripes" – a speckled pattern effect across the surface of the crema. The crema, however, is really just a by-product of brewing under pressure and the effect this has on the CO_2 in the coffee. It cannot tell you the quality of the

SEE ALSO
Espresso *p79*
World Barista Championship *p239*

coffee, but will instead indicate the freshness of the coffee (coffee loses CO_2 and therefore crema as it ages) and the darkness of the roast (a darker roast will produce a darker crema). In summary, the highest-scoring coffees do not produce the highest-scoring crema. The marking of crema at the World Barista Championship has become increasingly less important. So many other factors such as the quality of the green coffee, roast, and extraction are much more crucial to the cup's quality.

Cup of Excellence | COMPETITIONS

Cup of Excellence (COE) is a competition in which producers have their coffees graded and ranked according to their quality. The top lots then get auctioned off to the highest bidder around the world via an Internet auction. This hugely impactful programme was created by the US speciality coffee pioneer George Howell along with Susie Spindler. The programme really helps to throw a spotlight on – and reward – quality, allowing producers access to international buyers prepared to pay for the best. Countries like Rwanda have had their coffee-growing fortunes dramatically altered by this programme, which brings attention to the quality of coffee that a country can produce. Not all coffee-producing countries host the Cup of Excellence, and other auction systems have also popped up, such as the Best of Panama.

Cupping | TASTING

Cupping not only has a humorous name but is also accompanied by a slightly unsettling chorus of various pitched slurps. Cupping is the pre-eminent method for grading and buying

SEE ALSO
Panama *p169*

coffee. In order to achieve the most consistent results, the "cupper", or taster, has to follow a very specific, though in reality quite simple, set of procedures. You grind the coffee in a bowl, smell the ground coffee, top it up with hot water, wait for four minutes, then break the crust that has formed with a spoon and stir three times. You smell the aroma as this is happening and lastly wait for a further six minutes before tasting.
In order to taste the coffee, each cupper dips their cupping spoon, which is much like a soup spoon, into the bowl without disturbing the grounds at the bottom and then slurps the coffee from the spoon, aerating it as they do so. The procedure is then for the taster to return to each cup two more times within the ensuing ten minutes. The main benefit of this procedure is that it enables the cupper to taste a lot of coffee at once. It is often advocated that cupping is the ultimate way to taste coffee, and that when making espressos or filter we are focusing on an aspect of the coffee that we tasted on the cupping table. This does not make sense to me. Cupping is just another way to make a cup of coffee, and when made the primary assessment tool it can actually be a hindrance. This is because the cupped coffee does not fully translate to how we actually make and consume coffee in everyday life.

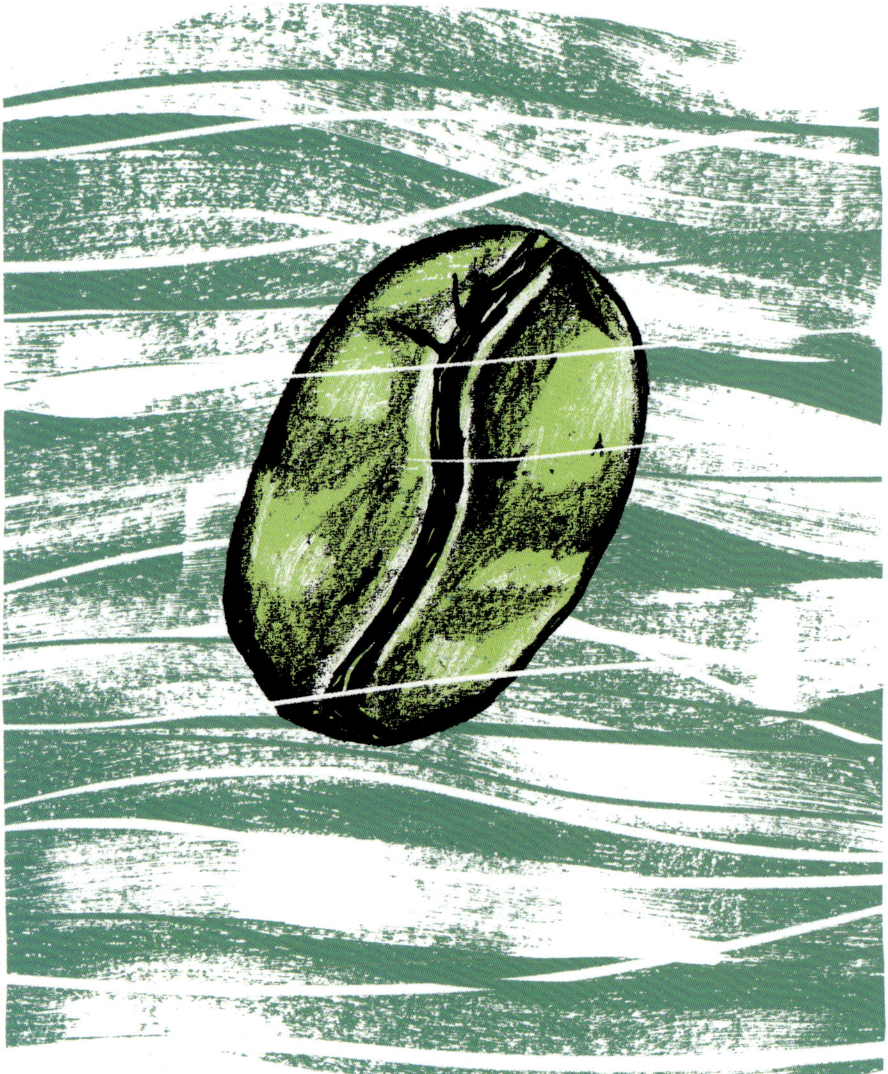

Decaf | PROCESSING

All decaffeination processes take place when the coffee is in its green state, before it is roasted. Various methods exist, the two most notable being the patented Swiss Water Process (SWP) and the CO_2 Method. In SWP, a batch of green coffee beans is soaked in hot water, which as a consequence becomes saturated with caffeine and flavour compounds. The now caffeine-free and flavourless beans are discarded and a new batch of beans added to the solution. This time the caffeine is removed but a large amount of the flavour compounds remain, as the water is already full of them. The CO_2 Method involves forcing carbon dioxide into coffee beans at pressures of around 1,000 pounds per square inch to draw the caffeine out of the coffee into a water solution. Decaf coffee is often made from older green coffee that has not sold very well, so has not had the best start in life. Although it has so far proved impossible to remove caffeine without affecting flavour, with a fresh, carefully roasted coffee, decaf can be made much more pleasant than it often is.

Defects | GROWING; HARVESTING

There are many aspects of coffee flavour that are relative: do you prefer a chocolaty, round

Antioquia Colombian to a fruity Huila Colombian bean? Regardless of preference, however, we can safely correlate better versions of both of these coffees with their having fewer defects. Defects are mainly caused by problems with the cherries' growth on the tree or arising during the harvesting and processing. Typical causes of defects include insect damage and fungal build-up. Most defects can be detected either by the astute, educated eye or by the use of clever technology such as UV lights and LED sorting machines. But even modern technology cannot currently catch everything. "Potato defect", for example, is very prevalent in Rwandan and Burundian coffee and almost impossible to spot until you make the coffee: when ground, it gives off an unmistakable waft of raw potato. The cause of potato defect is a contentious one, but it is widely considered that a kind of stink bug is behind it.

SEE ALSO
Rwanda *p194*
Species *p202*

Democratic Republic of Congo | ORIGIN

The Democratic Republic of Congo is the second largest country in Africa, and the conditions in eastern parts of this country produce ideal growing conditions for coffee. The area around Lake Kivu borders on the well-known Kivu growing region in Rwanda. We are only just starting to see some great coffees come out of Congo on a regular basis. The country has endured much turmoil and the coffee trade has been directly affected by this. Different roasters, sourcing companies, and certifications are operating in the country to improve production and help realize the country's coffee-production potential. The best cups are complex and full of citrus fruit flavours with wonderful acidity

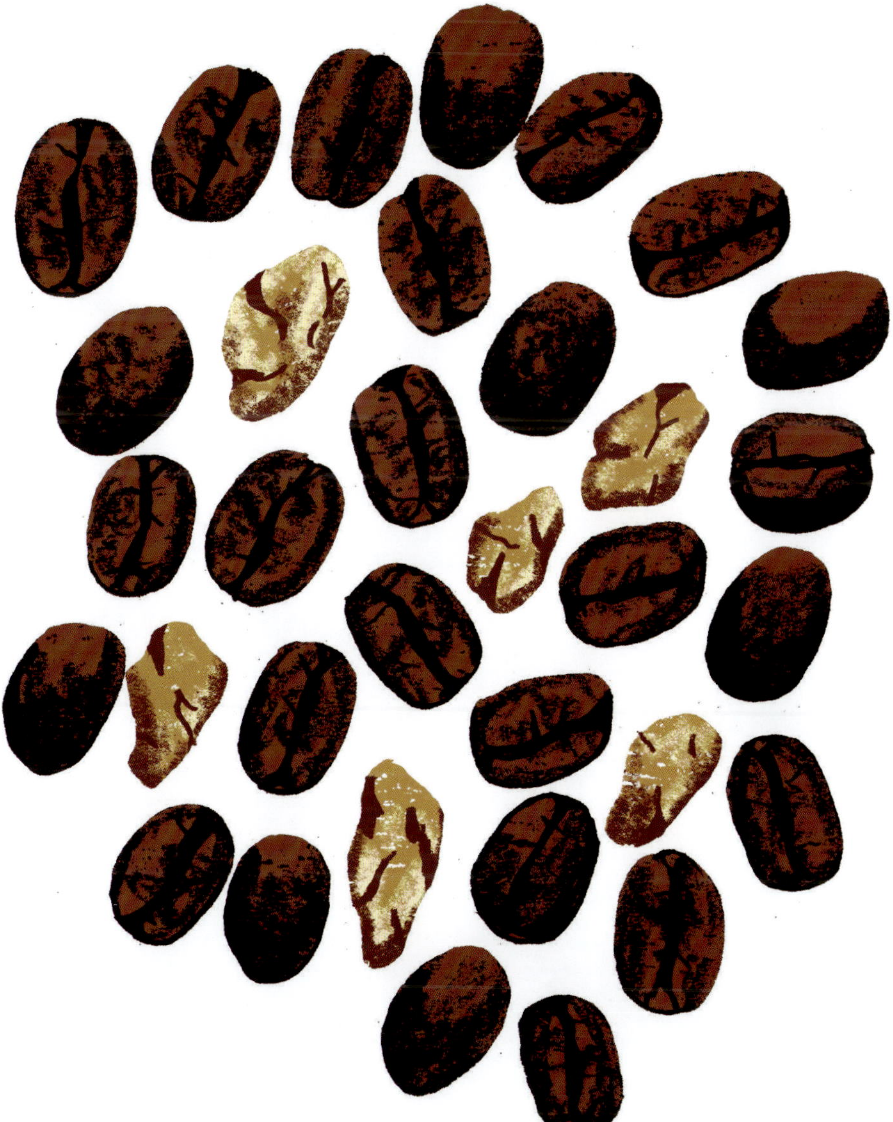

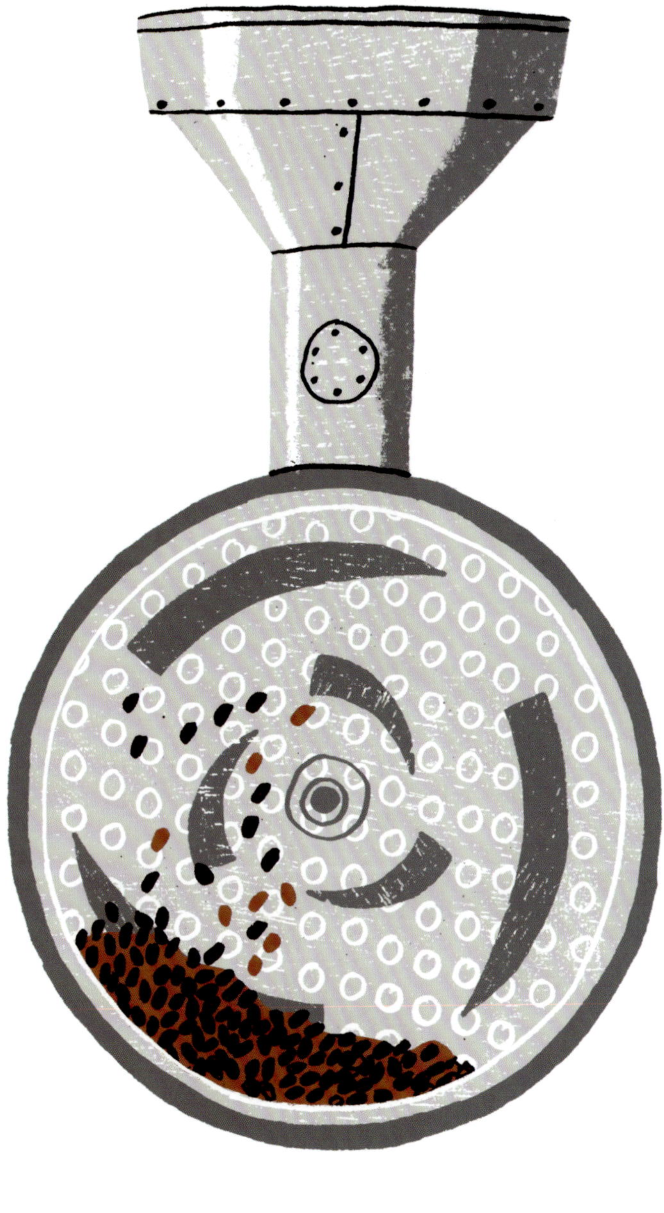

and round chocolaty notes. At this point in time, however, the country's Arabica production is far outstripped by Robusta crops.

Density table | SORTING

Also known as the Oliver table, this is a method of sorting coffee that uses vibration. Tilted at an angle, the dense beans move to the top side and the less dense to the bottom side. There is a correlation between the quality and the density of the beans: less dense beans often represent a less well-developed seed. Pieces of technology like this can have a huge impact on improving cup quality in lots. Hand and eye sorting can get you a long way, but certain pieces of technology assess what we cannot, so can be invaluable.

SEE ALSO
First crack *p93*

Development | ROASTING

The term "development" in coffee is used almost exclusively when discussing roasting technique. It can refer, on the one hand, to a very particular period during the roasting process and, on the other, to an overall concept of how well cooked the coffee is. When a coffee is roasted, many processes and chemical reactions occur. If we are not able to develop enough of these in the bean, then the coffee can taste grassy, sour, and insufficiently complex. Alternatively, we can develop unwanted processes by roasting the coffee too far. Upon tasting a coffee, the drinker may be able to pick up on the impact of the roasting process and could state that the coffee was "under-" or "over-" developed. "Development" time refers specifically to the amount of the overall roasting time that took place after "first crack". It is wise to discuss this in terms of a percentage. Just to confuse things,

SEE ALSO
Brew ratio *p36*
Extraction *p86*

however, a coffee that has not received adequate heat early on in the roast may still not be "well" developed, even if the development time is long.

Dose | BREWING

Dose is a simple technical term that commonly refers to the amount of ground coffee used to prepare a given cup of coffee, though it can also be applied to other aspects such as the amount of water used. The dose would be recorded and discussed as part of the "recipe" used to make a cup of coffee. Coffee is applied chemistry and physics in action. We dissolve coffee into water to create a beverage. There are several parts of this process that define the recipe and they have a huge impact on what the end cup of coffee tastes like, often alarmingly so. I often see customers who, while intrigued by coffee, are equally frustrated by the seemingly erratic nature of the cups of coffee they make. "I do the same thing every day, but it tastes different." Coffee has many "moving parts" and the search for relatable quality has been at the heart of the modern speciality field. However, the reality is that tiny changes in the recipe can make coffee taste very different, and by simply being aware of what aspects of the recipe affect flavour one can achieve far more consistent results and unravel the mystery.

Drum roaster | ROASTING

Turning coffee from a green seed into a complex flavoursome brown seed relies on the act of roasting. The most traditional – and still the most prevalent – way to roast coffee is on a drum roaster. Although there are various machines on the market, they usually share a rather simple

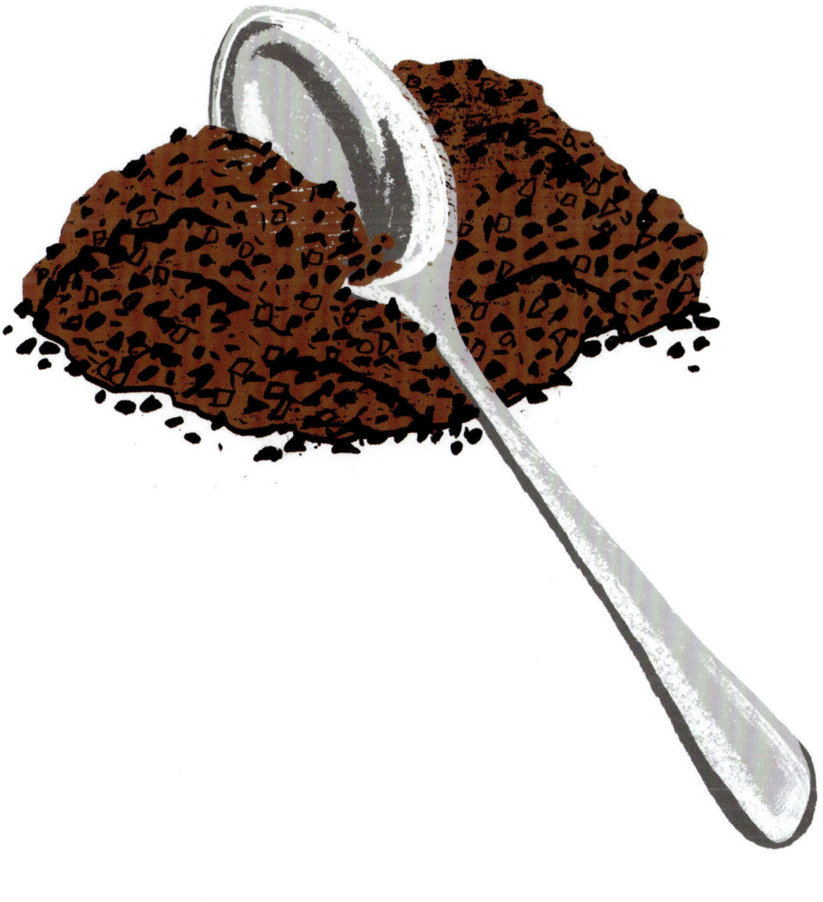

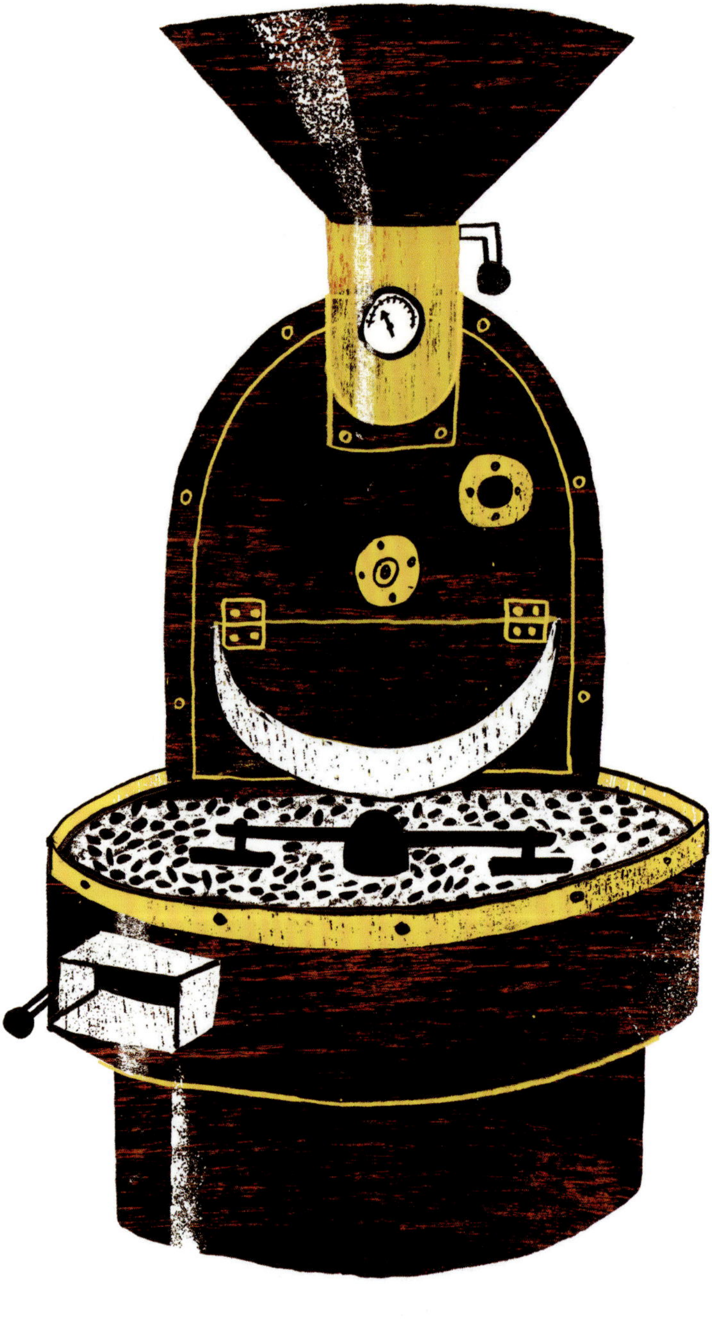

principle: a big rotating metal drum that has heat applied to the outside, often from below, much like a spit roast, and with air flowing through the drum to remove unwanted roasting fumes. Depending on the system, the operator can vary many elements of the process. Air speed, heat application, and drum speed can all be adjusted. Roasted coffee consists of several hundred flavour compounds and it is astonishing how even small changes in the roasting process can affect the flavour of the coffee. The other prevalently used roasting process is fluid air roasting, in which the coffee is suspended and roasted on a bed of hot air.

Dry aroma | TASTING

Dry aroma refers to the aroma given off by the coffee when it is ground but before any water is added (at which point we smell the wet aroma). The coffee releases distinct aroma experiences at each point. You may often have heard people say, "I love the smell of coffee but not the taste". Of course, we do not know whether an individual has tasted a wide range of coffees and finds all tastes undesirable and all dry aromas preferable, or whether their opinion derives from an altercation with a dark-roast commercial coffee that smelt rich and chocolaty but tasted like ash, earth, and batteries. Either way, there is a huge difference between the dry aroma and the experience of the beverage itself.

Dry distillates | TASTING

Coffee is made up of all sorts of compounds. It is quite common to break these compounds up into flavour groups – fruit acids, aromatics, sugar browning, and dry distillates. The term "dry distillates" is, in essence, a fancy name for woody, smoky, or burnt flavour groups that are the by-products of high-temperature processes. Interestingly, most of these are heavy compounds and it means that they are a little harder to get out of the coffee than the fruity and aromatic flavours. This is why a coffee that is brewed too hot or for too long, or with too fine a grind will display more of these heavy and potentially harsh flavours.

E

Ecuador | ORIGIN

SEE ALSO
Vietnam *p231*

This country falls into the "full of potential" category. A great coffee from Ecuador can be complex and sweet, with sought-after fruit notes, a medium body, and a pleasing and unique acidity. These coffees are becoming more likely, but they are still few and far between. Investment from the speciality sector is proving that great coffees are hiding in the country and are worth seeking out. Internally, instant coffee is most popular and, due to costs, is mainly imported coffee from Vietnam. Coffee production has been steadily growing in Ecuador and the multiple microclimates provide varying opportunities for exceptional coffee.

El Salvador | ORIGIN

SEE ALSO
Bourbon *p35*
Pacamara *p169*

Back in the late 1970s El Salvador was the third largest coffee-producing country in the entire world – quite something for the smallest country in Central America. It accounted for almost 50 per cent of the country's export revenues. Then came civil war and land reforms, and coffee production has never hit those kind of heights again. Coffee now accounts for around 3.5 per cent of the country's exports. Owing to economic, political, and agricultural factors, El Salvador is moving towards being a more speciality-

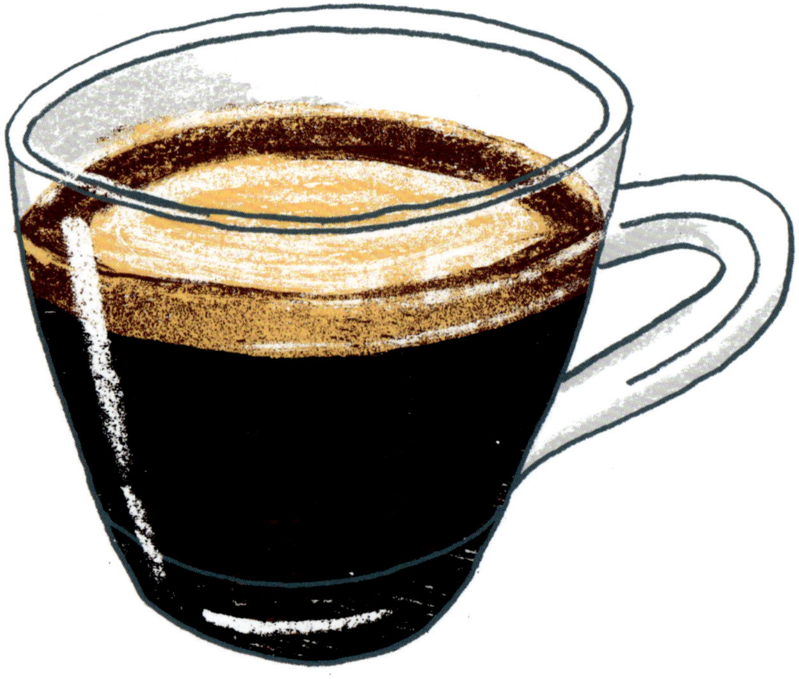

focused producing country, focusing on the higher-altitude growing regions and boutique productions. On my visits to the country, even with various problematic factors affecting coffee production, I have found very passionate farmers who are excited by their coffee, engaging in experimental processing, and setting up varietal gardens. The country is probably best known for washed-process Bourbon varieties. Forward-thinking El Salvadorian producers have developed and introduced unique varieties to the coffee world, such as the Pacamara variety. This large bean is a cross between the elephant Maragogype variety and the Pacas variety. Good El Salvadorian coffee often has a sweet chocolate body, combined with berry-like acidity.

SEE ALSO
Crema *p63*
Pressure *p179*
Strength *p206*

Espresso | BREWING; DRINK TYPE

The espresso – where to start? Espresso is iconic. It is essentially an intense, highly concentrated coffee beverage of a short measure. It is brewed under pressure, which creates a layer of foam on the surface of the drink, called the "crema". It is also the driving force behind the modern coffee shop phenomenon that has spread around the world. Espresso is finicky and hard to make well, which is surely where a lot of its romance and intrigue come from. Italy can lay claim to the invention of the espresso machine and for many years largely defined what a good espresso was. Back in the day, and in many cases to this day, espresso quality was defined by specific strict criteria, such as the visual appearance of the crema, the "correct" brew time of 25 seconds, and the "correct" volume of liquid. This narrow definition has been broadened in recent years upon the realization that to optimize a coffee's quality as espresso the rules may need to bend and move to suit the coffee. This is undoubtedly positive, but there is also the question, then, of when coffee is *not* espresso. You can achieve amazing results by brewing a very long filter-like coffee through an espresso machine. For me, espresso has to be a concentrate. Below 7 per cent strength I think it starts to become something else – it may well be great, but it is just not espresso.

Ethiopia | ORIGIN

Ethiopia is often rightly heralded as the birthplace of coffee. Technically, there is dispute as to where Arabica really originates. Ethiopia and Yemen are the two hot contenders, but it is Ethiopia that is home to the most incredibly diverse natural array of Arabica varieties. The Ethiopian Highlands offer the perfect habitat for Arabica to flourish. So much so that these highlands house nearly all of the world's diversity of Arabica varieties. Due to this, Ethiopia has the potential to produce a wide range of characteristics and flavour profiles. Most coffee in Ethiopia is not grown in the farm-like situations typical of the Americas. Instead, the coffee is cooperatively grown. Many smallholders, sometimes hundreds, will mix their small lots together and deposit them at a central processing mill. It is naturally more difficult to achieve traceability under these circumstances. You may buy a coffee from a mill in Ethiopia and then buy what appears to be the same coffee. However, different lots pass through the mill at different times, so any coffee will be dependent upon which parts of the cooperative are harvesting at any particular time. Washed coffees from the Yirgacheffe region

SEE ALSO
Terroir p214
Variety p228

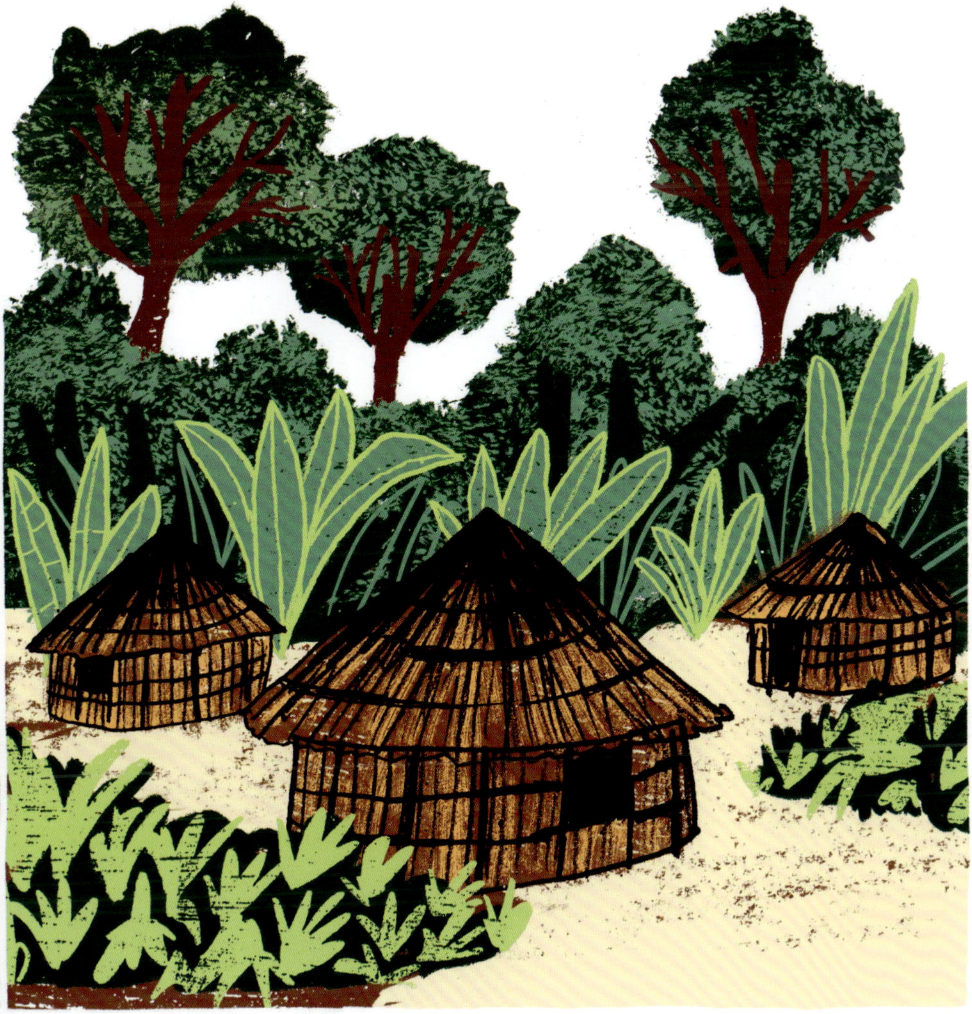

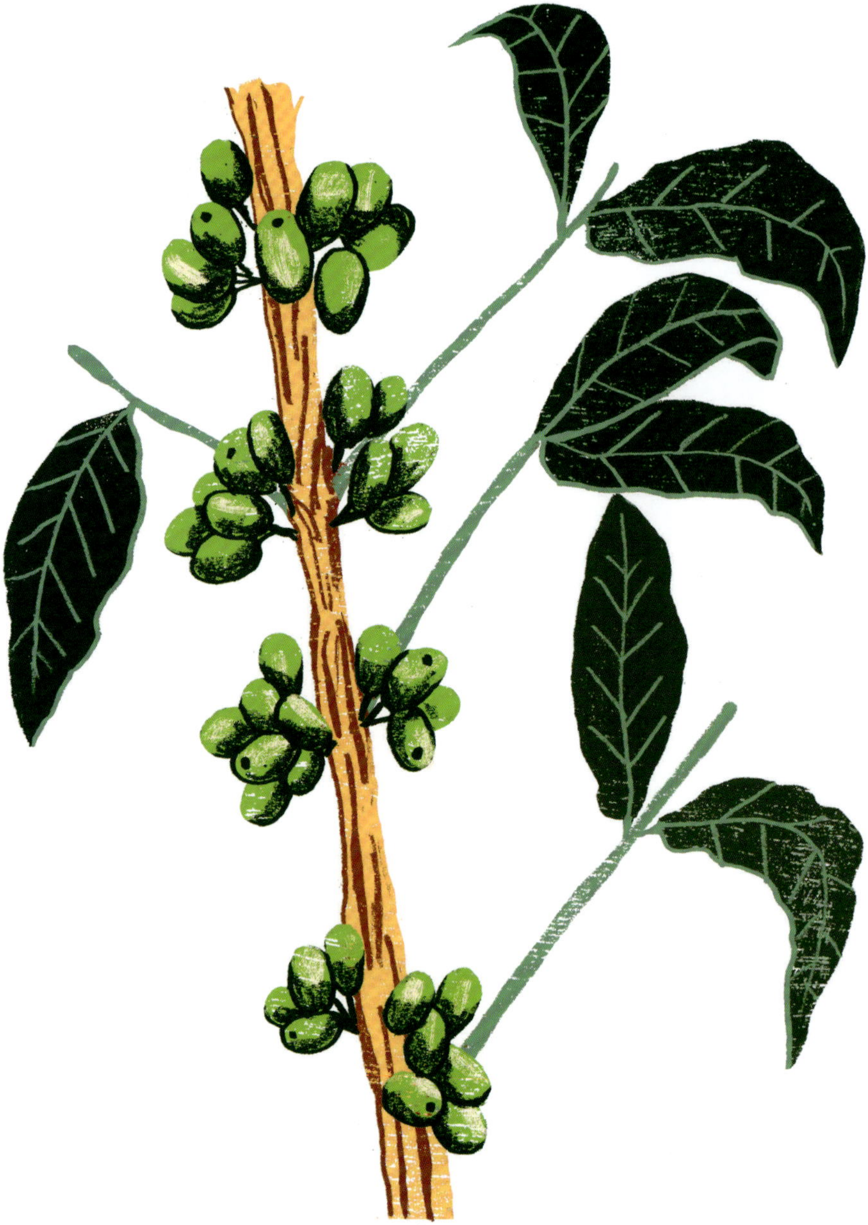

can be intensely floral and aromatic with tea- and citrus-like notes. A western Ethiopian washed coffee can be more densely floral and fuller bodied. In stark contrast, natural coffee from Sidamo and Harar can be bold, chocolaty, and chock-full of ripe fruit.

Eugenioides | SPECIES

Robusta may be known as the commercial and inferior relative of Arabica, but without it we would not have Arabica at all. Robusta is actually the parent plant of Arabica, and the species Robusta coupled with to produce Arabica is called *Coffea eugenioides*. This species is barely propagated for coffee drinking at all and has come into the spotlight only recently. Colombian producer Camilio Marisande has been experimenting with unique and rare varieties in recent years. The Sudan Rume that he produced with Saša Šestić for the World Barista Championship win was grown at Finca Las Nubes in Colombia. A few miles down the road on the small plots at Finca Inmaculada, Eugenioides is being grown, and with great success. Geoff Watts of Intelligentsia Coffee presented the coffee on a blind table to US Brewers Cup champion Sarah Anderson. Sarah chose the truly unique coffee to take to the world championships where she finished fifth in 2015. I was lucky enough to taste this coffee in Gothenburg at the competition. It is very unusual. The typical citric acidity you would expect in high-quality Arabica crops is almost not there at all. In its place is a lot of sweetness, so that it is almost sugary. The cup displays cereal-like qualities and is also described as being tea-like.

SEE ALSO
Arabica *p18*
El Salvador *p77*
Species *p202*
World Barista Championship *p239*

SEE ALSO
Barista *p23*
Espresso *p79*
Third Wave *p218*

Europe | COFFEE CULTURE

The history of coffee in Europe is rich and diverse. There is, of course, Italy and the espresso – a quick shot at the bar and on with the day – but there is an amazing coffee-house culture all over the continent. Long-held traditions persist. Generally, coffee shops open later in the day and all manner of sweet things accompany the coffee, each iconic in its own way. There is a wonderful variety of environments and atmospheres – from the ornate and grand to the tiny and cosy. You could indulge in a slice of Sachertorte in a grand Viennese café, or you may find yourself on a wicker chair on the pavement in Paris, drinking a black coffee and watching people go by. Interestingly, the so-called "third wave" movement is less ubiquitous in Europe, or at least it was until recently. Speciality coffee scenes full of passion have popped up all over Europe, often in major cities. It is intriguing to see how non-speciality areas of the world actually provide dynamic and enthusiastic speciality scenes, as a new-found interest in coffee drums up excitement.

SEE ALSO
Barista *p23*
Ethiopia *p80*

Evenness | HARVESTING; ROASTING; BREWING

The concept of evenness can be applied at many points throughout the coffee seed-to-cup journey. For the craft of the barista, and in coffee preparation in general, evenness is paramount. A more even grind, a more even distribution of coffee, a more even application of water, and so on, are all generally considered to be the goal. The same, however, also goes for roasting – the even roasting of the bean – and for harvesting, where grading is to a large degree dictated by the even sizing and shape of the raw seed.

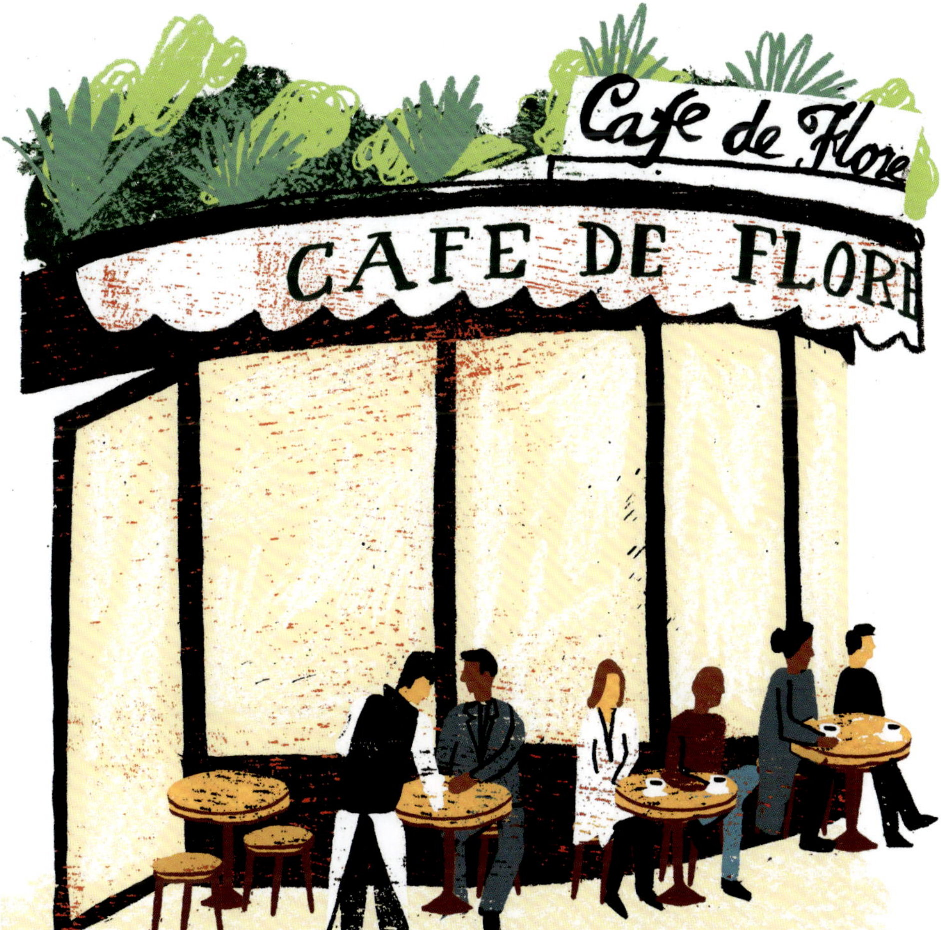
Cafe de Flore
CAFE DE FLORE

While there is definitely a correlation between quality and different forms of evenness, this does not always hold true. In 2015, World Brewers Cup champion Odd-Steinar Tøllefsen won on the back of a coffee that was intentionally dried unevenly to accentuate the character of the coffee. This coffee was a natural-processed coffee from Ethiopia called Semeon Abbay Nikisse, named after the maker who oversaw the processing, Semeon Abbay.

Extraction | BREWING

To extract is to "remove or take out, especially by effort or force". The principles of extraction are really the core concept of any brewing method or coffee-making process. Boil it right down and all cups of coffee are about using some water to take some flavour out of some ground coffee beans. It is the surprising complexity of this process that gives us so much of the intrigue as well as the frustration of making coffee. You could be forgiven for thinking that you make stronger or weaker coffee by extracting more or less from the ground coffee. The problem with this approach is that different compounds extract at different rates, so that extracting less or more from coffee results in different flavours. Sharper, acidic, fruity flavours tend to come out first, followed by the deep, heavier ones and, lastly, the woody, bitter notes. A well-extracted cup of coffee has a balance of these. The coffee industry utilizes a fancy bit of technology called a refractometer to measure the strength of the coffee and to speculate on the level of extraction. Unfortunately, the numbers provided by this machine are not the whole picture, as the evenness of grind, the pressure of water, the temperature, and other variables all affect

SEE ALSO
Refractometer *p189*

the type of extraction and how desirable it is. The optimum extraction that often gets cited is 20 per cent. This means that 20 per cent of the coffee was taken by the water, and the rest was chucked onto the compost heap. Quality of extraction is still ultimately decided upon by taste so this percentage can vary, but it is a useful marker all the same. The instant coffee world pushes extraction to the maximum through super-heating and multi-brewing. This allows for extraction levels of up to 60 per cent, making the instant coffee process the most efficient preparation method in the world, just not necessarily the most desirable.

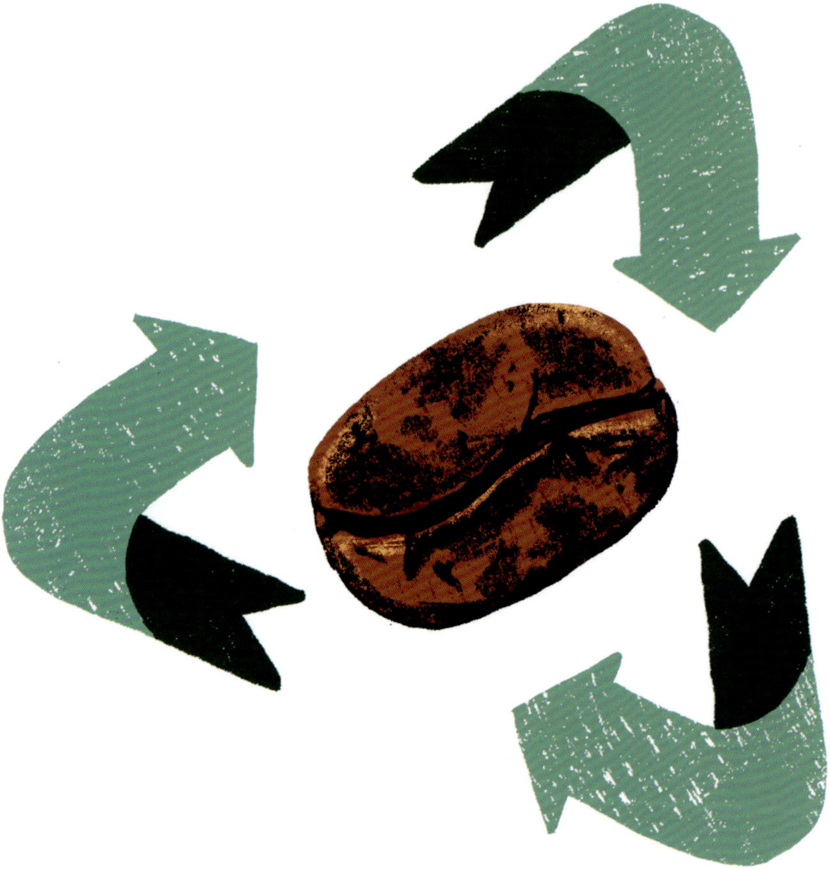

F

SEE ALSO
C market *p41*
Third wave *p218*

Fairtrade | CERTIFICATION

It is curious to note that the Fairtrade certificate is barely seen in the speciality coffee sector and the "third wave" shops and roasters around the world. This is really because Fairtrade was designed to safeguard growers against the whims of the commercial C market. In the speciality sector, where cup quality can offer prices over double that of the market price, Fairtrade makes less sense. This said, the certificate has its pros and cons in the commercial sector. The main tenet works in as much as Fairtrade producers will always get a price that at least meets the cost of production. The C market swings, so at certain times the market price can make coffee not worth growing at all. A study has shown that in certain areas Fairtrade deals can be arranged when the market is low and the growers then miss out on the high prices when the market takes an upward turn. It is a complex issue, but the goals of Fairtrade should be supported as it is a programme capable of making a real difference in the sphere of commodity coffee. Interestingly, in 2011 there was a split between Fairtrade International and Fair Trade USA, stemming from a difference in belief about whether to work with larger organizations or to work only with smaller cooperative farming groups.

SEE ALSO
Carbonic maceration *p47*
Natural process *p156*

Fermentation | PROCESSING

Fermentation has been used by humans since the Neolithic age to produce all manner of boozy beverages and pickles. Fermentation is defined as a metabolic process that turns sugars into acids, gases, or alcohol. It is often used broadly to describe the growth of micro-organisms. This is all extremely interesting because it can dramatically impact taste. Changes in temperature, time, sugar, and the type of bacteria will create different results. Coffee producers are always playing around with exactly how we ferment coffee during processing, as well as looking for a better understanding of existing processes and environments. Fermentation processes have the potential to have a positive impact on a cup, adding to its winey acidity and perceived body or sweetness. It also has the potential to detract from the coffee's character and quality should fermentation go too far.

SEE ALSO
Nordic *p159*
Third place *p217*

Fika | COFFEE CULTURE

This Swedish term for "coffee and cake" can be likened to the concept of a coffee break or afternoon tea, but is in fact rather unique to Swedish culture (though there is something similar in Finland, too). This daily ritual is often specifically important in the workplace where crucial social interaction takes place over a good cup of coffee and some form of baked goods. Cinnamon buns, sometimes even referred to as *fikabröd* ("*fika* bread"), are a particularly popular accompaniment. Although the origins of *fika* are rooted in coffee, today other beverages such as tea and juice have crept into the mix.

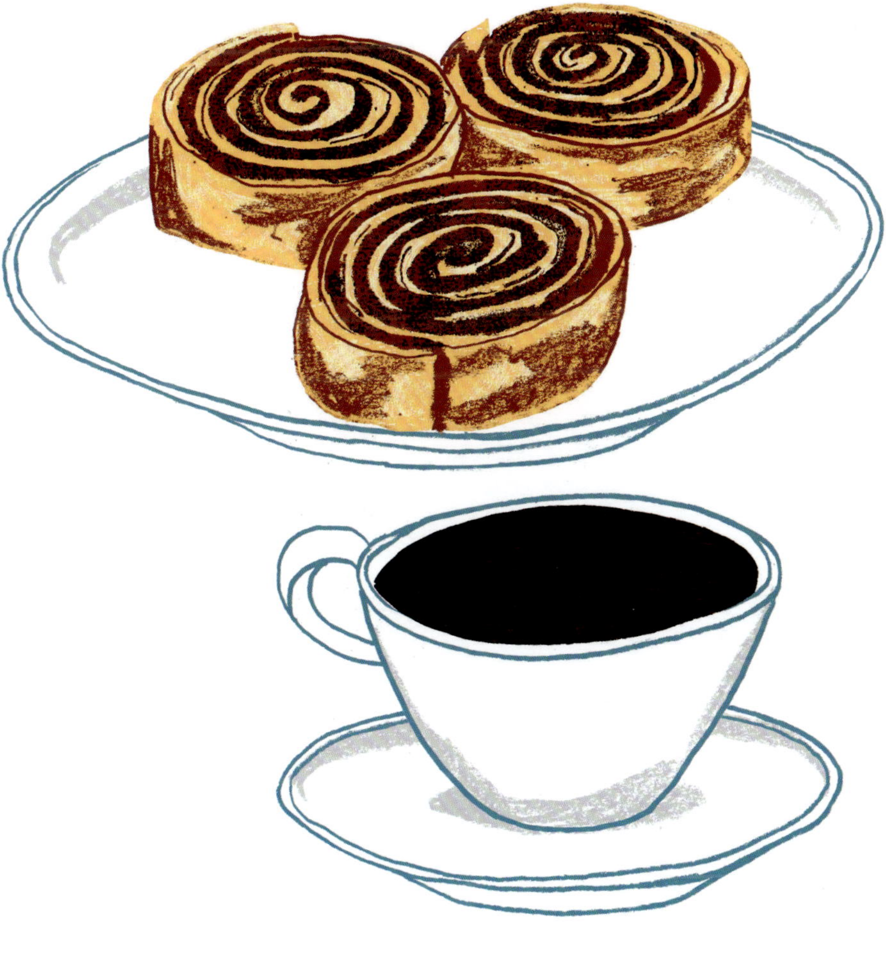

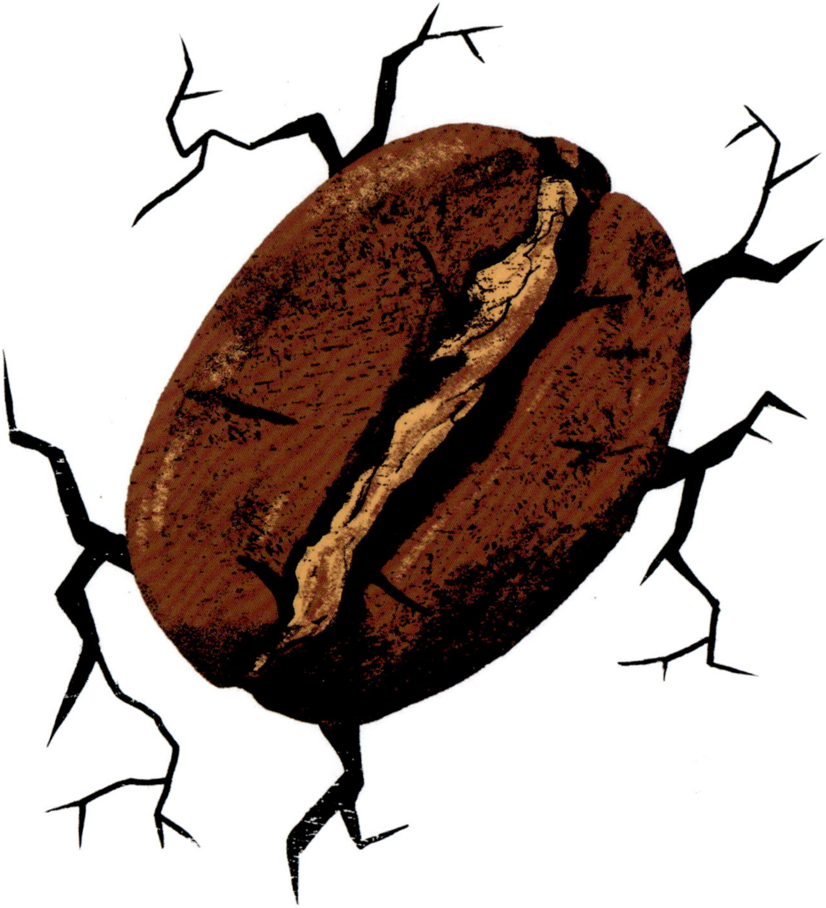

Filter

See "Chemex".

Fines

See "Grinding".

First crack | ROASTING

Roasting is full of interesting processes and sensory stimuli – the smells, the sounds, the tumbling visuals, the heat. One of the most notable experiences for the newly initiated is the audible cue of first crack. It is often likened to the popping of corn, although I would say that the first crack is more of a snapping sound than a pop. The name is linked to the physical process the bean is going through: it is cracking open and almost doubling in size, as the moisture in the coffee bean makes its escape. At this point it is a light brown and is releasing energy rather than taking it on. There is also a second crack that signals the build-up of gases in the coffee; this is when the coffee bean begins to break down and gets oily and dark.

Flat burr | GRINDING

Grinding coffee from whole beans into ground coffee can be achieved in a number of ways with various pieces of equipment. The flat burr and conical designs are the two predominant. Both styles are based on a system of two parts that are moved closer together or further apart to alter the space through which the coffee beans pass, crushing them as they do so. In terms of the flat burr, grinds inevitably vary wildly across different manufacturers, based on an

SEE ALSO
Development *p71*

SEE ALSO
Roller grinder *p193*

amazing variety of details such as rotations per minute (rpm), delivery of beans, and the material and diameter as well as the particular cut of the burr. All burr grinders are a massive improvement on the simple blade grinder, which hacks at the coffee like a juicing blender and gives a really inconsistent grind. Other grinding techniques are out there such as air grinding and roller grinding, but these involve expensive equipment. Grinding has an incredible impact on how good a cup of coffee is. More and more research is going into grinding in terms of our understanding of it and the equipment we use.

Flat white | DRINK TYPE

Who invented the flat white? We won't ever get a clear answer to that, but it was definitely somewhere Down Under. Next question: what exactly *is* a flat white? Well, it has espresso and steamed milk and is relatively strong. The specifics vary, a problem you will come across with all familiar drink types. They are interpreted in a variety of ways and these varying interpretations then become gospel, at least for a particular group of experts or aficionados. The definition of the flat white I am most familiar with is a double espresso shot with relatively flatly steamed milk poured into a 6oz cup. Traditionally, the cappuccino was a relatively small, strong, steamed milk drink, but over many years it has evolved to be larger and larger, so that in many countries it has become synonymous with a frothier latte. The flat white's success relies on its strength, and it has become commonplace in many coffee shops around the globe, as drinkers rebel against the increasingly oversized drinks that dominate the market and take more interest in the coffee itself.

SEE ALSO
Espresso *p79*

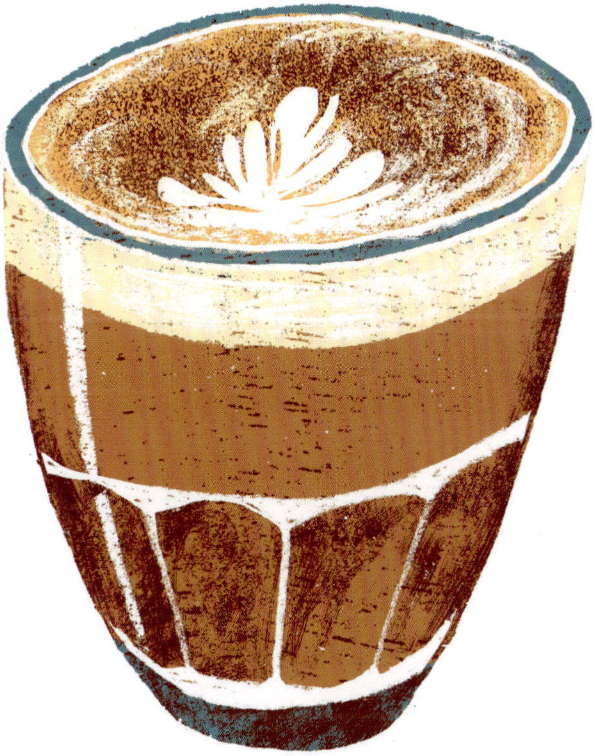

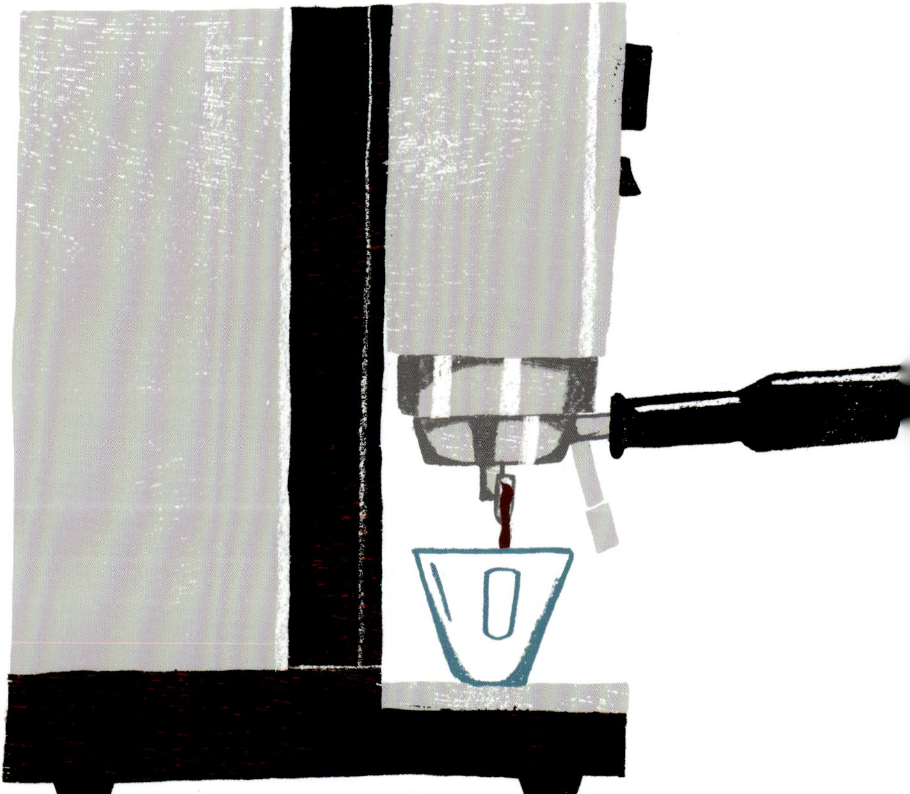

SEE ALSO
Body *p31*

Flavour notes | TASTING

A list of descriptive flavour notes, whether on a label or spoken about during a discussion, can be a little bit scary. Firstly, tasting something and being able to describe it analytically is both difficult and requires specific experience. Secondly, there is no such thing as perfect flavour notes; even though they are often presented in a factual way, they are in reality highly subjective. Certain elements of a coffee are easier to spot objectively and agree on, such as body, mouth feel, and overall style. We can, for example, quite easily concur whether a coffee is light and aromatic or full-bodied and sweet. Like all taste-based disciplines, experience is the real key. Tasting lots of coffee and beginning to grasp the range of flavours possible and to link words and language to those flavour experiences will increase your ability to notice and describe flavour notes. It is really useful to talk about flavour, to discuss it with others and to build reference points, and it can be really fun and interesting as well. There is a speciality coffee flavour wheel (updated in 2016) that outlines the industry language for both negative and positive coffee flavours. A pre-set language is very valuable for a global community so that it can find common ground.

SEE ALSO
Flat burr *p93*
Full immersion *p103*

Flow rate | BREWING

Flow rate is often discussed in relation to time – quite simply, the time it takes for the water to pass through the coffee and into the cup. The only method of brewing coffee when you would not reference flow rate would be a full-immersion method. In these instances we would still be interested in measuring time, but it would be in

F

97

terms of "steep time" – how long the coffee and water sit together before the brew is finished. It is arguable that flow rate has most impact with espresso. This is because flow in espresso is directly linked to grind. If the coffee is ground finer, it will be trickier for the water to pass through it and the flow rate will slow down. Conversely, as the grind gets coarser, there is more room between the particles and the flow rate will speed up. Grind also affects flow rate in pour-over filter methods. Like all the variables in brewing coffee, we have to consider flow rate as part of a bigger equation and it is difficult to offer up hard-and-fast rules. You may hear that a perfect espresso has a flow rate of 25 seconds. This just does not hold up: depending on the coffee and the grinder, as well as the recipe, flow rate can range dramatically if optimal results are to be achieved.

Flower

See "Blossom".

Freezing | STORAGE

"Stick your coffee in the freezer" is a common bit of kitchen advice offered to prolong the quality of your coffee for as long as possible. It turns out that this advice has legs. Freezing is used to preserve many different food types. There is a question over whether the freezing and expansion of water content in the coffee can damage it. The answer is "possibly". As the water in any foodstuff freezes, cell walls get ruptured; you see this most dramatically in fruits and vegetables with high water content, like tomatoes, which defrost into a mushy state. Green coffee has around an 11 per cent moisture

SEE ALSO
Extraction *p86*
Flat burr *p93*
Grinding *p109*

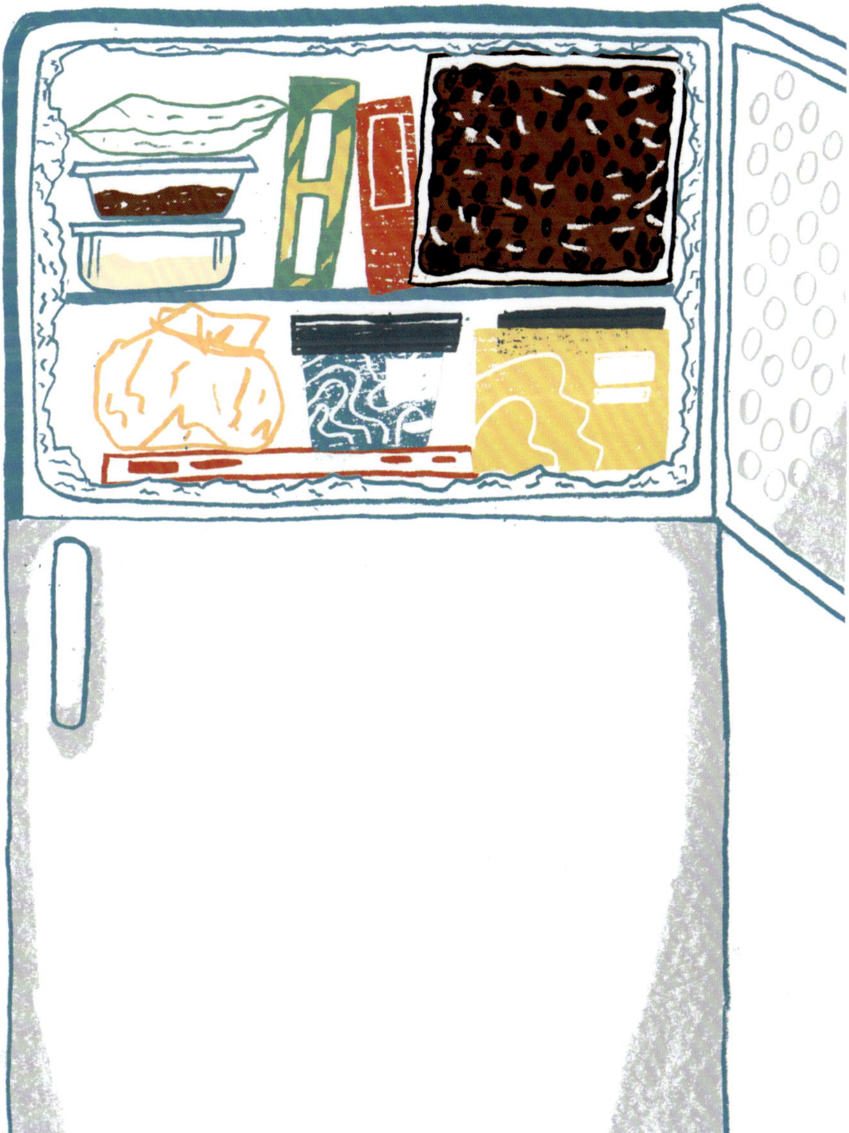

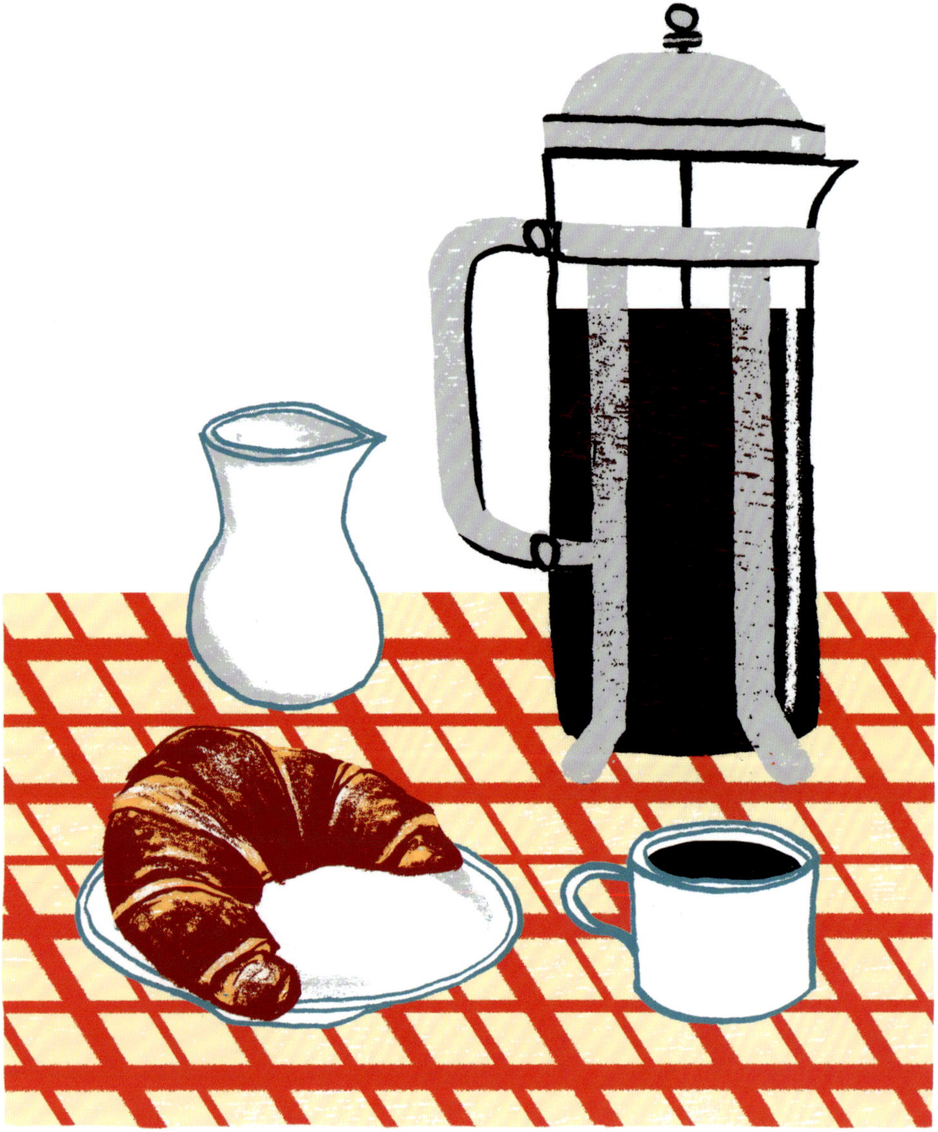

content, which makes this less of an issue. (Compare that to the 94 per cent water content in the tomato.) Roasted coffee has even less moisture and there would be almost no difficulty with frozen water content. Storing green coffee frozen has proved very successful in preventing it from tasting at all "agey", and it also introduces the idea of vintages, which up until now has been non-existent in coffee due to its perishability. A recent academic study also showed that frozen roasted coffee beans are more brittle and that beans grind differently depending on their temperature. This solves the mystery of why coffee flows differently throughout the day in coffee shops as they get busier and equipment changes temperature. Frozen beans also retain more volatile aromatics, which can lead to a better-tasting coffee. The key, however, is to freeze the coffee in a sealed bag with as little oxygen as possible and to grind immediately (while still frozen) before the beans attract moisture.

French press | BREWING

The French press, also known as a cafetière or plunger, is a classic and widely used brewer. In essence, the method is a jug in which you steep the coffee in the water before pressing down a metal-mesh filter that pushes much of the crust and sediment to the bottom of the jug before decanting. The mesh filter is pretty coarse and this means that the resulting coffee often contains a fair amount of sediment, so a bold, full-flavoured cup is produced. A hot tip if you are less keen on sediment is to scoop the crust off the surface of the coffee just before you plunge. Another thing to be aware of is the coffee settling early in the brew, therefore not allowing the

SEE ALSO
Full immersion *p103*

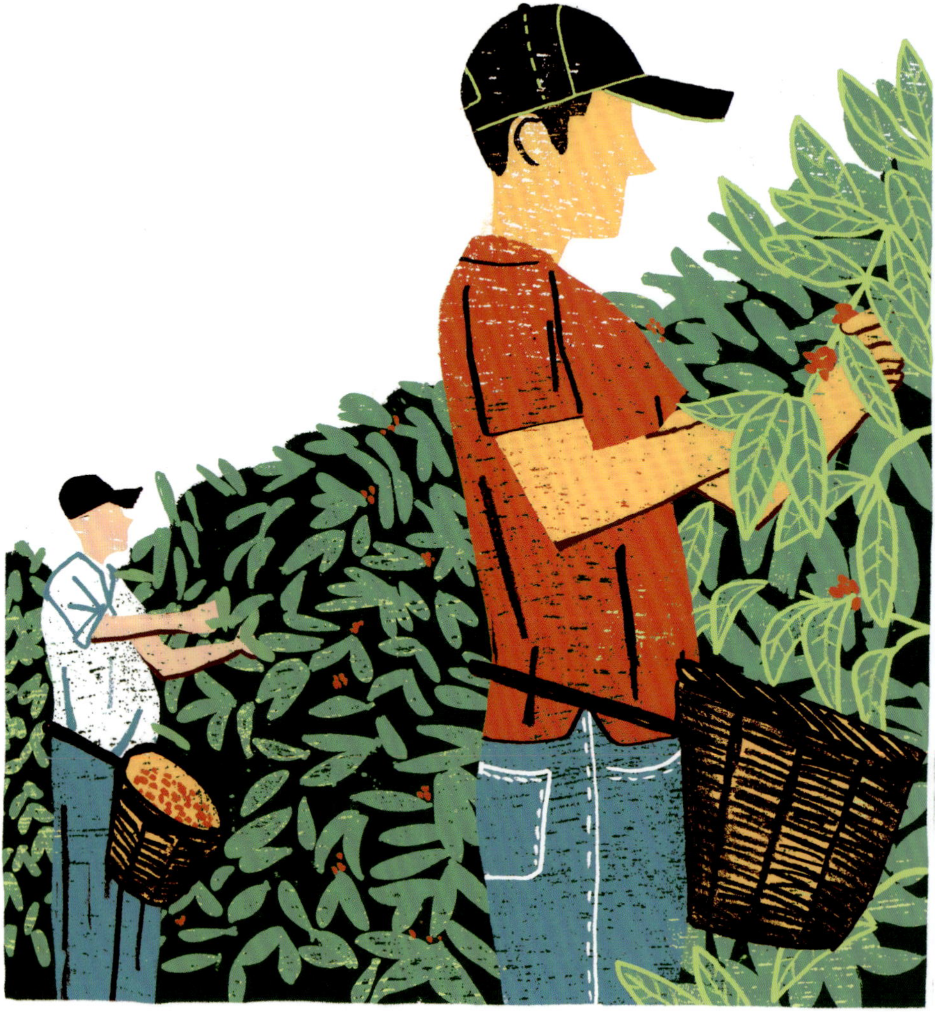

water to access it all. Simply give the solution a stir midway through the brew to avoid this. Though I always scoop off the crust, I am a big fan of the French press for its simplicity and the ease with which a great cup can be brewed.

Fresh crop | HARVESTING

SEE ALSO
Colombia *p60*
Kenya *p135*
Past crop *p172*

Coffee harvesting is essentially a fruit harvest. And, like all fruit, there is a flowering phase followed by a fruiting phase, which means that harvests come and go depending on the climate and the time of the year. The plant flowers following the rainy season and then begins to produce fruit. In high-grade coffees, the fruit typically takes nine months to ripen before it is ready to pick. Harvesting time can be a brief, strictly demarcated time in some countries but can stretch out for months in others. Countries like Kenya and Colombia typically produce a main harvest and a smaller "fly" harvest that comes later. Most coffee is still handpicked, and farms need more workers at harvesting time. The different harvesting times that occur either side of the Equator dictate speciality coffee consumption patterns, as roasters and drinkers move with the fresh harvests to get the best possible flavours.

Full immersion | BREWING

SEE ALSO
Aeropress™ *p13*
Cupping *p64*
French press *p101*

There are many different filter-brewing methods, enough to fill all the cupboards in your kitchen with equipment, and each has its own unique point of difference. Broadly, however, they can all be grouped under two headings: "full immersion" and "pour-over". In the first, the water and the coffee sit together and "steep"; and in the second, the water passes through a bed of coffee. In the first, all the water and coffee are together for the duration of the brew, whereas in the second, the water is effectively split up, each bit spending time with the coffee during different parts of the extraction. It is a pet peeve of mine how often the varying filtration methods get focused on. I think that, if any method is managed well and understood, it can produce a wonderful cup, and that it is the origin, roast, and water that determine quality more than the method. Having said that, there are differences to be noted between the various methods. Aspects of the method's design, such as the filtration barrier (paper or metal mesh) or the mechanics of decanting, will have an impact on the resulting cup of coffee. Take a French press, for example: there is a tendency for the ground coffee to settle at the bottom and not be used properly by the water. In the case of the Aeropress™, the water has to pass through the coffee to exit, so this is not a problem. It is also worth noting that full-immersion methods, although arguably more consistent than pour-overs, produce slightly less coffee, as you lose a small amount of the brew in the grounds at the end.

G

Gear | BREWING

A fetish for, and fascination with, equipment is prevalent in many areas of life. The term "gearhead" may come from the world of cars, but coffee brewing, and especially the making of espresso, have their own legions of gearheads. Jump onto an online coffee forum and take a look. There is a host of beautiful equipment and curious tools to discover, and there are vexed issues to become embroiled with, whether it is the motor speeds of grinders, or the use of flow restrictors or shower screens. Gear in coffee ranges from the classic and rudimentary to the super hi-tech and cutting edge. As we learn to value quality in coffee ever more, very small differences in variables become meaningful. I often compare it to Formula 1. Half a second is nothing in an ordinary day, but it is quite a different matter on the racetrack.

Geisha | VARIETY

No relation to the traditional Japanese hostess, the Geisha variety is actually named after a town in Ethiopia around which the variety is widely grown. Although cultivated in other countries, it was the introduction of Geisha to Panama in the 1960s that began its real journey to the top of the tree. This elegant, long-leafed plant

SEE ALSO
Ethiopia *p80*
Panama *p169*
Variety *p228*

is low-yielding and needs the right conditions to really shine. The cup profile is often more comparable to great Ethiopian coffee than to American lots. A great Geisha is immensely aromatic, with layers of floral notes and balanced juicy sweet acidity. Geishas have been grown in other countries with varying success. The top Geisha lots come at a premium price and repeatedly sell for more than any other coffee variety in the world. There is some contention around the success of Geisha, with the feeling that one coffee should not get so much of the limelight and that context is required for the quality to be understood. There is some truth in this, but I never fail to be blown away by a top Geisha. They are some of the most magical cups of coffee I have had, and at a blind tasting, when a Geisha is on the table, the words "Wow, that one is incredible" will often come to the lips.

God shot | ESPRESSO

"Most shots of espresso are a bit rubbish, but every now and then you strike gold and the coffee is beautiful, and you don't know why." Or so the "God shot" rationale goes. This romantic notion, while delightful, is problematic. On the one hand, it is true that coffee will vary inherently due to its nature as a harvested crop, and because each lot is made up of many individual beans. On the other hand, it is a notion that turns espresso making into something of a dark art, with inconsistency and low quality as more a matter of chance than anything else. The past decade has seen a wave of critical thinking, scientific inquiry, and better technology, and the notion of the god shot has slowly lost ground in favour of a focus on the provenance and flavour of the coffees being brewed rather than on an artisanal

SEE ALSO
Barista *p23*

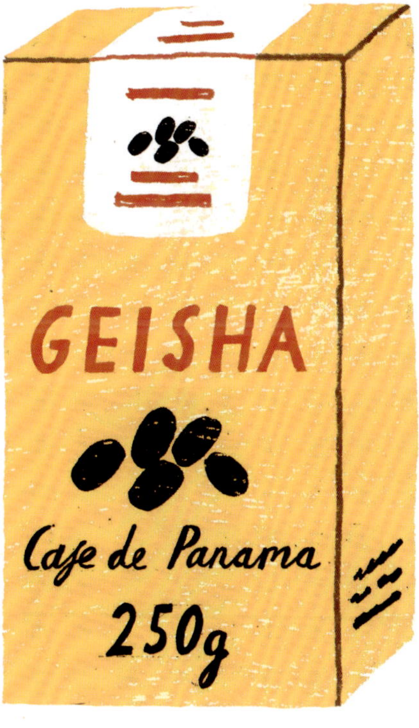
GEISHA
Cafe de Panama
250g

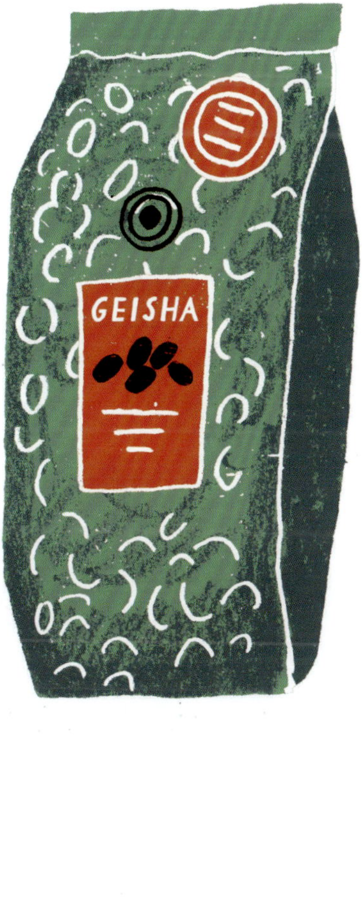
GEISHA

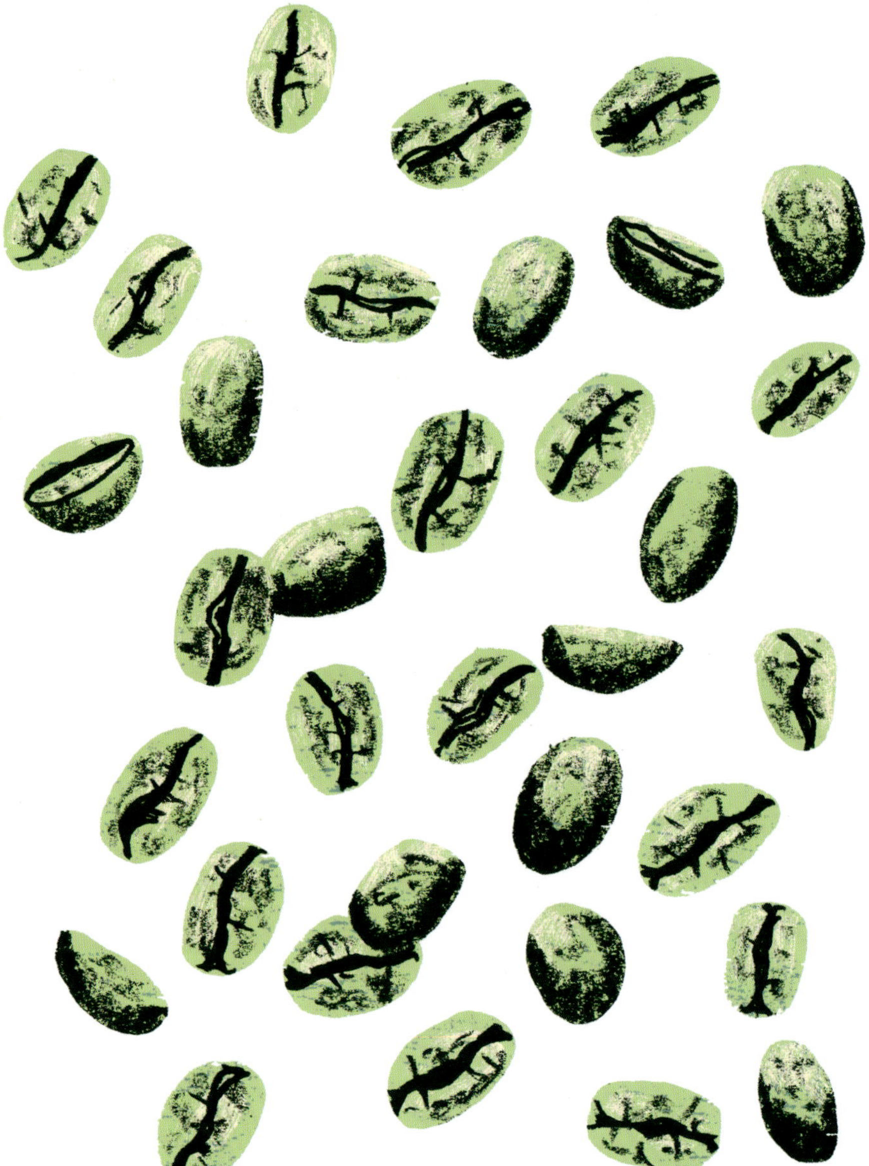

notion of a raw, "feel"-based process. There is some resistance to the introduction of science in coffee and its pursuit of a more consistent, better quality of coffee. Some feel that it takes away what is so special about coffee, and that it de-crafts and disenchants coffee. My response to that would be that we actually increase the potential and romance of coffee if we allow more people to engage with the flavours of great cups of coffee by making more of them.

Green | UNROASTED COFFEE

SEE ALSO
C market *p41*
Freezing *p98*
Silver skin *p198*

"How old is the green?" and "How much did you pay for the green?" are a couple of industry examples of where you may come across the term "green coffee". Mainly, it is a term used in the industry for unroasted coffee, which is how the world trades coffee, though not how we drink it. When coffee is harvested and the cherry and parchment have been removed, we are left with the raw bean. These beans typically have a greenish colour, hence the name. The type of coffee, and especially the processing, can alter the exact hue of the bean, with many appearing more yellowish. What is fascinating is that we often discuss the quality of the green coffee versus the quality of the roast. You could, for example, have great green coffee that is badly roasted or a dodgy green that is very well roasted. It takes a little while to become adept at tasting for these differences.

Grinding | PROCESSING

SEE ALSO
Freezing *p98*

Grinding coffee is simultaneously both very simple and incredibly complex. On the one hand, we are simply crushing coffee up into smaller pieces; on the other, we are creating different distributions of particle sizes and different-shaped pieces of coffee at different temperatures. It is a wonderful example of finding a world in a detail. It is impossible to break coffee up completely uniformly, so all grinds are a mixture of different sizes. By using a hi-tech piece of equipment called a particle analyzer, we can record exactly how many pieces we have of each size and how many different-size pieces there are. The really small pieces are called "fines" while the really big ones (relatively speaking, of course) are "boulders". A fine is defined as a coffee ground smaller than 100 microns. A micron is one-millionth of a metre, which is ridiculously small. For example, the size of a water droplet in a mist is 10 microns and a typical sheet of paper is 100 microns thick. The finer the coffee grounds, the easier it will be for water to dissolve its contents.

Grooming | ESPRESSO

This term refers to the moving around of the grounds in the basket before they are tamped and brewed in the portafilter. The concept behind grooming is to spread the coffee throughout the basket, allowing for a more uniformly distributed bed, which in turn allows the water to more evenly extract from all the coffee. There are varying techniques. For many years, the "stockfleth" was mastered by many a professional barista. In this technique, you effectively use your forefinger and thumb to spin and spread the coffee round. With the "north, east, south, west" method, you use the index finger to move straight atop the coffee in each direction. Both these are less common now. In the world of laying sand and cement, vibration is the most effective levelling technique, and

SEE ALSO
Barista *p23*
Espresso *p79*
Extraction *p86*
Portafilter *p176*
Tamping *p213*
World Barista
  Championship *p239*

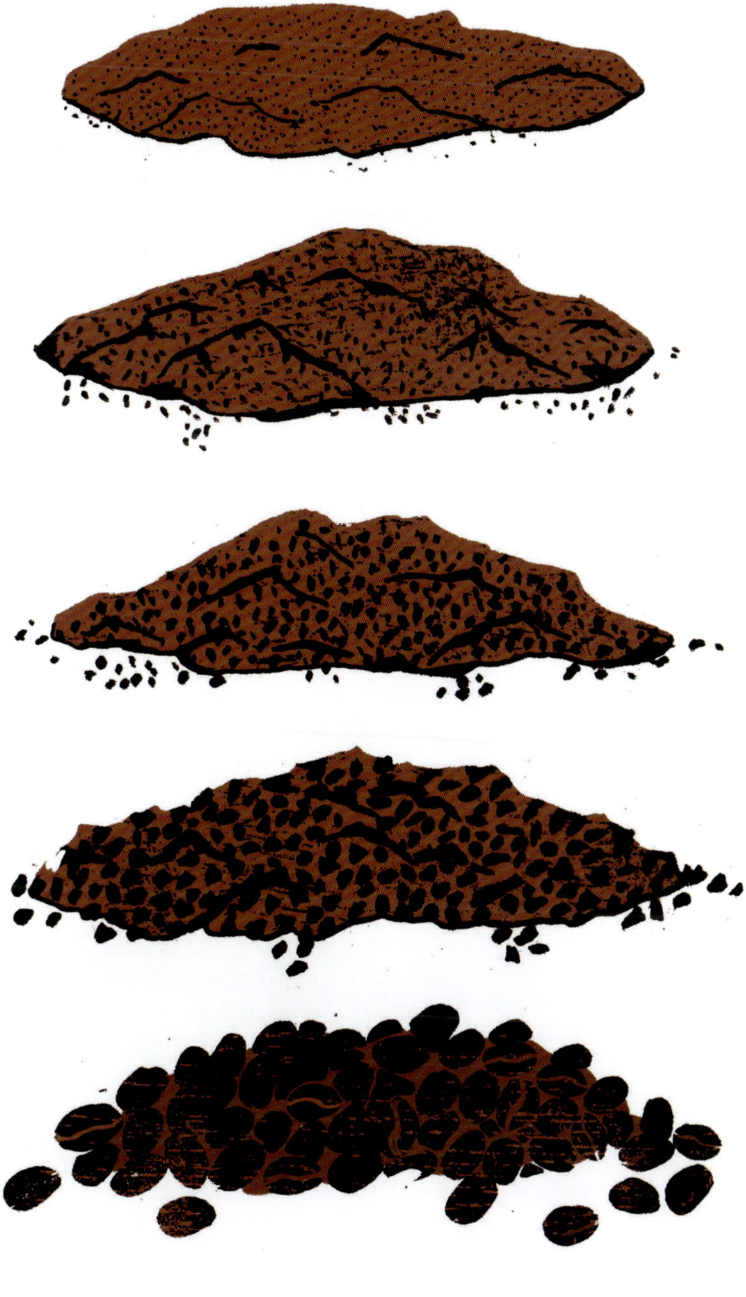

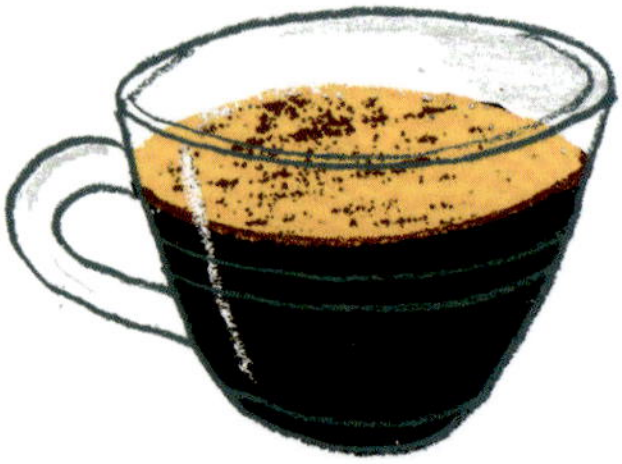

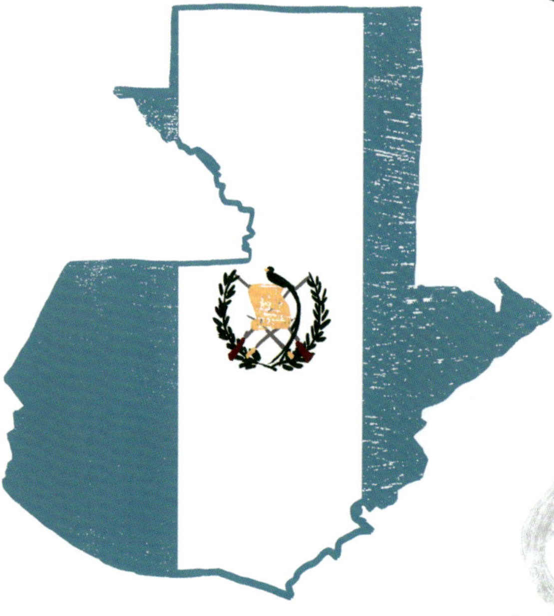

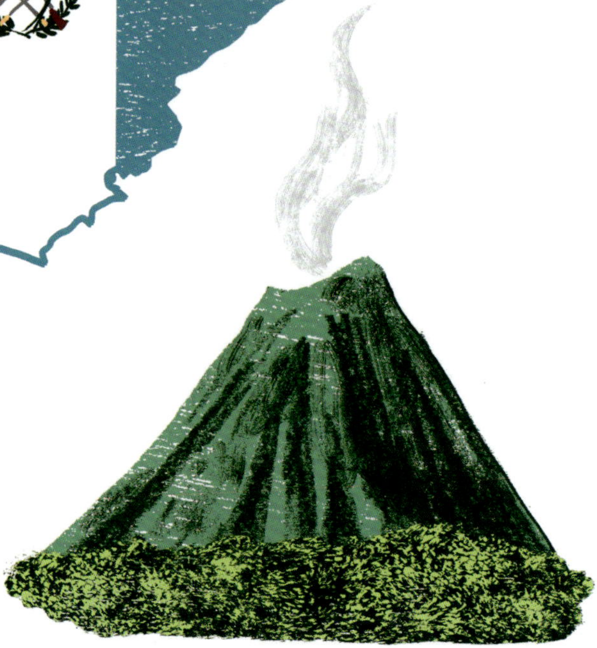

simply tapping the basket horizontally and vertically is very effective. It also neatly avoids the busy barista having a constantly brown finger. Specific tools have also been created. The Ona Coffee Distributor was created by World Barista champion Saša Šestić: you place the tool, which resembles a disc with a propeller-like base, atop the portafilter and spin the device to level the coffee for you.

Guatemala | ORIGIN

Guatemala is a country well known for its quality coffee and is one of Central America's biggest producers. Geographically, it sits at the top of the region, above El Salvador, and, as for most of its neighbours, coffee is a valuable export. Within Guatemala, there are many coffee-producing regions, but the best known is Antigua. This region can produce some stunning cups but, like any long-established growing region, prices tend to be on the high side. Huehuetenango is also seen very often in the speciality sector and some truly excellent coffees are grown there. Great Guatemalan coffees often have a bright and complex juiciness to them with a chocolaty centre. Unfortunately, crops have recently suffered dramatically from leaf rust.

SEE ALSO
Leaf rust *p140*

Gustatory | TASTING

When we eat or drink something we put it in our mouth and taste it. Gustatory is the technical term for this, referring to the experiences in our mouth that relate to taste. It is, however, a joint venture with our nose and in fact most of our ideas about "flavours" actually have more to do with the olfactory system. (You have likely heard of the big five tastes the tongue is responsible for:

SEE ALSO
Body *p31*
Olfactory *p163*
Super taster test *p210*
Umami *p223*

sweet, sour, salt, bitter, and umami. In the past, a "tongue map" was frequently touted showing which part of the tongue was responsible for which taste, but this idea is now much disputed.) The mouth is more responsible, however, for "taste feelings" as opposed to aromas and flavours. Astringency, smoothness, silkiness, and stickiness are all the domain of the gustatory system. A truly exceptional coffee experience engages and excites both the mouth and the nose.

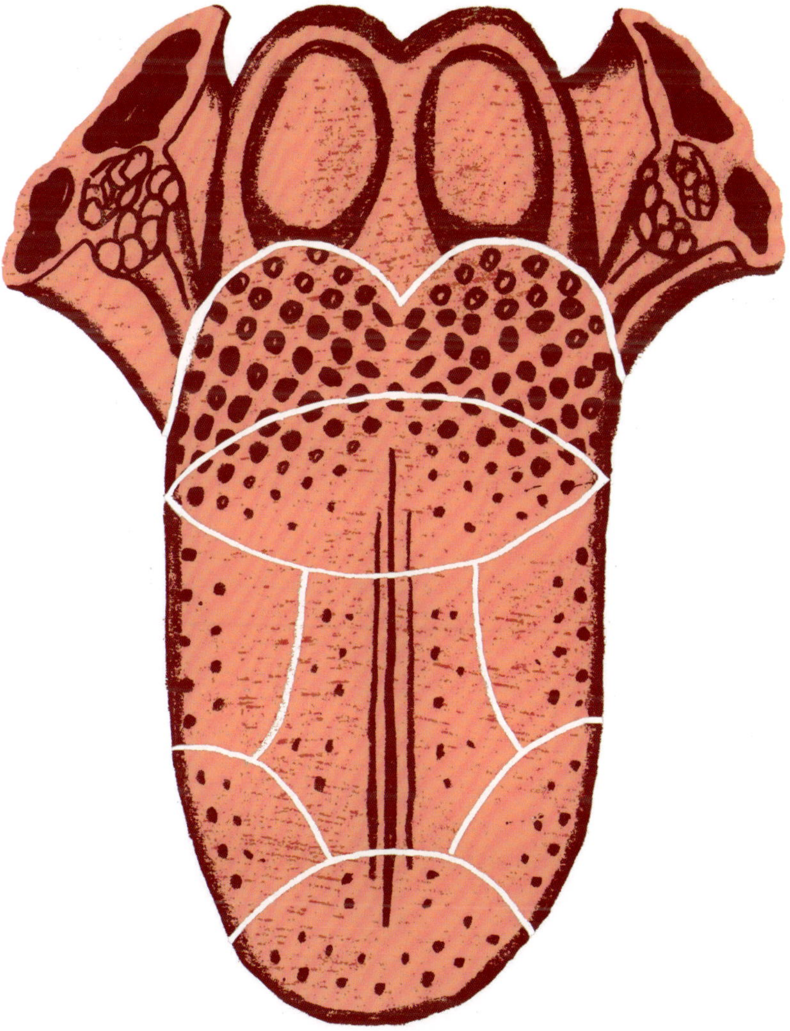

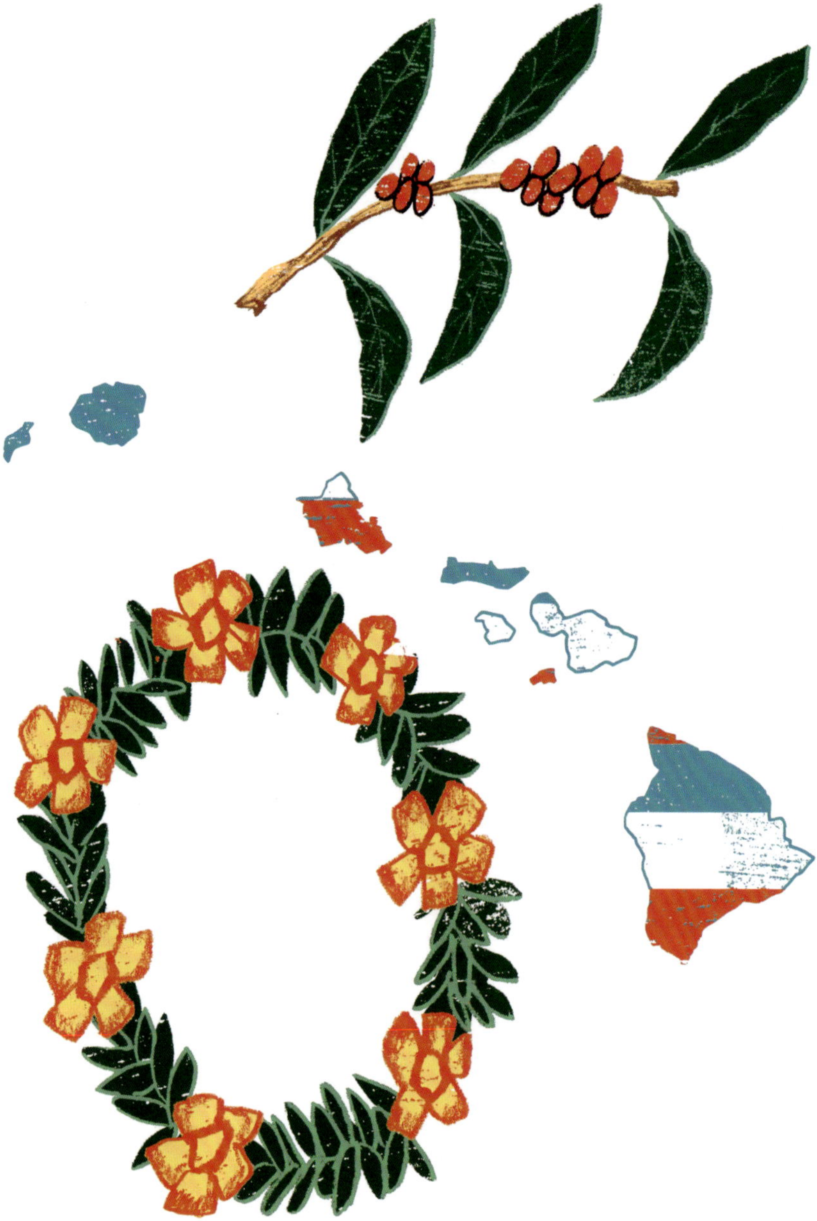

H

SEE ALSO
Brazil *p35*

Hawaii | ORIGIN

Hawaiian Kona is a long-revered name in the world of coffee. You are, however, unlikely to see it in the world of speciality coffee. Hawaii is rare in being a first-world coffee-producing country. This means that the coffee is relatively expensive for the same quality of coffee grown elsewhere, due to significantly higher labour and production costs. These costs mean that Hawaii has had to be pioneering in terms of introducing automated technology, and even the agronomist at Brazil's famous Daterra Estate has made trips to Hawaii in order to observe operations and take away fresh insights. Hawaii offers relatively low altitudes for coffee growing and produces cup profiles that are round, smooth, and complex.

SEE ALSO
Espresso *p79*
Multi boiler *p151*

Heat exchanger | BREWING

Espresso machines tend to heat the brewing water in one of two ways. The options are a thick metal boiler that is heated with an element (the most advanced of these will regulate the temperature to within a degree) or a heat exchanger. In a heat exchanger, a small tube with a very narrow diameter sits inside a hot boiler. When you brew a shot, fresh water is pulled through the tube and the "stretched-out" water is heated almost instantaneously. Heat

H

SEE ALSO
Green *p109*

SEE ALSO
Fermentation *p90*
Natural process *p156*
Silver skin *p198*
Washed process *p235*

exchangers are clever but have a few potential problems. If you are not brewing for a short while, then the water in the heat exchanger can get too hot. Additionally, the heat exchanger will still require a body of very hot water to act as the heat source – if this temperature drops when the machine is receiving heavy use, the brew water will have less heat to draw upon and will drop also. La Spaziale, an Italian espresso manufacturer, has an ingenious patented heat exchanger that uses steam instead of water, thereby providing a more stable heat source.

Honduras | ORIGIN

Coming relatively late to the Central American coffee-growing party, Honduras is now the largest producer of coffee in the region. In my experience, excellent Honduran coffees have outstanding complex (often tropical) fruit and acidity. Green buyers are often wary of coffee from this origin as, although the conditions are excellent for growing coffee, they are not always so good for drying it once the coffee is harvested. This is simply to do with the amount of rainfall. Problematic drying means that a coffee can taste awesome when it is fresh from harvest, but that the flavours quickly fade away. This issue is being heavily focused upon, especially with more coffees being grown for the speciality market. This is an exciting coffee origin.

Honey process | PROCESSING

First of all, there is no honey involved. The name refers instead to the sticky flesh of the coffee cherry called mucilage. When coffee is processed and dried, you can choose to leave all the cherry on (called the natural process) or remove all of

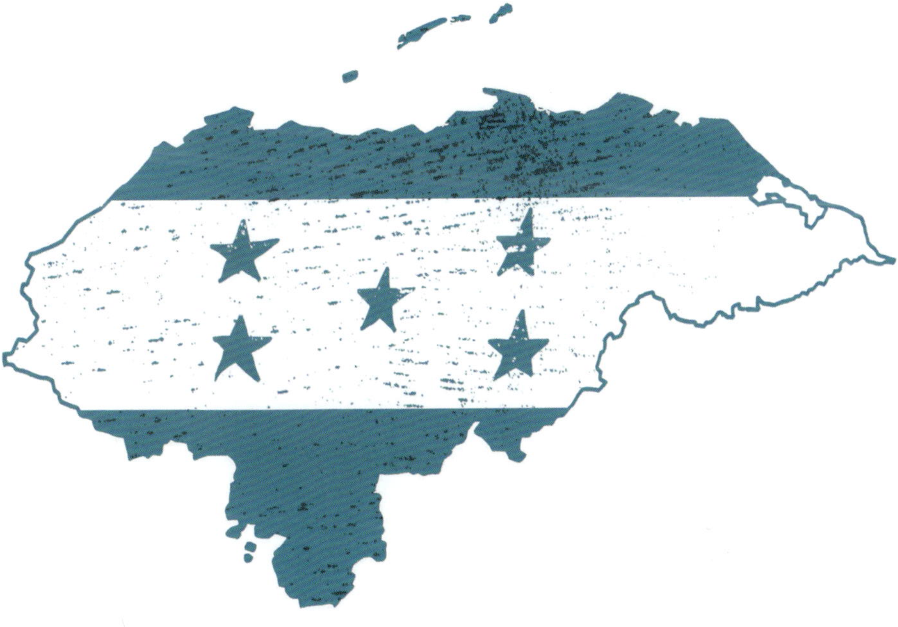

the cherry using the washed process. The honey process sits somewhere between the two and is essentially the same as the pulped natural method. Honey processing has caught on in Central America, and it is common to hear about a range of honey processes: black, red, and yellow, with less common labels of white and gold also existing. These labels imply slightly different things in different coffee-growing regions but, in general, refer either to the percentage of mucilage left on the bean or the amount of light and heat to which the mucilage is exposed. The heat and light are controlled by either the depth of the coffee layer or the frequency with which the parchment is turned, which in turn has an impact on how quickly the beans dry and the amount of fermentation that takes place in the interim. The black honey process universally implies more mucilage and a slower drying time, which results in a heavy, rounder, sweet cup with softer acidity. Each successive honey process (black, then red, then yellow, gold, and white) represents less mucilage and quicker drying times, or more frequent turning, resulting in brighter and lighter-bodied cups. The white honey process is intriguing as all the cherry is removed using water jets, which makes it possibly the most "fruit"-free process, even more so than washed processing.

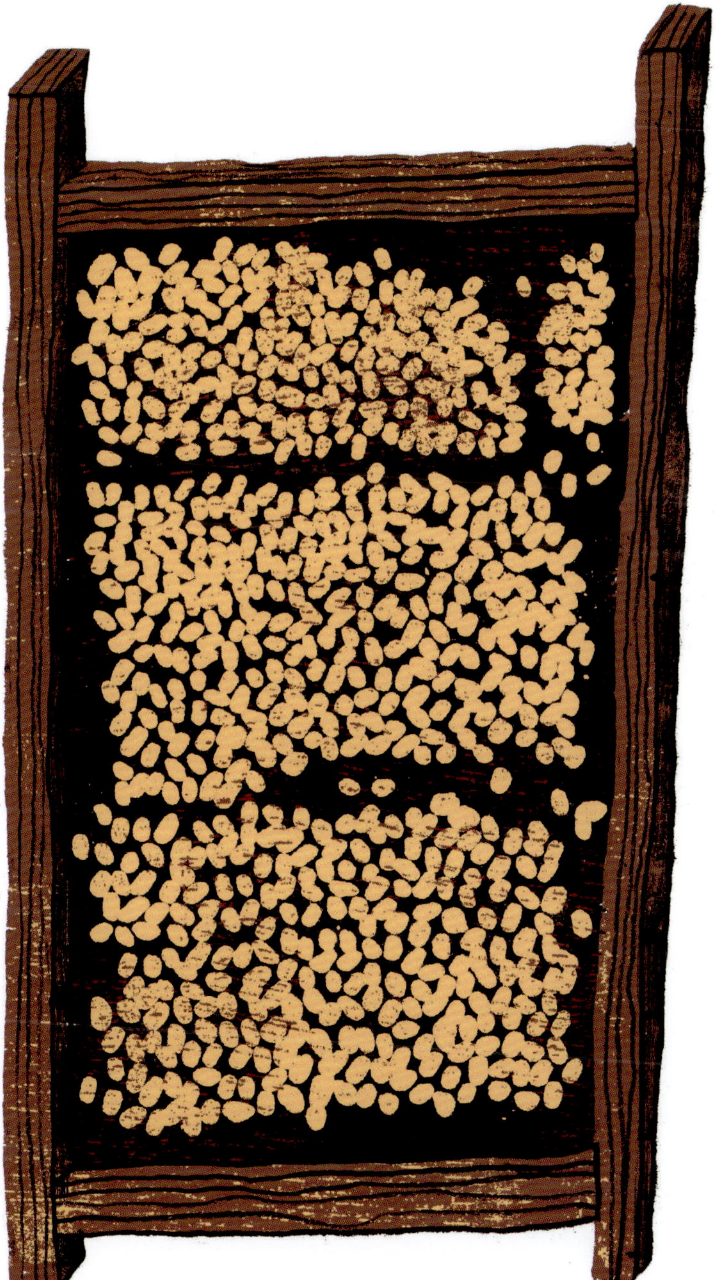

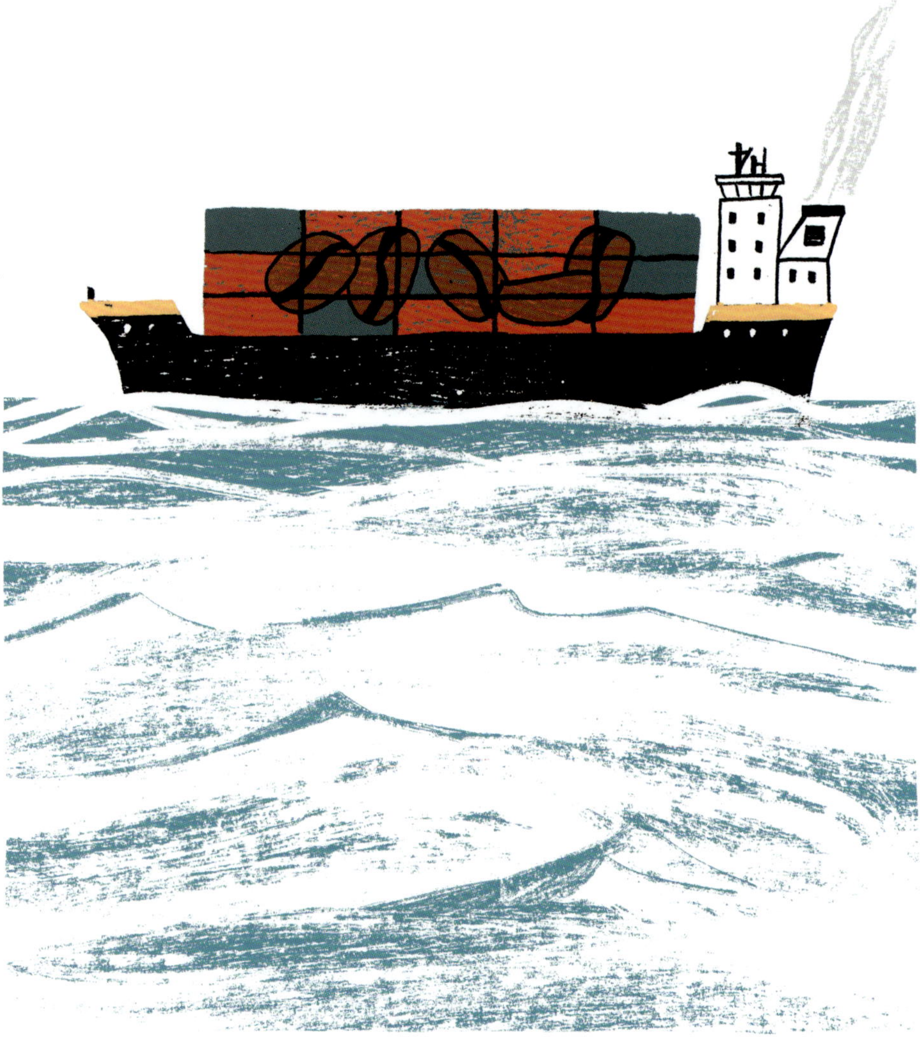

SEE ALSO
Cupping *p64*
Defects *p67*

Ibrik coffee

See "Turkish coffee".

Importing | TRADING

It is possible for coffee companies to source and import their own coffee, but what is more common is for specialist exporting and importing companies to act as intermediaries. Buying, shipping, and storing coffee is a big operation. Sourcing coffee directly provides a lovely narrative, and in times gone by, when the speciality industry was less prevalent and used less transparent practices, it was a great way to sidestep a bunch of limitations. Working with an importer has a number of benefits that small, quality-focused roasters can take advantage of. Hauling coffee across the world in container ships and through warehouses means that the coffee that turns up can often vary greatly from what you tasted on the cupping table at origin. If you are buying direct, this is a risk you have to stomach. Importers also have the benefit of specializing in their part of the supply chain, allowing them to focus on superior networks and relationship building. Boutique importers do now recognize the need for more unique coffees and are able to respond to trends for certain styles and processing. In doing so, it is becoming more common for programmes and competitions to be initiated by importers. Direct buying does have its benefits: it is easier to secure exclusive coffee and obviously you can save a bit of money.

Independent coffee shops | COFFEE CULTURE

The term "independent coffee scene" technically just encompasses all the non-chain coffee shops around the world, and thus a huge range of coffee-serving establishments of varying qualities and styles. However, the term has come to embody a sense of values, especially with regard to the coffee. The "third wave" and speciality movements are rooted in independent coffee culture and the correlation makes sense due to this. At the same time, I find the term and its use a little irritating at times. Many independent coffee shops have no focus on artisanal coffee, and, perhaps more interestingly, exceptional coffee is not solely the remit of independent coffee companies. Defining exactly when a coffee company is no longer independent can be tricky, but I have definitely seen growing, ambitious, quality-driven coffee companies producing and furthering the case of speciality coffee.

India | ORIGIN

India is a country known for many things: it has a lively mix of cultures and an incredible history, and is a booming modern nation. And, although it is definitely better known for the quality of its teas, there is also a fair amount of coffee production. In speciality circles, the country is known for growing some of the best Robusta coffee. Arabica is less well suited to

SEE ALSO
Third wave *p218*

SEE ALSO
Species *p202*

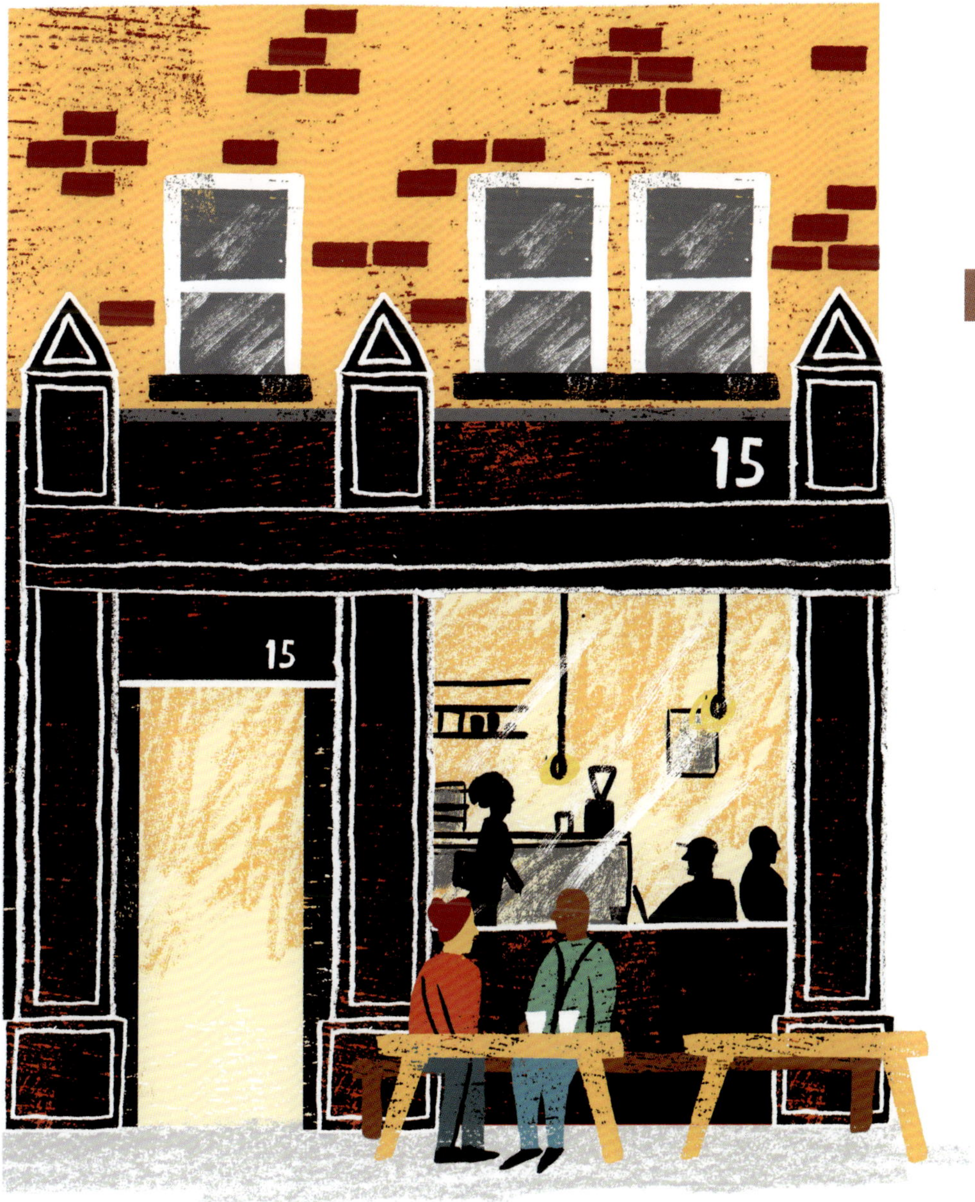
15
15

the growing conditions in India, though, that said, there are some impressive lots that display a round and creamy body with pleasant, spicy notes. Monsooned Malabar originates from the south-west coastal region of Kerala. In earlier times, coffee was transported in wooden boxes on seafaring vessels. During the monsoon season, the green coffee making its way across the seas would soak up a lot of moisture and create a coffee that was low in acidity and slightly musty, with a very round body. A preference for this evolved and so, when transportation improved, coffee began to be put through an artificial monsoon process to mimic the flavour. The cup profile can be divisive as acidity and nuance are lost. A strong market for the coffee continues to exist, however.

Indonesia | ORIGIN

Earthy and spicy are the notes that this part of the world is best known for when it comes to coffee. This can mainly be attributed to the unique wet-hulled processing method, also referred to as Giling Basah. This is a two-stage process. The coffee has most of the cherry removed and is dried to 30–35 per cent moisture (for export it would be completely dried, to 12 per cent moisture or below). This drying phase is carried out with the mucilage still intact, much as in the honey process. Afterwards, everything, including the parchment, is removed from the beans before they are dried further. It is unusual to remove the parchment this early and the process tends to give the coffee a bigger body and lower acidity. Fully washed Indonesian coffees are available and will tend to have more acidity. Although there are some exotic coffee stories from this part of the world, such as Kopi Luwak

SEE ALSO
Honey process *p118*
Kopi Luwak *p136*
Old Brown Java *p163*

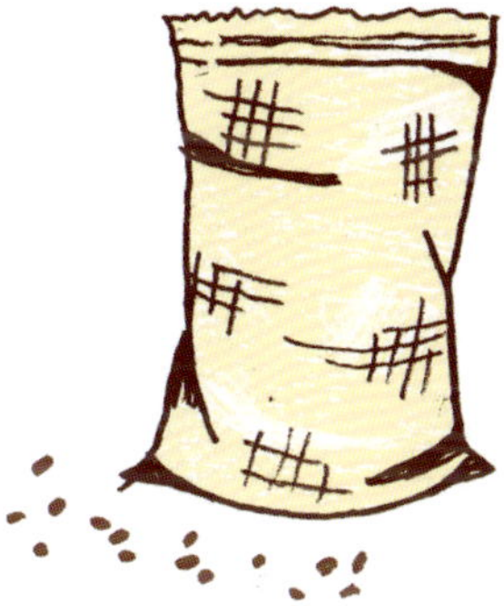

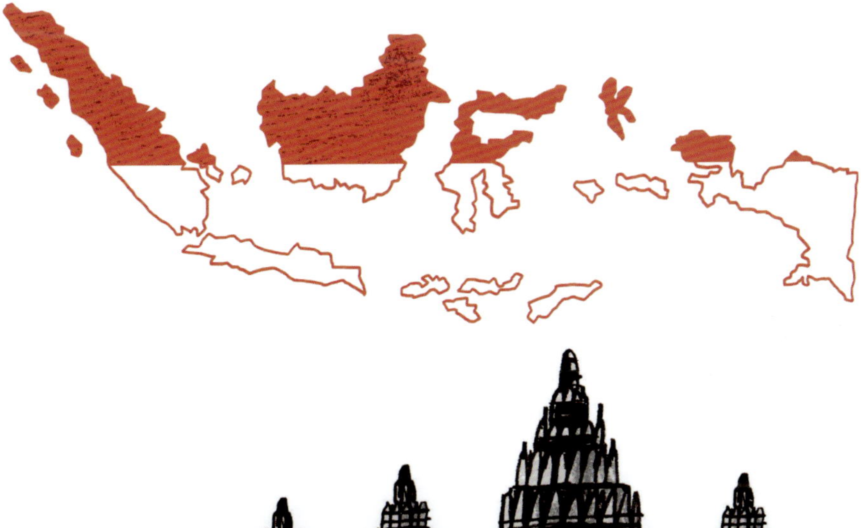

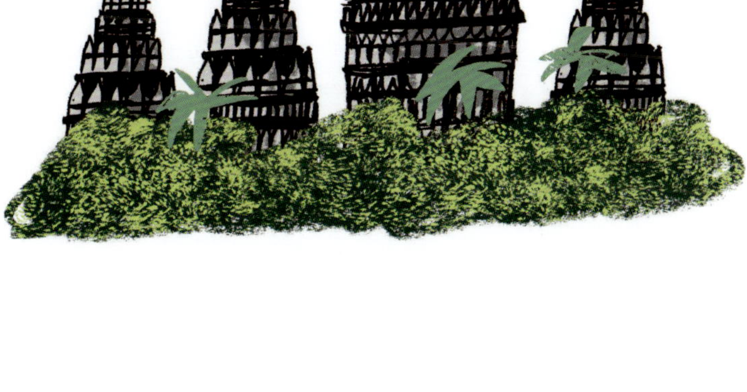

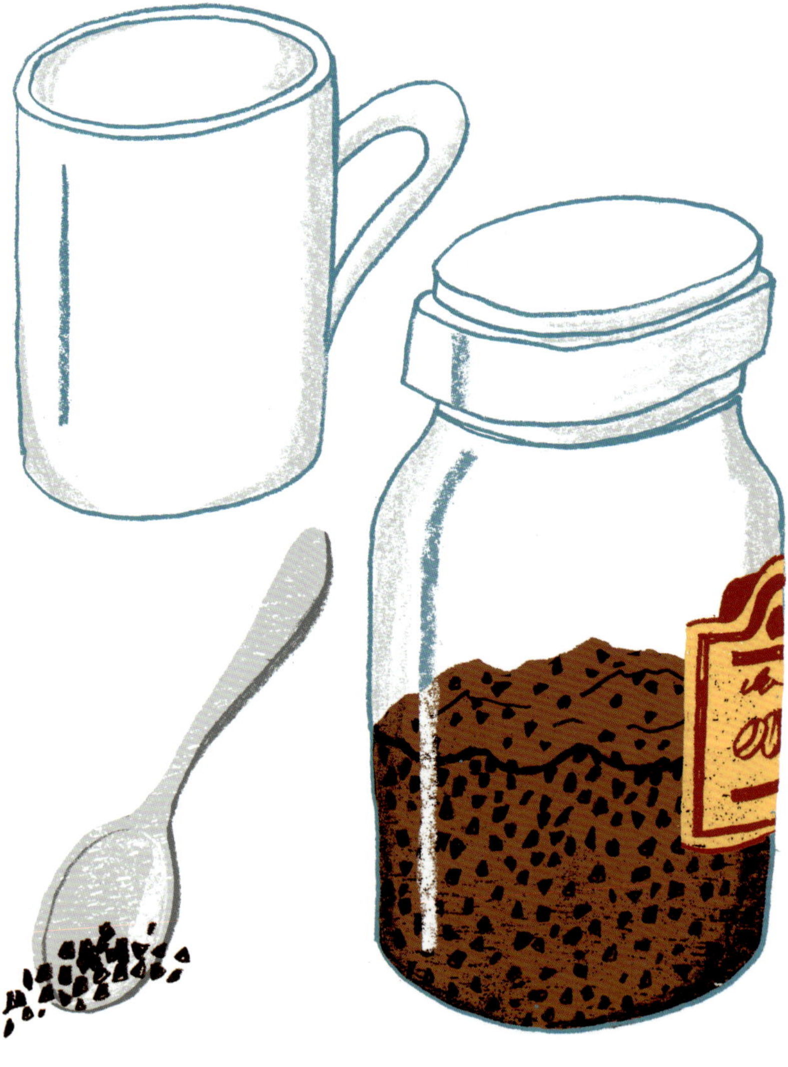

and Old Brown Java, for me the best coffees from this region are washed coffees with aromatic and spicy qualities. The rounder Indonesian coffees are more often found in espresso blends looking to achieve a full-bodied and less acidic profile. Note that many locations and islands come under the Indonesia bracket, including Sumatra, Sulewesi, and Java.

Instant coffee | COFFEE CULTURE

SEE ALSO
Extraction *p86*
Freezing *p98*

Instant coffee is also known as soluble coffee, which in layman's terms means "just add water". It is said that instant coffee was first invented in the late eighteenth century in England. The first registered patent, however, belongs to New Zealander David Strand from Invercargill. The instant preparation method has been hugely successful. Although there are varying methods, the principle is to brew coffee and then to get rid of all the water. This leaves you with a coffee powder that is just waiting to be rehydrated, and, *voilà*, a cup of coffee in an instant. There are many commercial benefits to instant: a long shelf life, a lower shipping weight than bean or ground for the same amount of coffee, and, of course, its convenience and ease of preparation. However, "instant" has become a byword for cheap, low-grade coffee that provides a caffeine hit but fails to offer quality. This may be changing. In 2016 two-time Finnish Barista champion Kalle Freese founded Sudden Coffee – taking exceptional speciality coffees and making, brewing, and producing them as instant. The challenge here is maintaining aromatics, but having tasted Kalle's coffees I think it fair to say that instant coffee has the potential to display the character and flavour of high-quality coffee.

SEE ALSO
C market *p41*
Producing *p180*

International Coffee Organization | TRADING

The headquarters of the International Coffee Organization (ICO) can be found on Berners Street, Fitzrovia, in London. Set up in 1963, the ICO – in collaboration with the United Nations – began to improve relations and cooperation between coffee-producing and coffee-consuming countries. From the late 1960s to the early 1990s international agreements agreed under ICO auspices put in place a quota system to stabilize coffee prices as markets fluctuated. The idea was that, if more coffee was produced than the demand of the market warranted, coffee would be withheld from the market; the opposite applied when demand increased. While the ICO no longer plays any significant role in stabilizing coffee prices as it once did, it is still an important and influential body that today focuses on research and education for the benefit of all its members.

SEE ALSO
Espresso *p79*
Gear *p105*
Grinding *p109*

Invention | TECHNOLOGY

On the one hand, a great cup of coffee can be made very simply; on the other, the endlessly complex variables involved in making a cup of coffee mean that things can get pretty hi-tech. A focus, for example, on the impact of temperature in an espresso machine requires much research before new technology can be developed. Patents for "unique" designs get filed left, right, and centre. At seminal trade shows around the world, new projects are unveiled and rival companies circle booths. While some inventions either do not work or just do not take off, others will end up changing the coffee industry forever.

SEE ALSO
Barista *p23*
Espresso *p79*

Italy | COFFEE CULTURE

The Mediterranean nation of Italy is the home of espresso and can lay claim to a coffee culture that has been exported more than any other. Many a billboard or marketing campaign has made reference to this heritage, and the country undoubtedly represents a broad global brand. The Instituto Internationale Assaggiatori Caffè (IIAC), based in Brescia, is an institution that defines espresso down to the colour of the crema and specific flavour notes. Despite this, coffee styles vary throughout the country, with a Neapolitan espresso being more Robusta laden and served shorter and hotter than the longer, more Arabica-driven espresso of northern Italy. It is fair to say that Italian coffee-drinking culture is sophisticated, but the coffee itself tends to be more commoditized and speciality coffee is still rarely represented. Espresso machine companies have popped up around the world, but Italy is still the heartland of espresso machine production, even if the market for the top-end versions tends to be elsewhere.

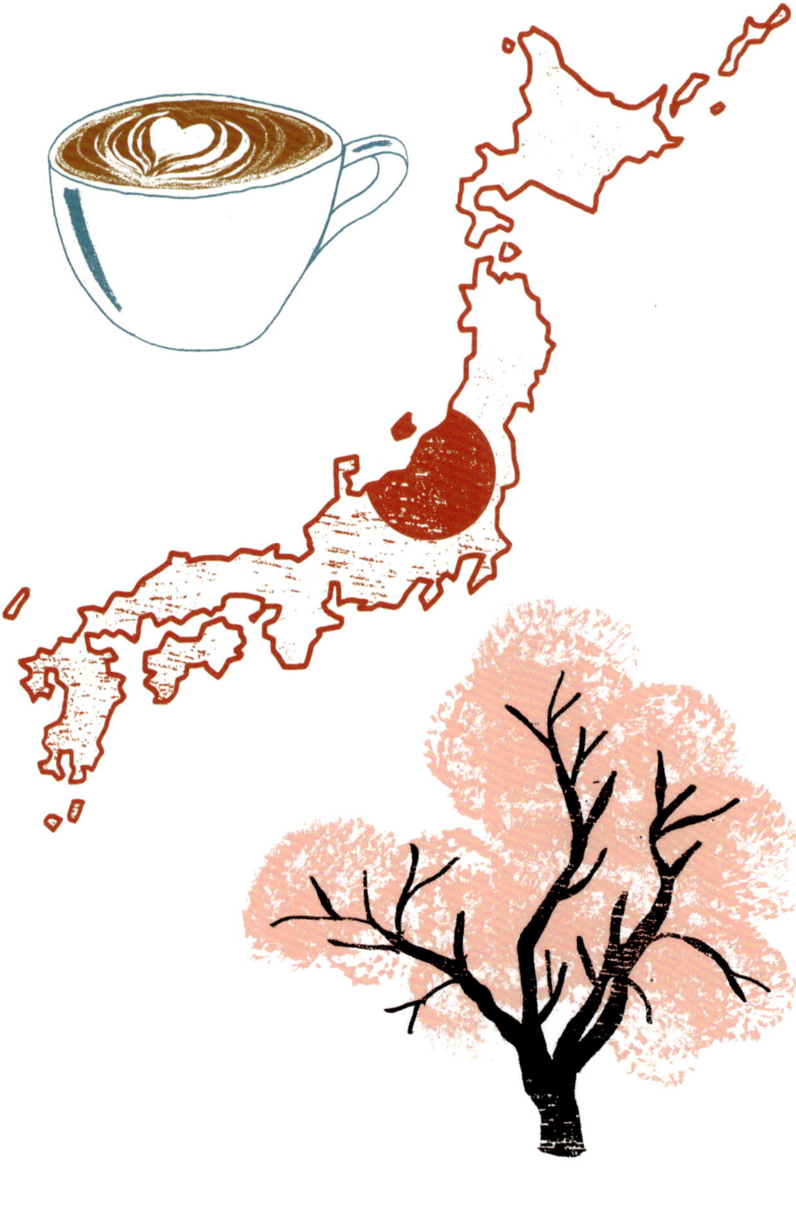

J

SEE ALSO
Cup of Excellence *p64*

Jamaican Blue Mountain | ORIGIN

Historically, Jamaican Blue Mountain is synonymous with expensive, gourmet coffee. More recently, it is developing a new reputation as an overpriced coffee that showcases how good marketing is often more valuable than cup quality. This Jamaican coffee gained its reputation back when well-processed coffee was harder to come by, but nowadays simply cannot compete with the best coffee.

SEE ALSO
Cold brew *p59*
Cup of Excellence *p64*
Green *p109*

Japan | COFFEE CULTURE

Coffee is big in Japan. In fact, Japan is one of the world's biggest coffee importers, and the country embraces a diverse range of coffee offerings and cultural approaches. Coffee lounges in Japan have long been established, evolving from traditional Japanese tea rooms. Coffee boomed in the country after World War II and is now a staple, with hot and cold canned coffee available from vending machines. (Japan was truly ahead of the cold brew craze now emerging in the rest of the world.) The concept of exceptional, rare, and carefully brewed coffee is also well established in Japan. It is a common occurrence in the world of green coffee buying and sourcing to lose out to Japanese coffee buyers on the high bidding prices paid for the best coffees.

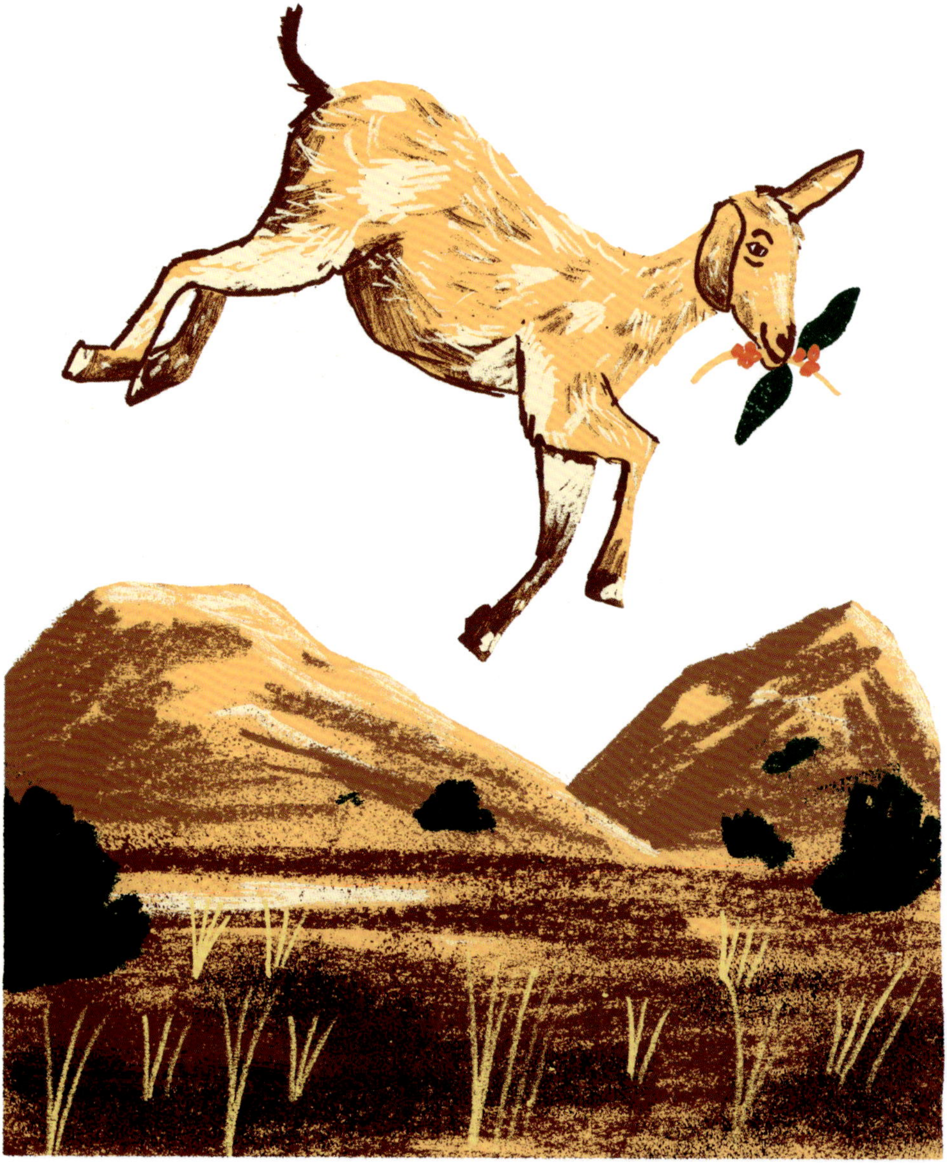

K

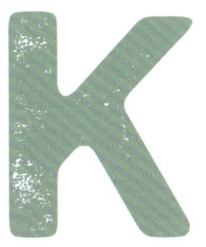

Kaldi | COFFEE LEGEND

The unanswerable question: who first discovered coffee? Well, there is a nice little folk tale that tells one side of the story. Kaldi, an Arab Ethiopian goatherd, is said to have found his goats dancing in the forest in south-west Ethiopia sometime in the ninth century. Noticing that the goats were nibbling on the bright-red cherry of a nearby bush, Kaldi took one for himself and noticed the stimulating effect and began to dance along with his goats. It is said that he then took the seeds to a nearby monastery. A monk disapproved of their use and threw them onto a fire. The aroma they gave off was so enticing that the beans were raked from the fire and ground and dissolved in water to create the first ever cup of coffee.

Kenya | ORIGIN

If you want to showcase how delicious fruit notes in coffee can be, you can do little better than to get hold of a great complex Kenyan coffee. The country produces some amazingly berry-like cups with soaring acidity and a big round body to boot. I adore the best Kenyan coffees. The country is a developed coffee producer with an auction system that helps to reward quality. Kenyan coffees are often graded on bean size, and, although there is a correlation with the

SEE ALSO
Peaberry *p175*
Variety *p228*

larger-sized AA grading and quality, it is not absolute, and AB lots (which are a combination of smaller screen sizes) can score very highly. The sorting of peaberries for separate sale is also popular in Kenya. The two most oft-cited focus points of Kenya's speciality coffee production are the SL varieties 28 and 34 and the Nyeri district. "SL" stands for Scott Laboratories, which produced these experimental varieties. They now account for most of the high-grade coffee in the country, and, apart from the odd appearance elsewhere, are relatively unique to Kenya. Nyeri is located in central Kenya, around Mount Kenya, and gives rise to many of the country's most desirable lots. Much excellent coffee is grown elsewhere in the country, too.

Kopi Luwak | PROCESSING; ANIMAL RIGHTS

"Have you ever tried the coffee that gets … you know … 'passed though' an animal?" Some of the most expensive coffee in the world comes under the label Kopi Luwak, which translates as "civet coffee". The idea is that the little civet cat chooses only the best (most ripe) cherries to eat as it wanders the forest floor, and that the beans then undergo a special processing in the cat's digestive system. The resulting coffee is an exotic and sought-after rarity, or so the marketing story goes. The reality is far less fanciful. Animal welfare is a serious concern, as caged civet cats get force-fed low-grade coffee. To top it off, in blind taste tests Kopi Luwak coffees have never scored highly. A good story is a powerful thing.

SEE ALSO
Jamaican Blue
  Mountain *p133*
Hawaii *p117*

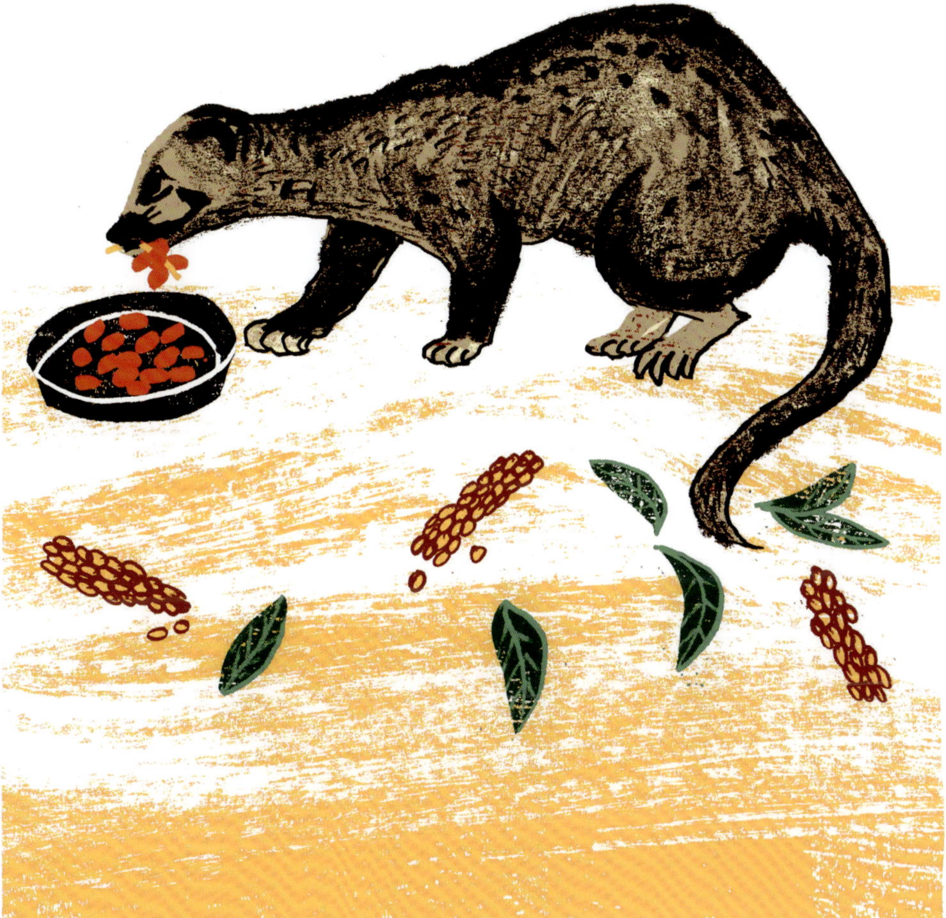

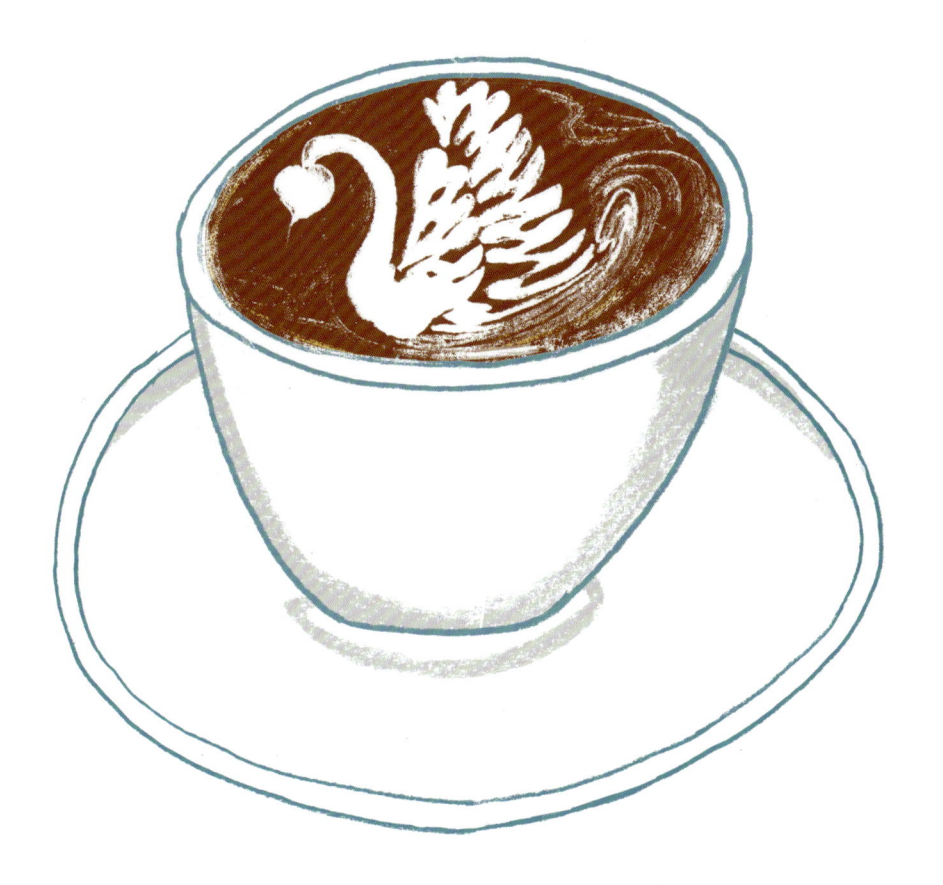

SEE ALSO
Flat white *p94*
Sensory science *p197*

Latte art | COFFEE CULTURE; PREPARATION

Patterns adorning the surface of your freshly prepared flat white have become ever more commonplace. This final flourish in coffee preparation often signifies to a drinker that staff know what they are doing and that they have taken care over the making of the coffee. A study I worked on with the Oxford University experimental psychologist Charles Spence indicated that customers are willing to pay more for a coffee with latte art on, not necessarily because they think it is qualitatively any better, but because they recognize that more energy and craft have gone into the preparation of the drink. The flipside of this is the illusion that a beautiful cup is always a good cup. The appearance certainly indicates well-steamed milk, but it tells us very little about the quality of the coffee within. Latte art is hard to master, and the feats certain baristas are capable of by simply pouring steamed milk into coffee can be quite remarkable. The World Latte Art Championship never fails to draw a crowd. The two main methods are free pouring and etching. Free pouring requires that steamed milk be poured into the espresso and a pattern created with no additional tools. It is a matter of timing, skill, positioning, and milk-steaming quality. Etching allows you to draw on the surface using a tool a lot

SEE ALSO
Defects *p67*
Olfactory *p163*
Q Grader *p183*

like a toothpick. A combination of the two can yield stunning patterns.

Le Nez du Café® | AROMA

This beautiful box of liquid aromatic solutions is the perfect dinner-party toy, albeit a relatively pricey one. The box contains 36 vials, each designed to represent one of the 36 most common aromas in coffee, both positive and negative (the latter the result of defects). Each vial has a number, and after smelling it you can have a go at guessing which aroma it is, detailed in the accompanying booklet. As with all such olfactory tasks, you get a lot better with practice. It is a brilliant game to play with a group of friends and it can be illuminating to see how differently people interpret the same smell when there are no visual or textural clues. The kit is used as an integral part of the Q Grader qualification. The same company makes similar boxes for the worlds of wine and whisky.

SEE ALSO
Castillo *p51*
Climate change *p56*
Guatemala *p113*

Leaf rust | GROWING; DISEASE

While its origins lie in East Africa, coffee leaf rust (CLR) is a fungus that has had a devastating impact on coffee-growing regions around the world. The first time CLR showcased its effects was during the late 1800s when the fungus reduced Ceylon's coffee production by 80 per cent. Before the fungus hit, Ceylon was the largest coffee producer in the world. Careful use of quarantine kept the disease from the Americas for a long time, though it was discovered in Brazil in the 1970s. The exact path the fungus took to make its way to the Americas is unknown, but the dust-like spores can easily travel on luggage, people, and plants. There

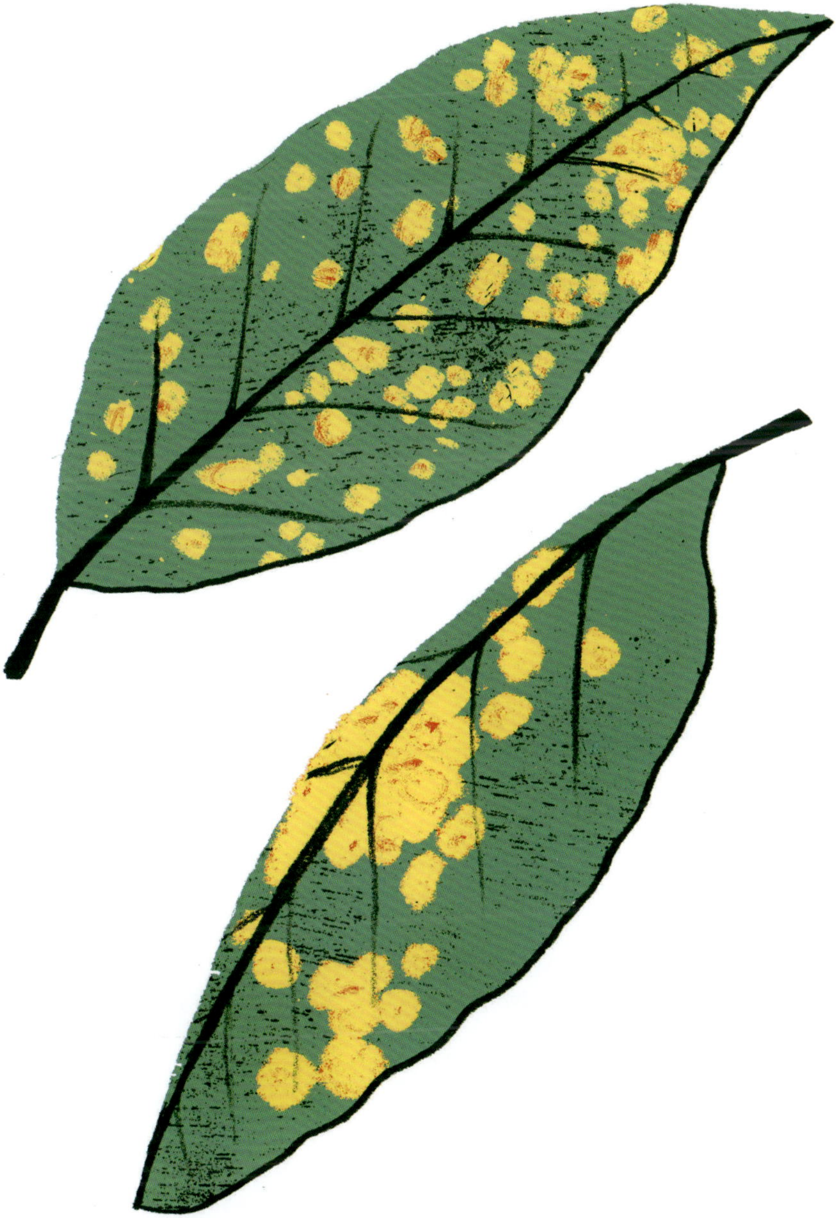

SEE ALSO
Espresso *p79*
Italy *p131*

are a number of ways to combat CLR, whether through farm management, quarantine, or use of fungicides. None of the combative solutions are foolproof, and the development of varieties resistant to the disease continues to be one of the most viable options.

Lever machine | EQUIPMENT; ESPRESSO

The concept of espresso is to brew coffee under pressure, the name meaning literally to "press out". It does not mean "express" or "quick", even though making an espresso is. The first espresso machines that began to appear at the end of the nineteenth century used steam to create the pressure. In 1945 the Italian Giovanni Achille Gaggia (1895–1961) invented and produced the lever machine. This took away the need for the steam to provide the pressure and it meant that the water did not need to be as hot. Levers work by the user providing all the pressure or with the user loading the reps using a spring. It is this action that gave rise to the saying "to pull a shot". The lever machine also largely defined the size of the modern espresso, as there is only so much water that can be held in the chamber to brew with. After this came the pump-driven machine, which now dominates the market. Levers have seen a resurgence in the artisanal movement as a more manual and "involving" machine. Modern programmable pump machines can now mimic the press changes of the classic lever machine.

SEE ALSO
Constantinople *p60*
Third place *p217*

Lloyd's of London | HISTORY

There is a strong association between the emergence of coffee houses and social, economic, and cultural change. In Europe, during the sixteenth and seventeenth centuries, the coffee

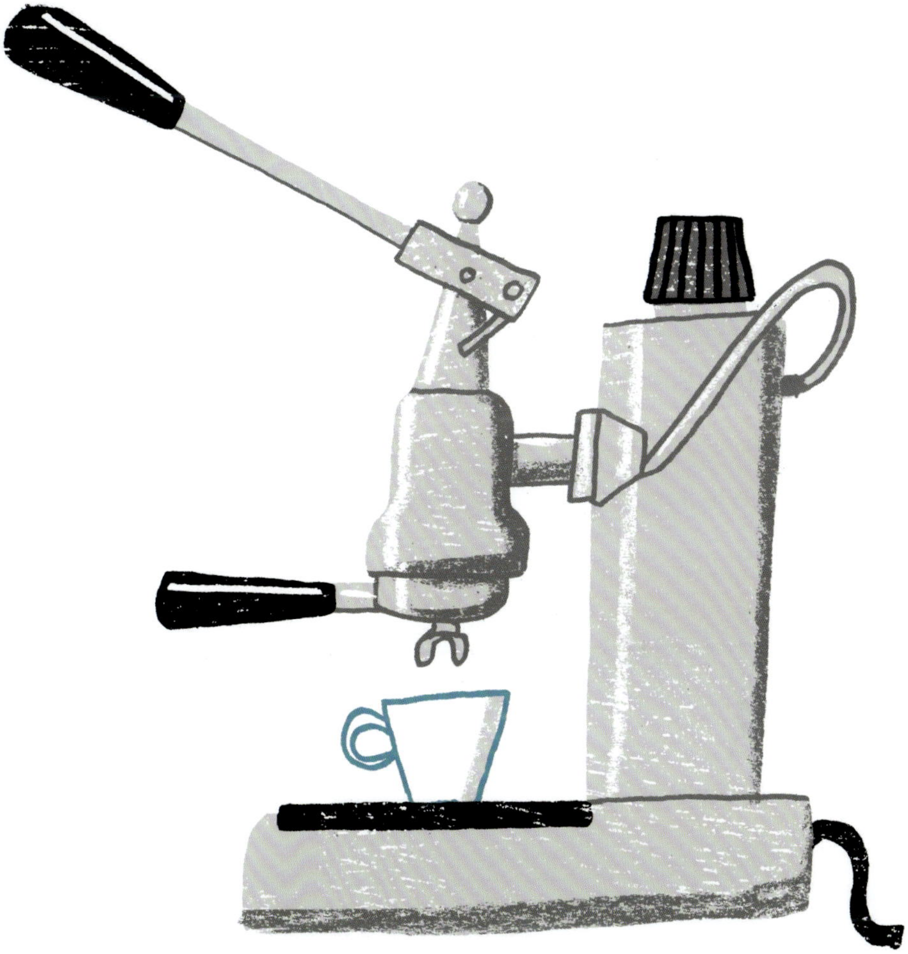

house offered a stark contrast to the prevalant alehouse. The nature of coffee – stimulating but not inebriating – meant that coffee houses were places that induced more discussion and exploration of ideas, and many historians have drawn a link between this vibrant coffee scene and the eighteenth-century European Enlightenment. As well as being centres of scholarly discourse and gossip, coffee houses also proved great places to do business. Lloyd's Coffee House on Tower Street in the City of London was established in 1688. The shop was frequented by sailors, merchants, and ship owners who received reliable shipping news at the establishment. The coffee house soon became known as the ideal place to obtain marine insurance, and so the Lloyd's of London insurance market, which runs to this very day in the British capital, was born.

SEE ALSO
Development *p71*
Drum roaster *p72*
First crack *p93*
Green *p109*

Maillard reaction | ROASTING

Unroasted, green coffee is not a flavoursome proposition, tasting a bit like grass and cereal. It is an unfinished ingredient that has flavour *potential*, and it is the roasting process that unlocks that potential through a series of complex chemical reactions. Coffee shares one of its main flavour-defining processes with many other food and drink items – the Maillard reaction. While the process is unpredictable, it generally involves the amino acids and oxygen-rich compounds (such as sugars) present in the coffee. Chemical reactions in the compounds occur at various temperatures in the roasting process – most rapidly between 140°C and 165°C – creating many flavoursome by-products. Other chemical reactions also take place during roasting and, of course, how these reactions occur and affect flavour depends on how you roast. Sugars will caramelize but, if roasted too long, will create a burnt taste.

SEE ALSO
Drum roaster *p72*
Raised beds *p186*

Mechanical drying | PROCESSING

A mechanical drier is somewhat like a roaster: it is a big rotating drum to which heat is applied. However, the temperatures involved are a lot lower, so perhaps the tumble dryer is a better comparison. Traditionally, most coffee is dried out in the open, relying on sunshine, whether on big concrete patios or raised beds. Mechanical driers are often used in countries where rainfall makes this difficult or to speed up the process. Mechanical drying is often seen as inferior, and this is not completely unwarranted as often the driers are too hot, which risks compromising the quality of the coffee. However, there is an argument that, used well, a mechanical drier offers the most controllable and quality-focused drying technique. There is also the belief that the "resting" provided by cool nights is beneficial to the drying process, too. The research appears inconclusive at this point in time.

Melbourne | COFFEE CULTURE

If you read the introduction to this book, you will notice that Melbourne saw the beginning of my coffee journey. It is fair to say that in recent years this city has influenced many coffee journeys and sparked many passions. The thriving café scene there as well as in other parts of Australia is diverse, characterful, and top notch. Apart from brilliant brunch options, it is the care and value that coffee is given that stand out, resulting in a real emphasis on the role of the barista. Reportedly, this results in Melbourne being the best-paid location in the world to work as a barista. This Australian approach to cafés and coffee has been exported around the world in the past decade. There are now many other exciting and influential coffee scenes around the globe, but Melbourne is still pretty special.

Mexico | ORIGIN

Due to close proximity to the United States, most of Mexico's coffee is sold to the country's

SEE ALSO
Barista *p23*

SEE ALSO
Guatemala *p113*
United States of America *p223*

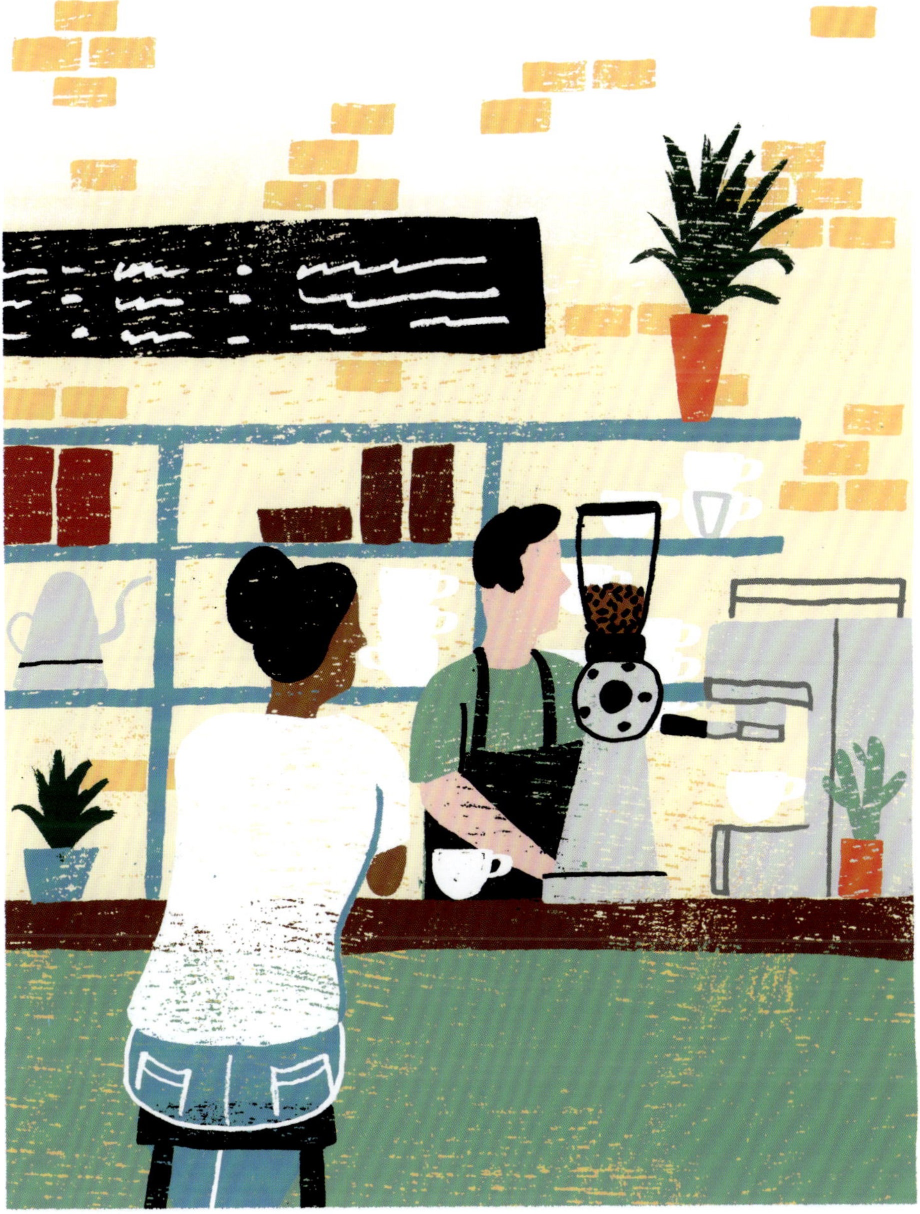

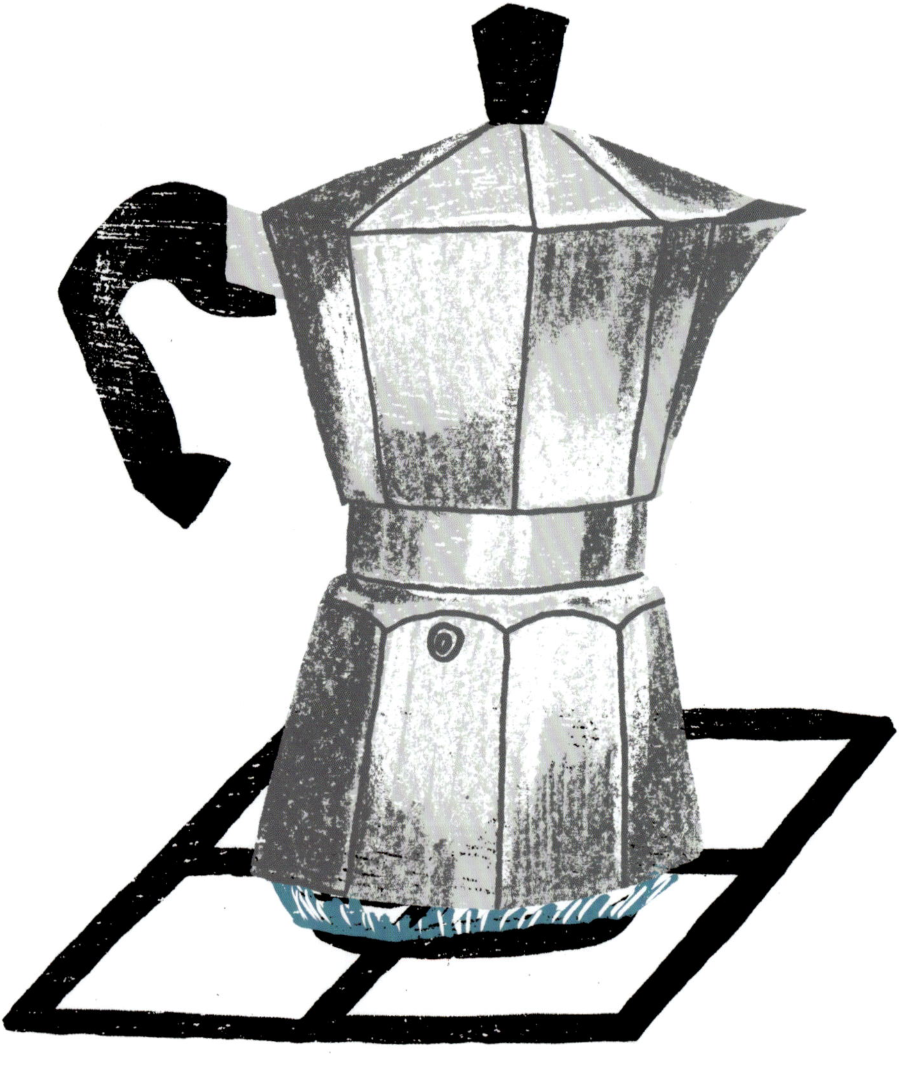

northern neighbour, and for this reason you do not see a lot of Mexican coffee around the world. The country is capable of producing a range of impressive, high-quality flavour profiles, from light and floral to ripe, toffee-like, and round. Mexico is one of the largest producers of coffee in the world and the crops are predominantly of the Arabica species. Even so, coffee production in Mexico is actually down from its heights, before the coffee crisis following the dismantling of the 1989 International Coffee Agreement. The highest-quality crops in Mexico come from the southern coastal regions bordering Guatemala.

Moka pot | BREWING

This stovetop brewing device has been around for the past 80 years, and, like espresso itself, was invented in Italy. Alfonso Bialetti (1888–1970) acquired the design (the work of Luigi De Ponti) in 1933, and Bialetti Industrie still produces the very same model under the trade name Moka Express. The moka pot has found great popularity due to its ability to produce an espresso-esque drink on the domestic stove. The design allows pressure to build up as the water heats in the bottom chamber of the pot along with steam. When the steam gets to critical point, it forces the water up through a bed of ground coffee and fills the top chamber with strong, freshly brewed coffee. Different designs require a different amount of heat and pressure before the water makes its way up through the coffee, and a common complaint directed at the pot is that the coffee can taste burnt. The reality is that the water has just got too hot and is over-extracting the coffee. A simple trick is to use less water in the bottom chamber; this means the build-up of steam is more quickly able to move

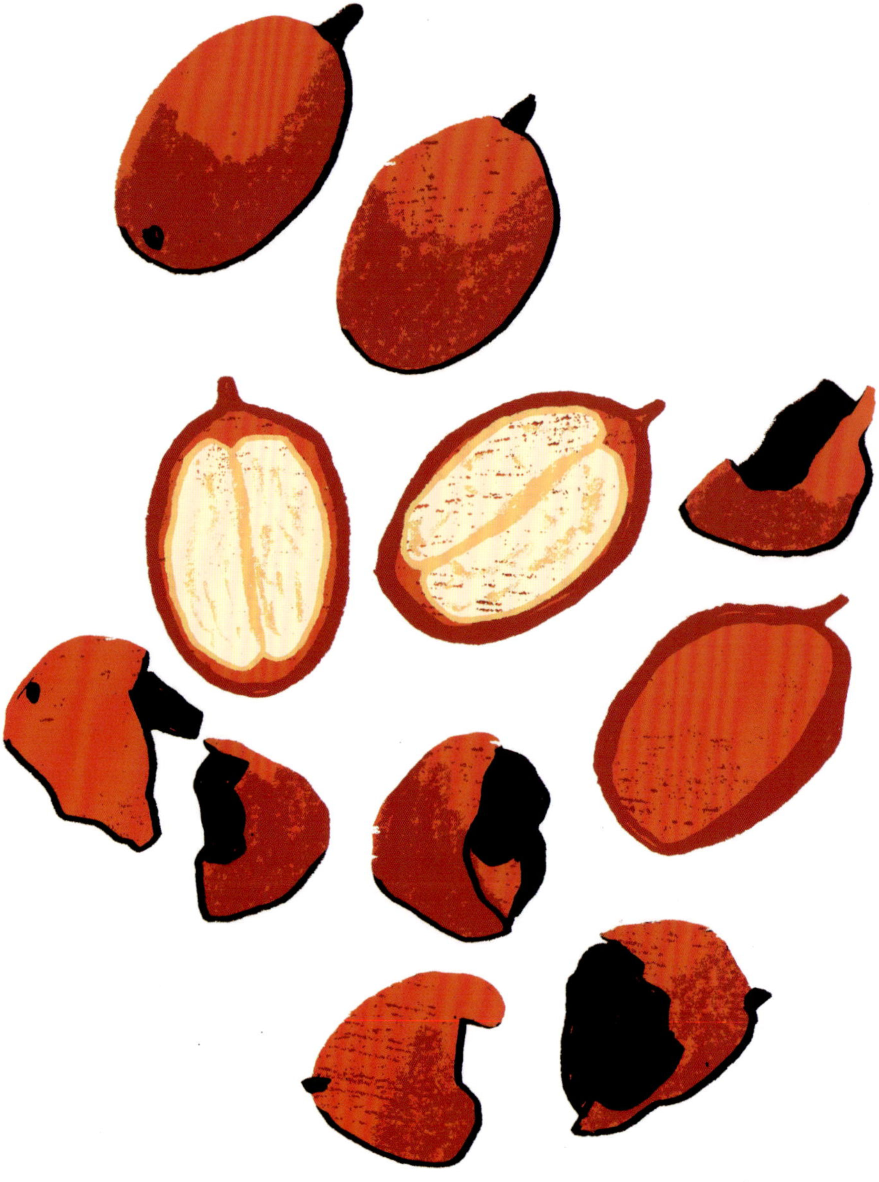

the water up and through the coffee before its temperature rises too high.

Mucilage | ORIGIN

Mucilage is the flesh of the coffee fruit that sticks to the parchment surrounding the coffee beans. This mucilage is very important in a number of ways. During the development of the cherry on the tree, it is this mucilage that will be measured for sugar content. When picking a ripe cherry off the tree and tasting it, it is always surprising to find just how sweet it is. A favourite experience of mine took place at the Finca Los Pirineos in El Salvador, where, wandering among the coffee plants, we tasted a huge range of ripe cherries from some of the famous coffee varieties grown there. The differences in the flavour of the mucilage were staggering. During the various processing methods it is this mucilage we are interested in, how it dries and affects the flavour of the bean.

SEE ALSO
Brix *p38*
El Salvador *p77*
Honey process *p118*
Natural process *p156*

Multi boiler | ESPRESSO

Perusing the espresso machine options available in the marketplace, you may well have seen the term "dual" or "multi boiler" among the technical specifications and selling points. Back in the day one big boiler would provide multiple services across the machine. The boiler would heat water for the heat exchangers, provide hot water for the spigot, and provide steam power for making the frothy hot milk. For this to be effective, you need a really big boiler, so that you can do all these things at once without them hindering one another. The idea behind the multi boiler is to split up these jobs. This concept was first introduced in the form of dual boilers – one

SEE ALSO
Heat exchanger *p117*

for brewing espresso and another for steam and hot water – but the idea has now gone much, much further, and you will see not only separate boilers for each group head on the machine, but also separate pre-heating boilers for each of these. The multi-boiler design allows the machine to store and produce water of varying temperatures at any one time and creates more consistency and precision in those temperatures.

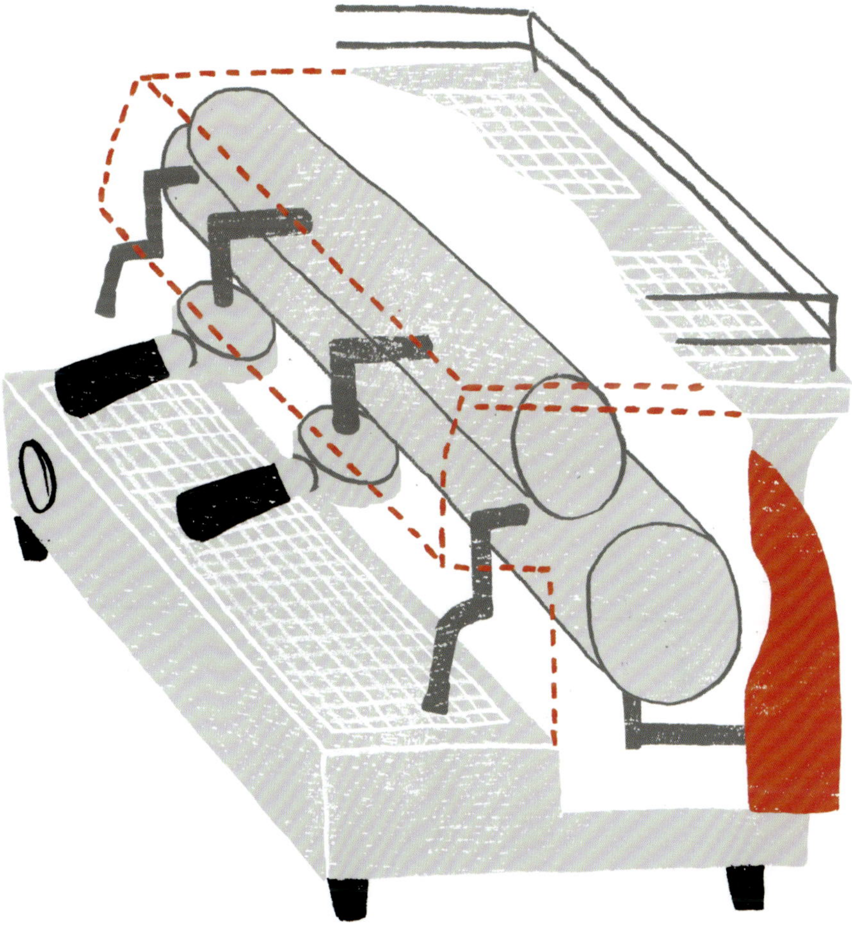

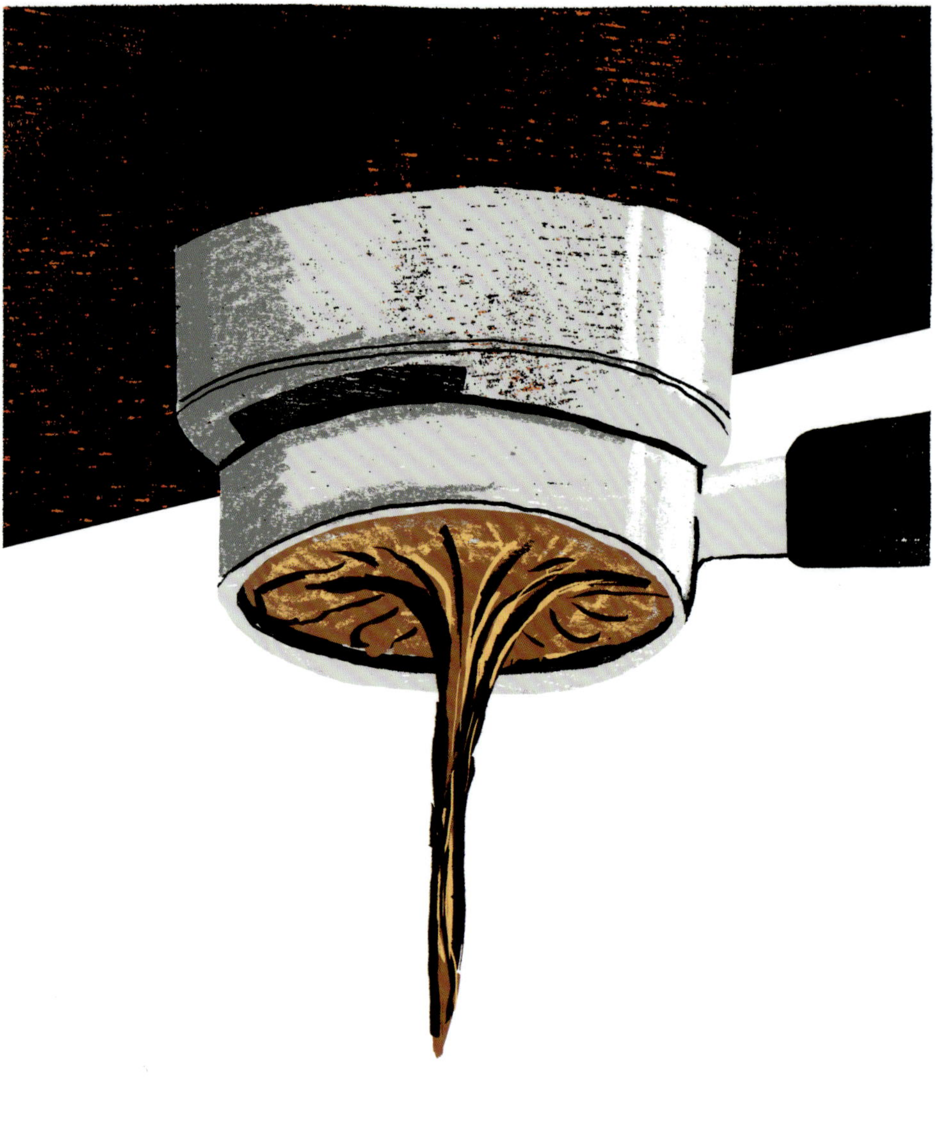

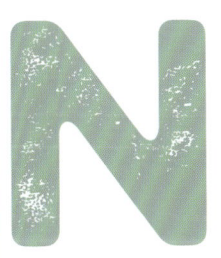

SEE ALSO
Basket *p23*
Channelling *p52*
Espresso *p79*
Portafilter *p176*

Naked shot | BREWING

The naked shot went through a period of extreme popularity that has now somewhat subdued. This term refers simply to the bottom of the portafilter being drilled out so that the coffee exits directly from the base of the basket and into the cup. This means that the mesmerizing pour of the espresso can be witnessed. An initial slow-mo-like exit of very dark liquid transforms into long, rich, flowing streams of espresso. As this is happening, the colour turns from brown to red and then a rich caramel. Midway through the shot, the streams converge into one central stream that becomes faster and blonder in colour, before the shot is completed. It really is rather pretty, if potentially a bit messy. Other than the aesthetics, there are a few benefits to the naked shot. It does allow you access to a better visual representation of how the water is flowing through the coffee and as such will help indicate channelling. The spouts of a standard portafilter also have the potential to build up coffee residue, which imparts negative flavours on the cup, so not having them helps to avoid this, though you can, of course, just clean the spouts. The same thought process suggests that a naked shot allows all the coffee into the cup, with valuable solids not being caught in the spouts. I don't think this has a particularly large impact on cup quality. Testing

SEE ALSO
Fermentation *p90*
Honey process *p118*
Silver skin *p198*

suggests that it is very hard to achieve two even versions of a single espresso when the shot is split through two spouts, suggesting a naked or a double shot is likely to be more consistent.

Natural process | PROCESSING

Natural processing (or dry-processed coffee) is the most ancient and straightforward processing method. The coffee cherry is harvested and then set out to dry with the fruit and skin intact and the coffee beans inside. The coffee bean and the coffee cherry dry together and are separated at the end of the drying process. This is a stark contrast to fully washed coffee, in which the cherry and the bean spend very little time together. The drying of natural coffee can take a long time and is labour-intensive, requiring continual raking and turning to avoid mould build-up and over-fermentation, which will result in off tastes. The exact drying times and temperatures correlate closely to quality; a common issue in natural-processed coffees is that they take too long to dry. These coffees can develop rotten or overly "funky" flavour characteristics. Pioneering work by Flavio Borém looks at water activity in drying coffee and shows that incorrect drying can compromise the cell walls of the beans, meaning that these coffees age and fade in flavour very quickly. It is often suggested that the coffee "takes on" the fruit flavour from the cherry. Though there are theories, the exact reason why the coffee develops winier, rounder fruit notes with the natural process is not precisely known. The natural process requires considerably less water than other processing methods and is, in this sense, environmentally superior. It also means that natural processing is more likely to be used in

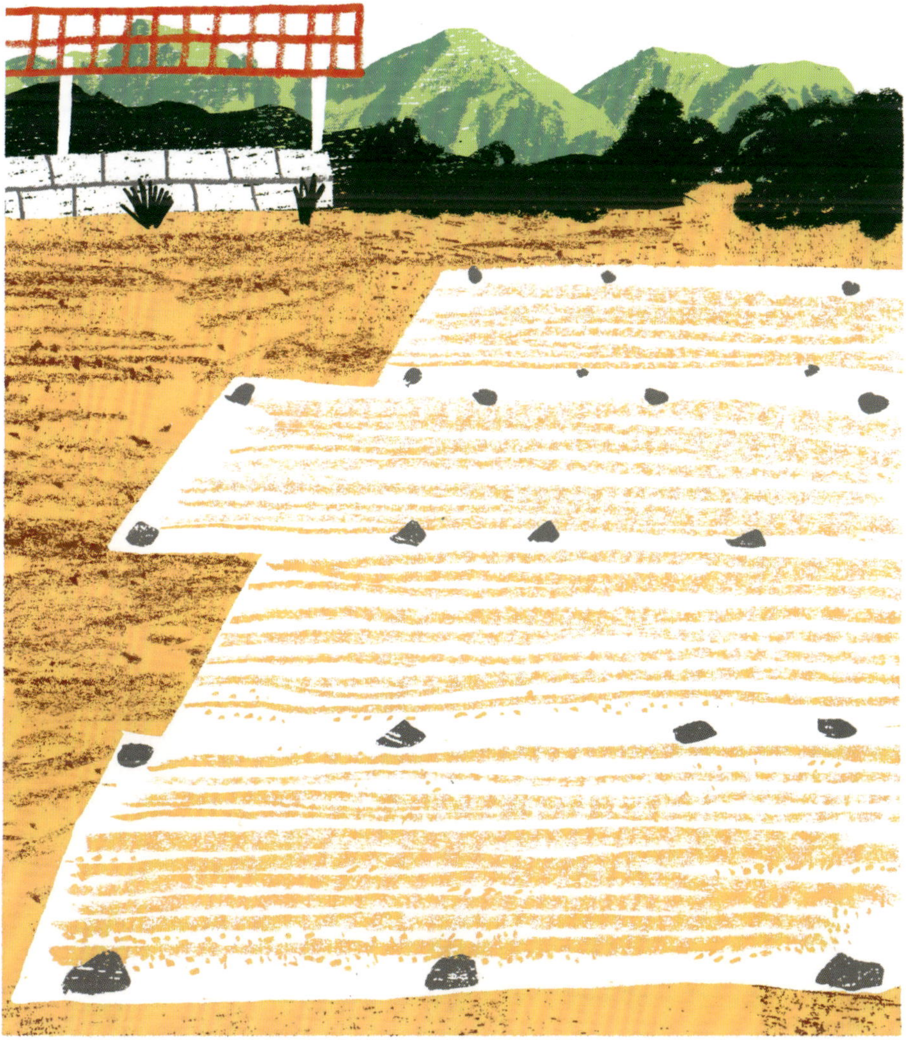

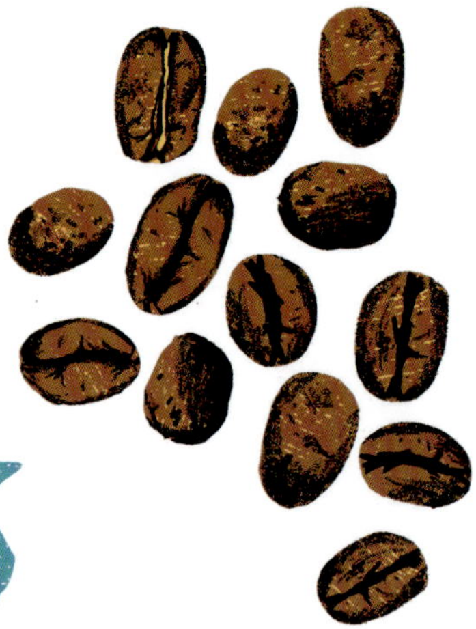

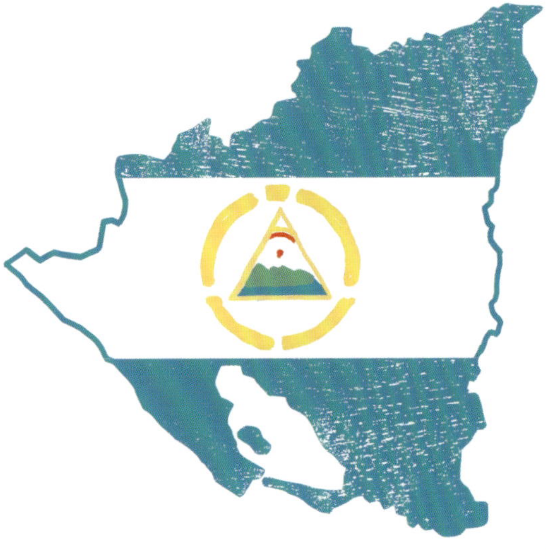

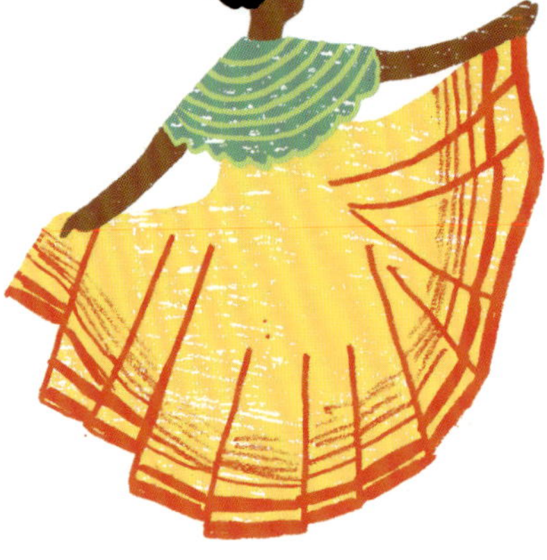

parts of the world with water shortages. It is not altogether unusual for roasters and coffee buyers to have a complete "no natural" policy. Personally, I think that, while there are many examples of "bad" natural-processed coffees that are earthy, woody, or sour, certain natural-processed coffees can have exciting and complex flavour profiles that are delicious. The natural process is actually very close to honey and pulped natural processing methods, and nowadays many experimental farmers are playing with various natural-style processes as a means of altering and improving the flavour characteristics of their coffee.

Nicaragua | ORIGIN

It has been a tumultuous century for Nicaragua and coffee growing is part of that journey, as it has inevitably got caught up in the country's political and economic events. Nowadays, though, traceability and high-quality cups are flourishing. A number of varieties grow very well in Nicaragua's various regions and produce a range of cup profiles, from rich and full bodies to juicy, fruity, and complex. The Cup of Excellence has been successful in the country and the Nueva Segovia region in the north repeatedly provides many successful coffees with outstanding cup quality.

Nordic | COFFEE CULTURE

Nordic countries will often head up the per-capita coffee consumption lists, with Finland sitting at the top, closely followed by Norway. Not only is a lot of coffee consumed in this part of the world, but provenance and flavour are key, as can be seen, indeed, in the whole Nordic

SEE ALSO
Cup of Excellence *p64*

SEE ALSO
Fika p90
World Barista Championship *p239*

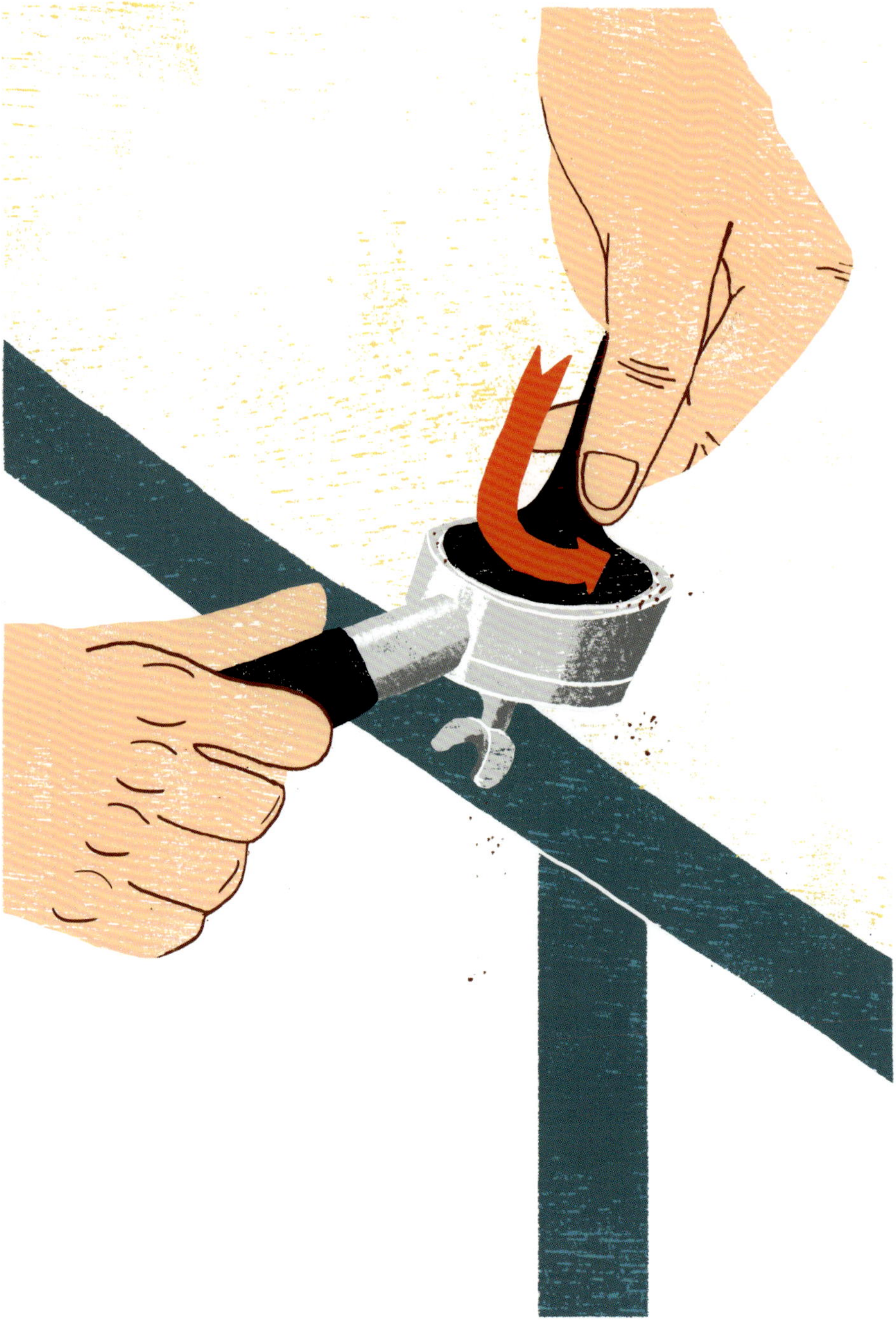

approach to cuisine. When the World Barista Championship began in 2000, the Nordic countries swept the board repeatedly for the first several years while everyone else sought to catch up. Many influential coffee companies and individuals are dotted around Scandinavia and Finland. In Sweden there is the daily ritual of *fika* and in the region as a whole the best restaurants incorporate the best coffee into their profile, as pioneered by the likes of Noma in Copenhagen and its collaboration with 2004 World Barista Champion Tim Wendelboe.

SEE ALSO
Barista *p23*
Extraction *p86*
Tamping *p213*

Nutate | ESPRESSO

Nutating is a relatively modern term to make its way into coffee. Popularized by Australian 2012 World Brewers Cup champion Matt Perger, it refers to a tamping technique. Normally, a barista would tamp down as levelly as possible in one smooth lowering movement until the ground coffee is compacted. The physics behind nutating is a lot like walking on snow. If you walk in traditional snowshoes (the ones like tennis rackets), your weight, and therefore force, is distributed and you will not compress the snow very much. Compare that to walking on snow with a pair of heels. Nutating allows you to compact the coffee bed to a greater degree by applying more concentrated pressure. To achieve this, the barista tamps the dose in a circular fashion with a swivel. One edge of one side of the tamper compresses the coffee first, you then roll it round to compress the rest, before ending up with a flat tamp. Although potentially a successful way of compressing coffee grounds, for an even extraction it also has high potential to be executed inconsistently or unevenly.

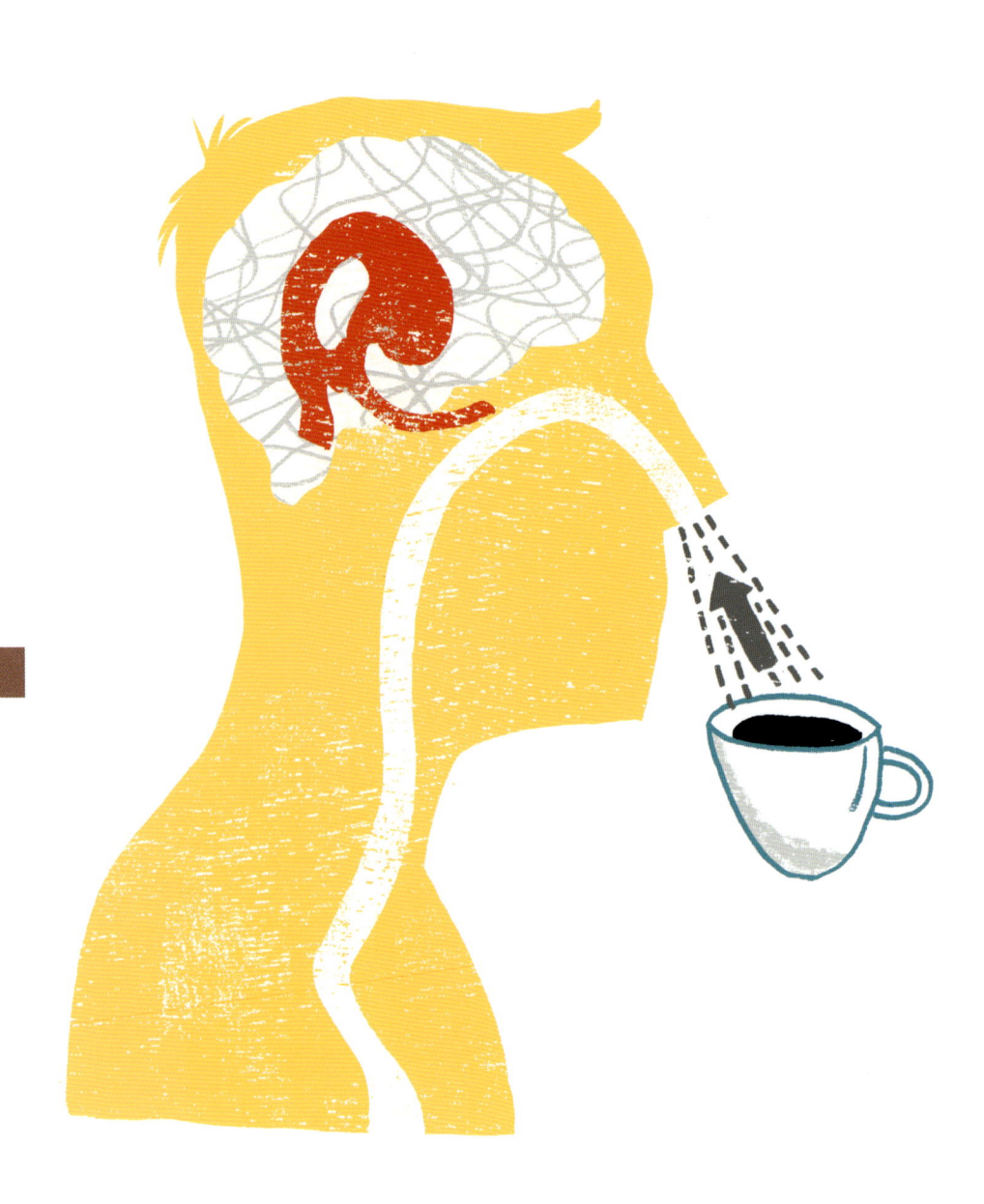

SEE ALSO
Green *p109*
India *p124*
Indonesia *p126*
Past crop *p172*

Old Brown Java | AGED COFFEE

The freshness of green coffee has become increasingly important to how we understand quality. A lot of the attributes we value, such as a clean cup, acidity, vibrancy, and sweetness, are present only in the freshly harvested coffee, and after several months these fade. Coffee becomes woody and flatter over time. Old Brown Java, a bit like Monsoon Malabar, breaks a coffee storage rule and is purposefully aged for up to five years, during which time the bean turns from a blue–green to brown. These coffees are pungent and woody with almost no acidity. There continues to be a market for these coffees.

SEE ALSO
Flavour notes *p97*
Gustatory *p113*
Sensory science *p197*

Olfactory | FLAVOUR

When we eat or drink something, our mouth and our nose work together and we experience taste and flavour. You just need to hold your nose while eating something to notice that much of the expected flavour simply disappears. In fact, it is our noses that are responsible for most of what we call flavour. This tasting system in our noses is called the olfactory system. Our mouths are known as the gustatory system and are responsible for sensations such as sweet, sour, and salty as well as textures like dryness and astringency. Other senses such as sight and sound feed into our tasting experiences as well, but are often forgotten about. The olfactory system, however, is undoubtedly the king of taste. Humans have varying sensitivities within their olfactory systems. Our sense of smell, and therefore taste, can be affected by a number of factors including genetics, age, or disease. This feeds into why the same drink can taste different to several people. We humans have a pretty decent smelling apparatus, but other mammals such as dogs have far superior ones, with up to 300 times more sensitivity. I have often smelt the intense perfumed notes of a very special coffee and wished at that moment that I had the nose of my dog Luca.

Oliver table

See "Density table".

One-way valve | PACKAGING

When you treat yourself to your favourite bag of beans it can come in a vast array of containers, made from varying materials, each with different storage properties. Once the beans are roasted they begin to change and age as they release carbon dioxide and are exposed to oxygen. The majority of coffee bags have a one-way valve that allows the CO_2 to leave while not allowing oxygen in, while others are simply top-folded paper bags. The paper bag style is simple and has a certain aesthetic appeal, but it will mean that the ageing of the coffee is much more rapid compared to the one-way valve bag. The valve, of course, needs to be part of a bag that itself provides an oxygen barrier (usually achieved with some kind of foil lining). Plant-based liners are becoming available. These

SEE ALSO
Green *p109*
Resting *p189*

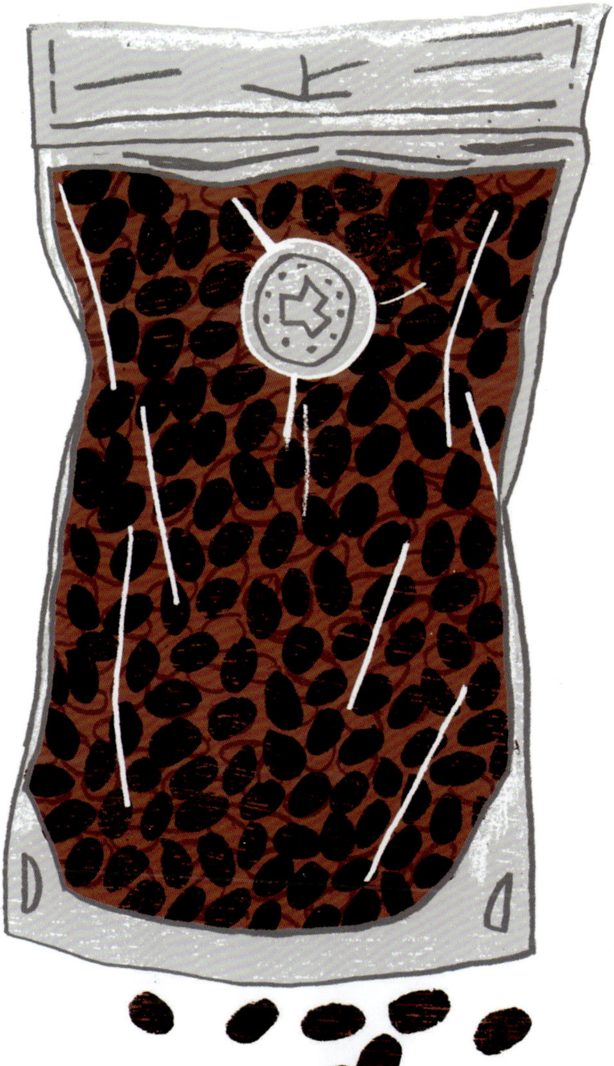

SEE ALSO
Blending *p27*
Espresso *p79*
Third wave *p218*

bags can also be flushed with nitrogen to limit the oxygen left in the bag. Nitrogen-flushed packaging, especially in the form of tin cans, extends the shelf life and freshness of the coffee considerably. This is alluring as it can give us more time to enjoy coffees when they are at their best in terms of green freshness and roasting.

Origin | PROVENANCE

Origin has become a commonly used term in coffee. I think it is valuable to point out the potential vagueness of the term. In essence, "origin" is a straightforward term. It refers to the point of origin of a coffee: "Where does it come from?" Historically, especially in the Italian espresso tradition, coffees from many countries have been blended together. In many cases, the exact origin of the components in the blend is the secret of the maker. Contrarily, the speciality and "third wave" movements place an emphasis on traceability and provenance, seeking to outline the origins of what you are drinking and to draw connections between flavour and the coffee's "story". The term "single origin" has become widely used and is becoming more prominent throughout the coffee-retailing landscape. The term implies quality and appeals to the drinker's curiosity to explore the flavour possibilities of coffee. However, a coffee from any single country is technically from a single origin, in as much as the coffee is from one country. The coffee, however, could be a blend of many diverse coffees from many farms. A number of speciality roasters now have almost exclusively single-origin offerings, and the term in this context is increasingly intended to denote a coffee from a specific variety of coffee plant, from a specific farm.

SEE ALSO
Resting *p189*

Oxidation | STORAGE

Oxygen is a very useful thing. However, it is also the scourge of shelf life and the perisher of food products. Coffee ages in two ways: it loses aromatics and it oxidizes. Oxidation is where oxygen comes along and steals electrons. Fruit going brown is a very visible example of this. Other forces have an impact upon a coffee's ageing, such as heat and light, but oxygen is the big daddy. If a coffee container can be made to contain less than 1 per cent oxygen, the freshness of the coffee is extended for amazing amounts of time. An aluminium container will give the longest life to the coffee by creating an extremely impressive oxygen barrier. With nitrogen-flushing and sealed containers, the life of the coffee goes from one month or so to several months, or even years. While freshness can be objectively measured from the moment the coffee is roasted, the optimal condition of the coffee – when the coffee's character it at its peak – is more subjective.

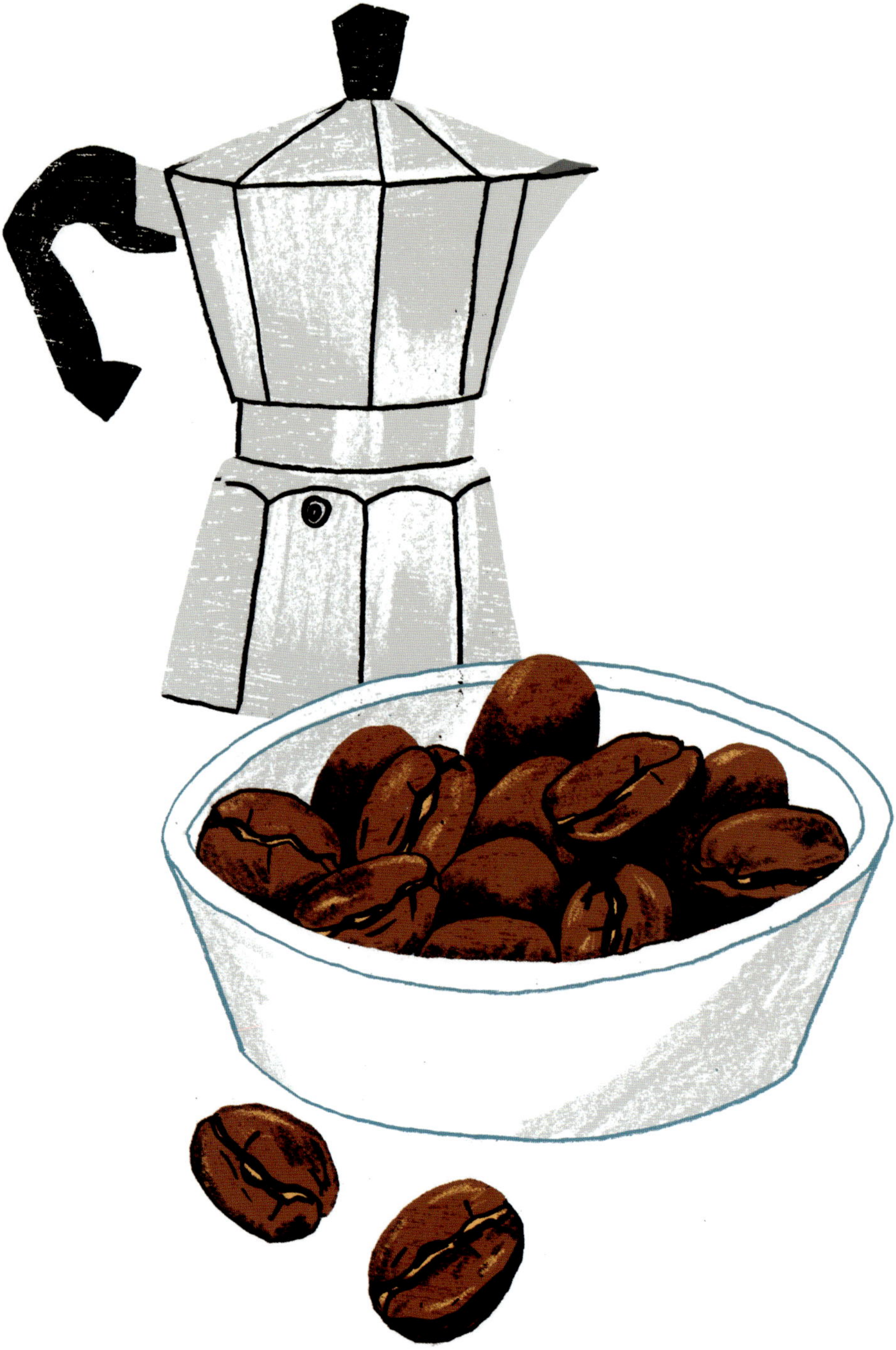

P

SEE ALSO
Bourbon *p35*
El Salvador *p77*
Variety *p228*

Pacamara | VARIETY

Pacamara is a coffee variety with a large bean size that is growing in popularity and is the result of the crossing of the Pacas variety and the Maragogype elephant bean. Pacas itself is a Bourbon mutation that originates in El Salvador and is named after a long-established family of coffee growers in the country. Pacamara, too, originates in El Salvador and, due to the high cup quality, has been successfully planted in other origins. Surprising not only for its size, Pacamara is capable of distinctive flavour characteristics. I often find floral and hoppy notes combined with a fair dose of chocolate and red fruit in Pacamara lots.

SEE ALSO
Bourbon *p35*
Cup of Excellence *p64*
Geisha *p105*

Panama | ORIGIN

The international reputation of Panama is intrinsically linked to the fame and success of the Geisha variety. Panama is likely the best example of a boutique coffee producer. Estates regularly focus on separating their crop up into individual lots, allowing for a focus on flavour variation within one estate. This means you will often be able to taste individual varieties processed in various ways all from one plot of land. Farms often develop a strong brand and identity to sell to the international market. Hacienda

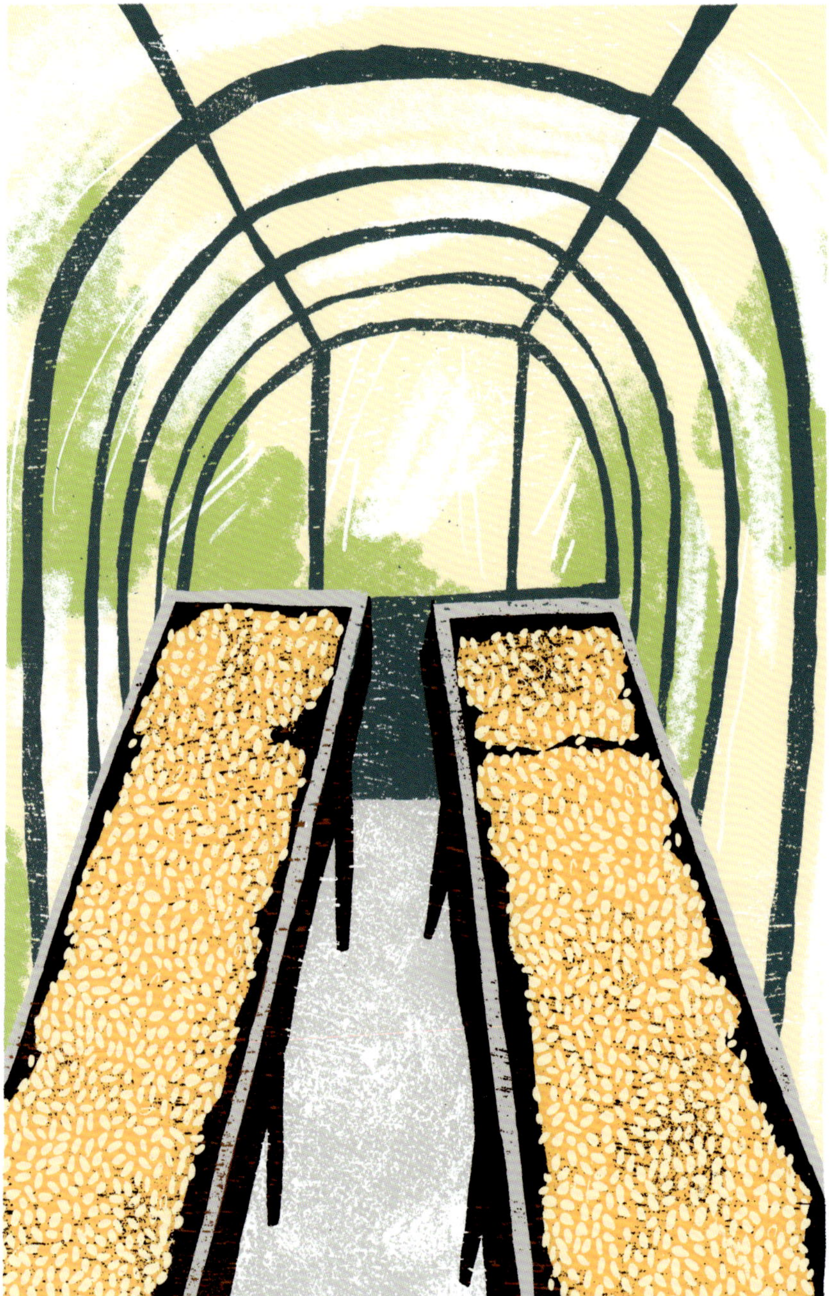

Esmeralda is well known for beginning the prominence of Geisha and establishing very high prices for the highest-scoring coffees through the Best of Panama competition. Esmeralda has won this competition multiple times. The Boquete and Volcán Barú coffee regions are known for producing exceptional coffee. It is not all about Geisha, though: there are other varieties that are grown very successfully in Panama, such as Caturra and Bourbon.

Paper

See "Chemex".

Papua New Guinea | ORIGIN

Papua New Guinea is popping up more and more on importers' cupping tables as well as in speciality coffee roasteries. Nearly all of the coffee is grown by smallholders. The potential problems with smallholdings – most notably, the lack of resources to process coffee well – can be countered by cooperative farming, which is all about bringing producers together and pooling resources as well as achieving market share. This origin is still very much in the "full of potential" bracket: some companies are actively working in the country to help improve quality, while many others are keeping a keen eye on the origin. Often, Papua New Guinea is filed under the Indonesia origin, but the cup qualities are unique. The good coffees are clean and bright with complex fruit and a creamy quality.

Parabolic | DRYING

Many drying environments can be used to dry coffee beans once they have been

SEE ALSO
Mechanical drying *p145*
Raised beds *p186*

harvested. Parabolic drying takes place inside an environment much like a greenhouse or polytunnel. As with all drying and processing techniques, it appears that parabolic drying is a multifaceted equation – the coming together of a number of variables defines the results. Parabolic drying, like mechanical drying, is most popular in countries with erratic rainfall. The polytunnel helps create a more controlled drying environment.

Past crop | OLD COFFEE

It is usually considered that fresh-crop coffee tastes better, though exactly when a coffee becomes "past crop" is not clearly defined, and a market does exist for some purposely aged coffees – Monsoon Malabar and Old Brown Java are good examples. Interestingly, a freshly harvested coffee can taste a little grassy, tight, and green, and so, while fresh is the rule, optimal flavour often requires some resting as well (much the same applies to freshly roasted coffee). Coffee from origins that struggle with drying will fade and taste like past crop more quickly. The widespread adoption of GrainPro Cocoons™ – plastic storage bags for green coffee – has prolonged the life and quality of coffee beyond what used to be possible. Even so, once imported, the environment in which green coffee is stored has a big impact on the speed of ageing. Heat and variable humidity are a problem. Regardless of how engaging and beautiful it is to have a roaster in the coffee shop, it is often not a great place to store green coffee. Temperature- and humidity-controlled environments are now becoming more prevalent as a means to extend the life of green coffee.

SEE ALSO
Freezing *p98*
Fresh crop *p103*
Green *p109*
India *p124*
Old Brown Java *p163*
Resting *p189*

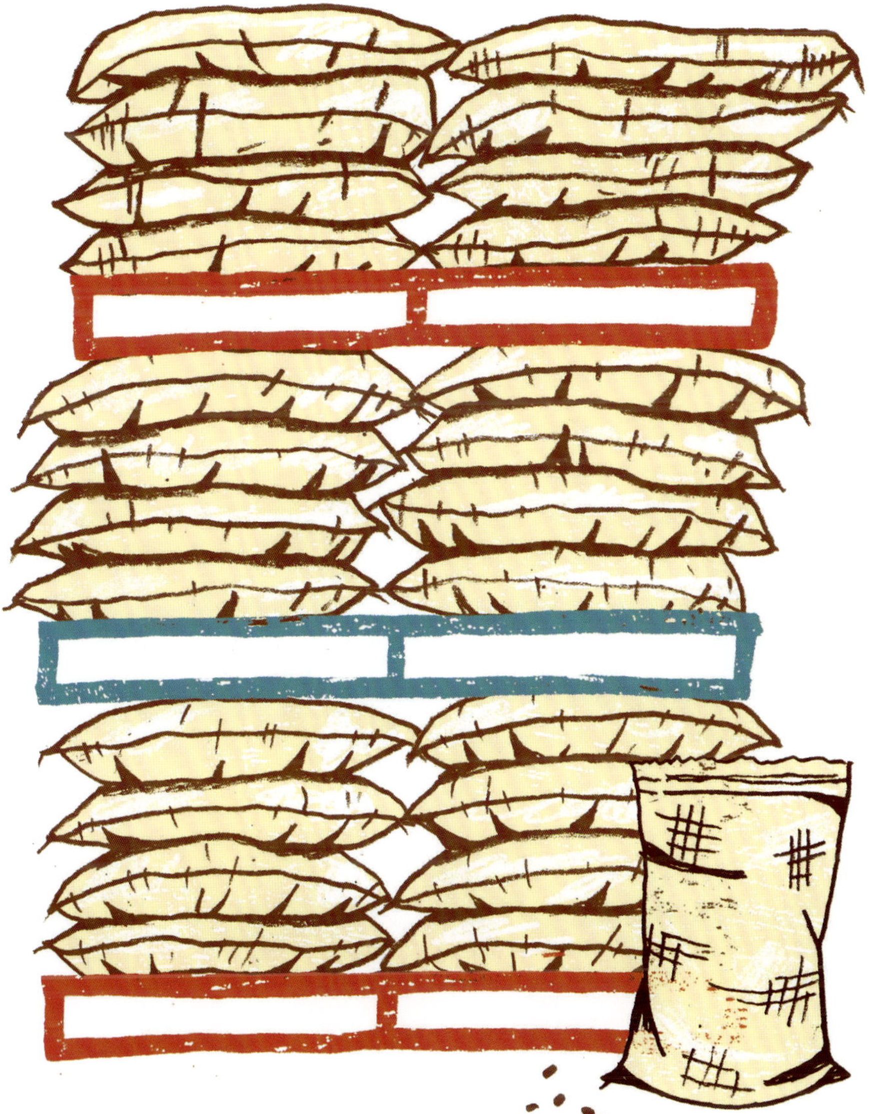

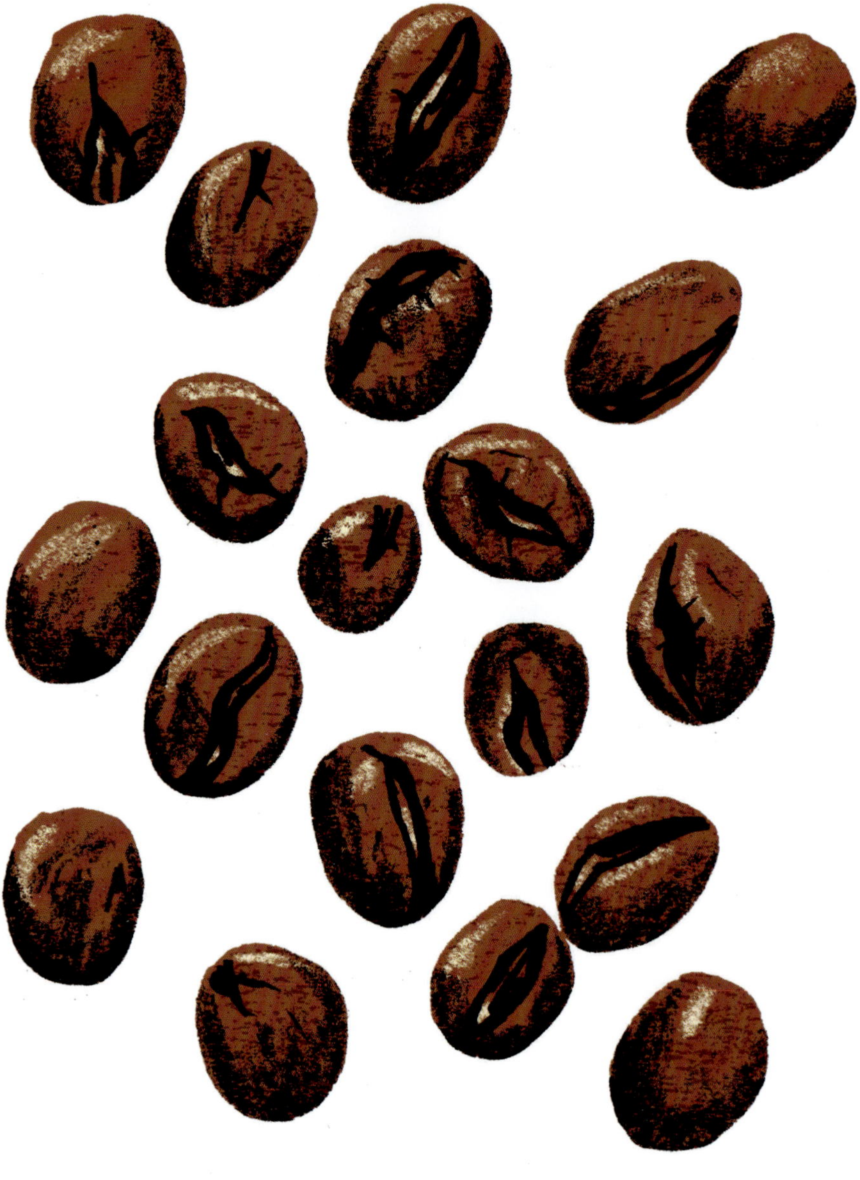

SEE ALSO
Defects *p67*
Kenya *p135*

Peaberry | COFFEE BEAN TYPE

There are many coffee terms and technical definitions that you will see on packets and websites. It can be overwhelming, and a few key terms often get confused. Peaberry seems to be one of those. You may see a Kenyan coffee that is labelled as a peaberry and you might be forgiven for thinking that this is a variety of coffee. This is not the case, however: all varieties can produce peaberries. The term refers to a natural anomaly that occurs inside the coffee cherry in which only one of the seeds is fertilized and so develops alone inside the cherry. Normally, two seeds grow next to each other, creating a flat side on each where they meet – this is what gives coffee beans their familiar shape. Without the second seed to grow against, the peaberry becomes almost spherical. Certain origins (most prominently Kenya and Tanzania) are more likely to sort the peaberries and sell them separately, whereas many others will not, which is why you do not see peaberries from all origins. Peaberries do taste different to the rest of the crop, and the theories as to what causes the difference are as follows: (1) the peaberry gets more of the cherry's nutrients; (2) the spherical shape and density of the bean means it can roast more evenly; and (3) the fact that the peaberry has to be so carefully sorted means that it is less likely to contain defects.

SEE ALSO
Fairtrade *p89*

Peru | ORIGIN

Peru is a large producer of coffee. The cup profile tends to be round and smooth, with lower acidity and a more nutty, chocolaty quality. The organic certification is very prevalent in Peru, as is the Fairtrade certification, though neither really leads to higher cup quality and many of the certified-organic coffees are still sold extremely cheaply. It is not common to see Peruvian coffees stocked and presented by speciality roasters but, as with many producing countries, increasing numbers of traceable and interesting coffees come from the origin.

Phosphoric acid | GROWING; TASTING

Coffee contains many flavour attributes and one of the most desirable and sought-after elements of a good cup is acidity. Acidity in coffee is not always good, however: a vinegary flavour, for example, would be attributed to acetic acid. It is rather the type and structure of acidity that we are after, and it is possible to link these flavour experiences back to specific acids within the bean. The roasting process alters acids in the coffee bean, but we still rely on them being present in the harvested green coffee. Citric acid is made by all coffee plants due to the process of photosynthesis. Phosphoric acid, however, can become part of the coffee only if it is present in the soil the plant grows in. Many East African coffees display phosphoric acidity, which presents itself as a sparkling, slightly fizzy sensation.

Plunger

See "French press".

Portafilter | ESPRESSO

Also referred to as the "braccio" (the arm), this word simply means "carry [a] filter". This term, along with the likes of "group head" and "drip tray", is a description of integral parts of all espresso machine designs regardless of the

SEE ALSO
Acidity *p13*

SEE ALSO
Basket *p23*
Espresso *p79*
Weighing scales *p239*

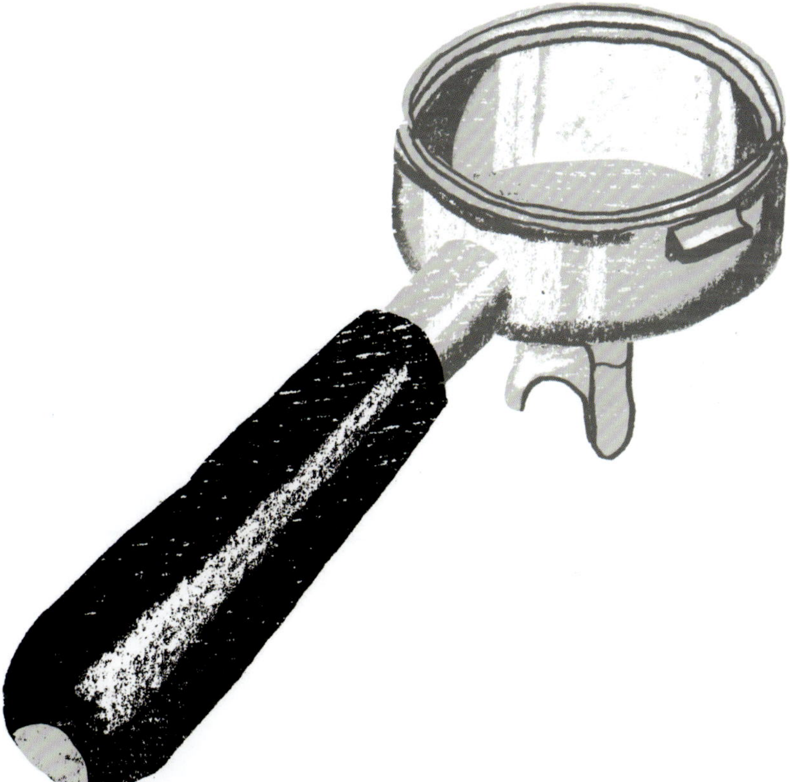

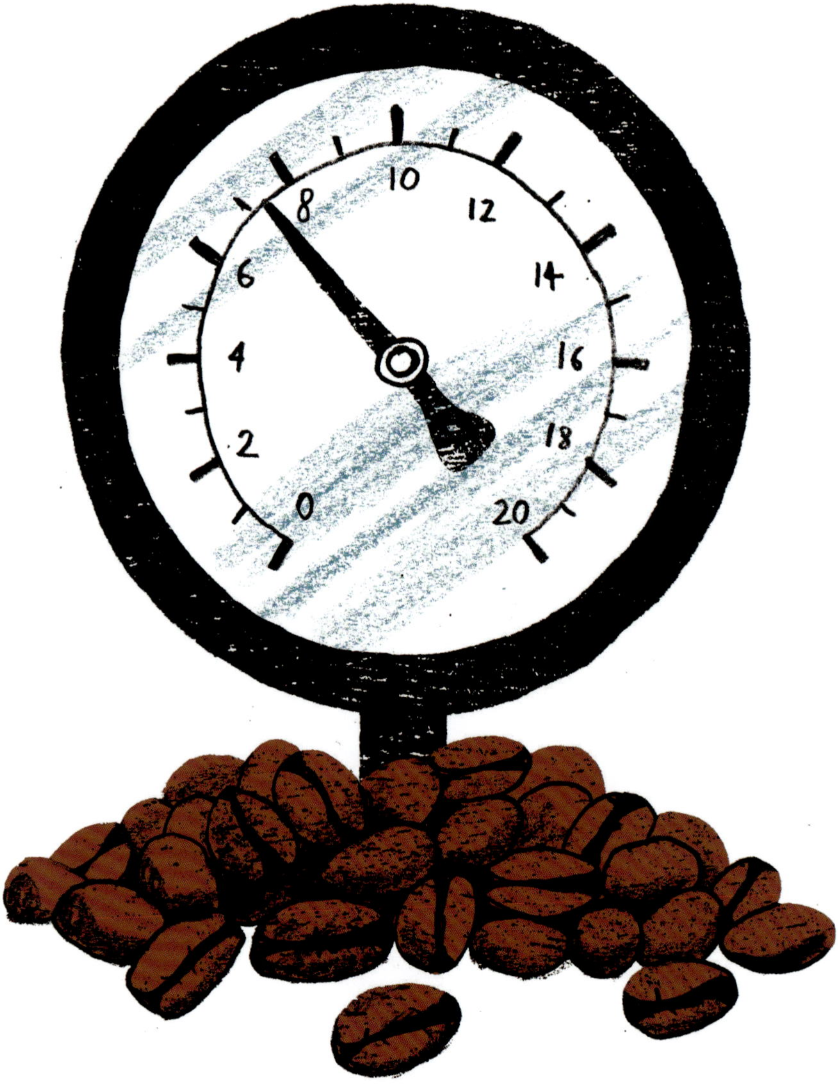
0
2
4
6
8
10
12
14
16
18
20

manufacturer. The portafilter is the handle that holds the basket. Like other parts of the espresso machine, it is relatively common for the portafilter to be customized with all manner of designs and materials. A pro tip is to add small weights or tape to the portafilter to allow multiples to all weigh exactly the same amount. This eliminates the need to constantly tare the scale when using an espresso machine with multiple groups.

Pour-over

See "Full immersion".

Pressure | ESPRESSO

SEE ALSO
Aeropress™ *p13*
Crema *p63*
Espresso *p79*
Moka pot *p149*

Espresso is a coffee brewed under pressure, but what exactly is the pressure doing to the coffee and the drink? Brewing espresso under high pressure drives the CO_2 out of the coffee, which then becomes the crema on top of the espresso. The pressure allows us to grind finer and increase extraction potential by having enough force to pass the water through the finely ground coffee. Without pressure, the water would just get stuck. It is fascinating to compare the flavours of the same strength beverage at two slightly different pressures, say 7 bar and 9 bar. The exact cause of these differences is hard to figure out as there are so many variables occurring at once. Pressure has an intimate relationship with the grinder, too: grind too fine and the water cannot pass through the puck, no matter the pressure. There might be a sweet spot, but this is one of many unanswered questions in coffee. Other methods like the moka pot and the Aeropress™ produce pressure but in much smaller and less measurable amounts.

SEE ALSO
Brazil *p35*
Colombia *p60*

Producing | GROWING

When it comes to coffee, the world tends to be broken up into consuming and producing countries. Do you grow or do you drink? For the majority of coffee's trading history, most of the coffee grown has been consumed outside the countries growing it. This is due to its value as an exported good. The irony is that the high-quality coffee is far too valuable to stay, and so the coffee consumed internally is the lower-grade gear. Things are a changing, though: as countries like Brazil and Colombia prosper economically and modernize, their café cultures are expanding and more and more coffee is being consumed within the countries of origin.

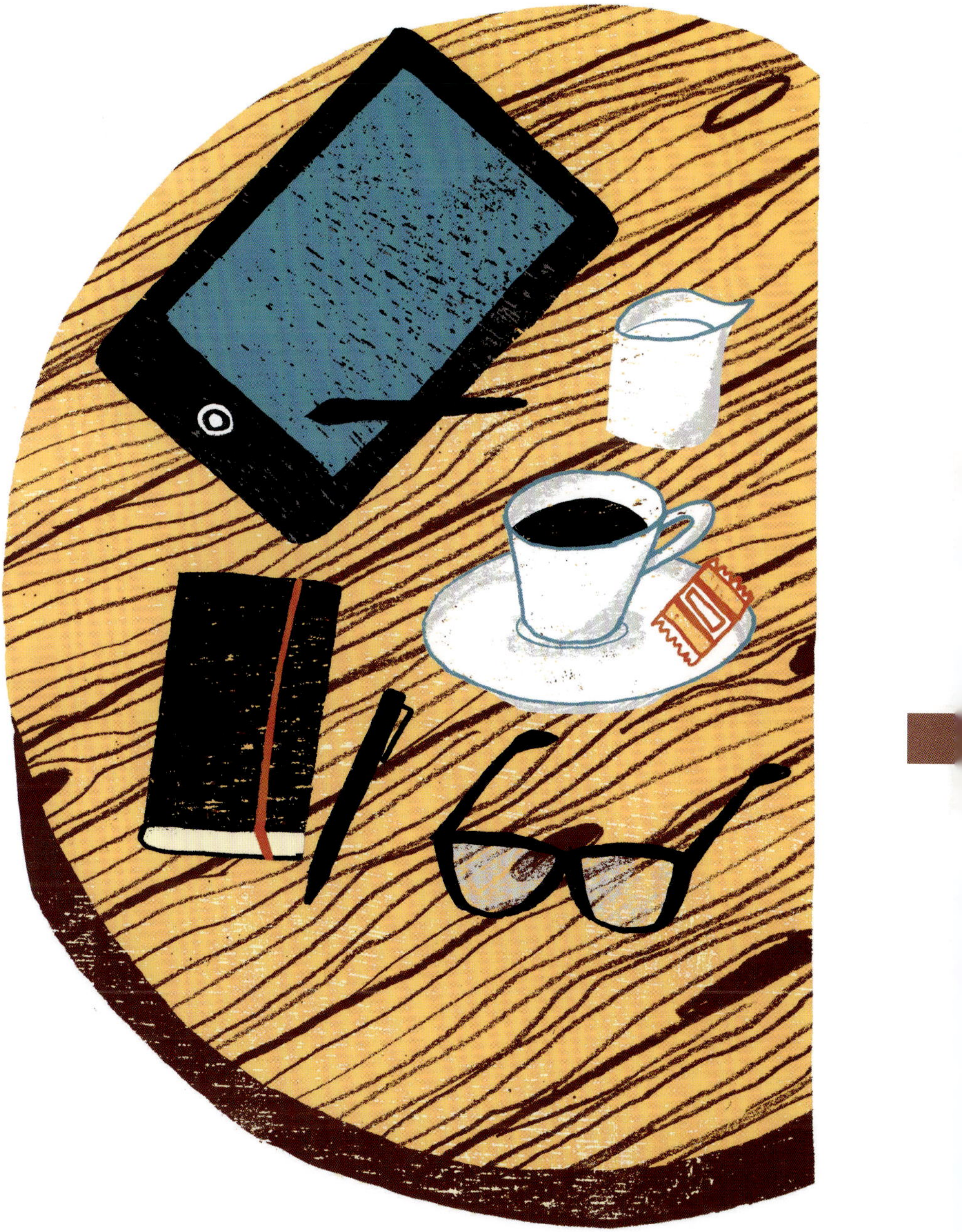

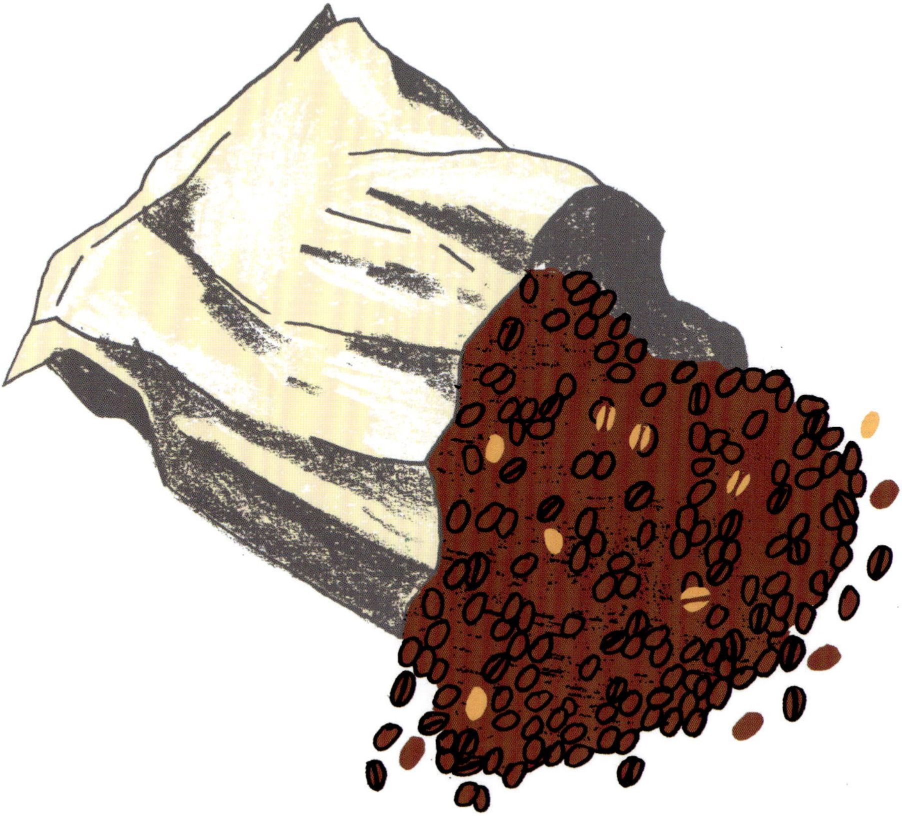

Q

Q Grader | QUALIFICATION

Administered by the Coffee Quality Institute, the Q Grader qualification is the most prestigious in the coffee industry. It consists of an intensive week-long course and exam that tests the individual's ability to taste and grade coffee. Twenty-two individual tests must be passed to become a Q Grader. These cover everything from picking out the amount of salt and sugar dissolved in test waters to general knowledge tests and coffee scoring. Qualifications in speciality coffee are becoming more prevalent as the industry grows and matures. The Q Grader qualification has applicability across all commercial coffee and not just speciality coffee. There is also an R Grader qualification, which focuses on the discipline of grading and understanding the Robusta species and the coffee it produces.

Quaker | DEFECTS

Have you ever spotted a very blond-looking bean among all the brown beans in a hopper or bag of roasted coffee? This is a quaker, and you don't want it to be there. This is a seed that came from an under-ripe cherry during harvesting. The wet-process method is able to almost eliminate quakers, as they generally float to the top when submerged in water. The natural processing method makes them harder to spot, and so it is often in coffees processed this way that you spot one. If you see a quaker, snatch it out of your dose or bag and chuck it on the compost heap – and enjoy a tastier cup of coffee.

Radiation | ROASTING

When you roast a coffee you are essentially cooking it and, just like heating food, there are various ways in which you can cook a coffee. The two most commonly used methods are convection and conduction: the application of heat either through the use of hot air (convection) or by making a container such as a drum hot (conduction), which then transfers heat to the beans. Different roasting machines can play around with the amount of each cooking force (you could, for example, have a roaster that is more air driven or one that is more drum driven), and the different processes alter the way in which the bean is cooked and how it tastes. The fastest roasters, though, are those that use convection. Less common is the use of radiation, as in the domestic microwave oven. The radiation vibrates the water molecules in the food, which then heat up and cook the food. What is especially interesting here is the potential for more even heating throughout the beans, as the centre gets heated at the same time as the outside. The exact differences in flavour radiation produces are not particularly well documented, but this roasting technology is increasingly being explored and with great results.

SEE ALSO
Species *p202*
Honey process *p118*
Natural process *p156*
Terroir *p214*
Washed process *p235*

Raised beds | PROCESSING

After coffee cherries are picked, the cherry must be removed and the seeds (coffee beans) dried. Coffee must be dried to the point of a 12 per cent moisture content before export. There is a variety of methods for the removal of the cherry and the drying of the bean, all of which come under the bracket of "processing". Even though the cherry has spent nine months maturing on the branch of a coffee tree (according to the *terroir*), this relatively short process has a huge influence on the taste and quality of the coffee. Raised beds can be used to dry the bean with varying amounts of cherry still intact. The main idea behind the beds is to help control the drying process by lifting the coffee from the ground and allowing air to circulate around all the coffee, enabling more even and predictable drying with less problematic fermentation. There is a strong correlation between raised beds and increased cup quality.

SEE ALSO
Development *p71*

Rate of rise | ROASTING

This technical industry term refers to the change in temperature of your beans as they get hotter, describing the rate at which the bean is heating up. Coffee expert and author Scott Rao has been influential in coffee brewing and roasting and has popularized the term "rate of rise". He draws a correlation between a continually decreasing rate of rise and a better roast. This means the bean takes on heat more quickly at the beginning and more slowly as the roast goes on. This requires a fine balance, however; if the heat of the roast begins to reverse and the beans start getting cooler, then we get something called a "baked roast", which tastes flat and bland.

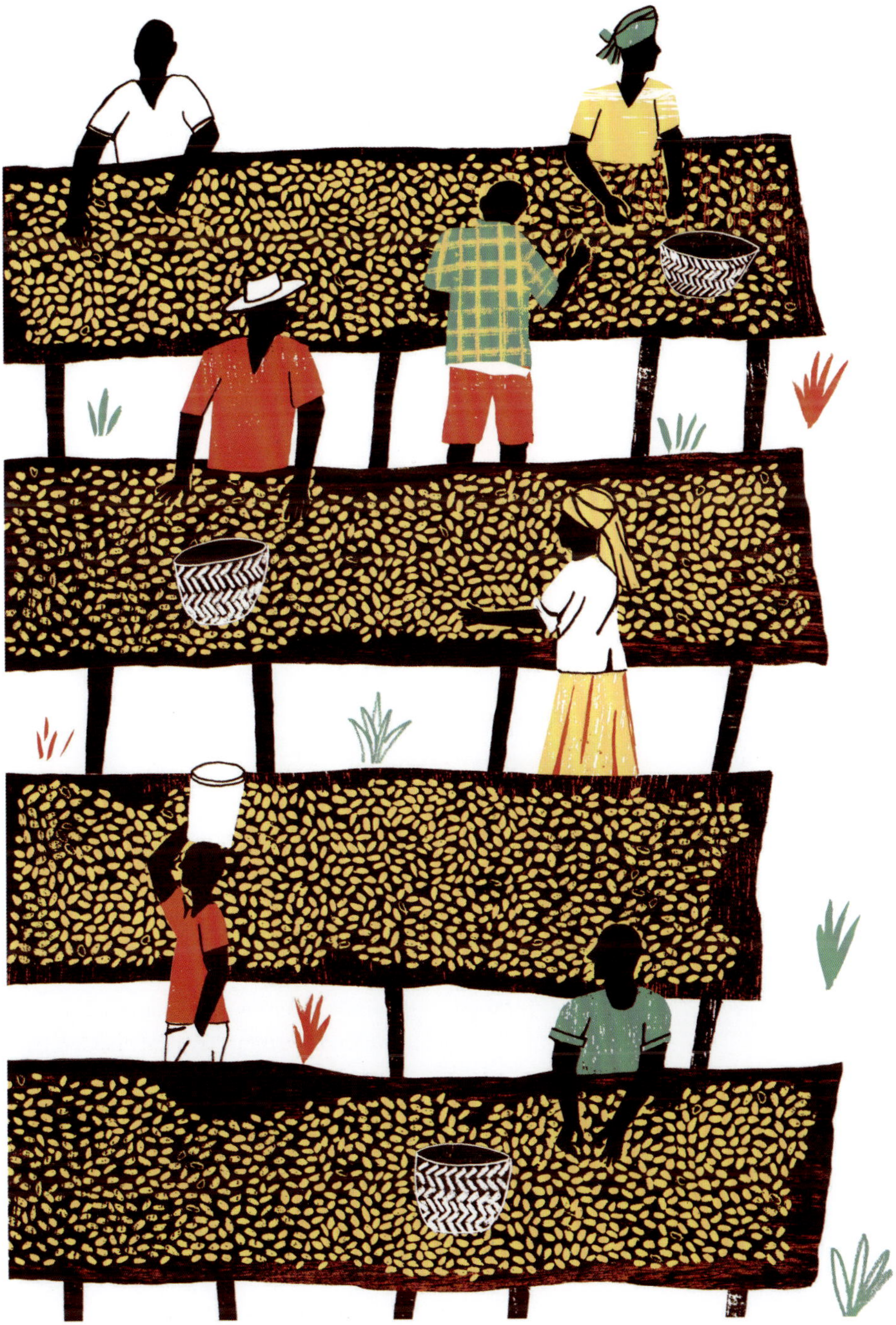

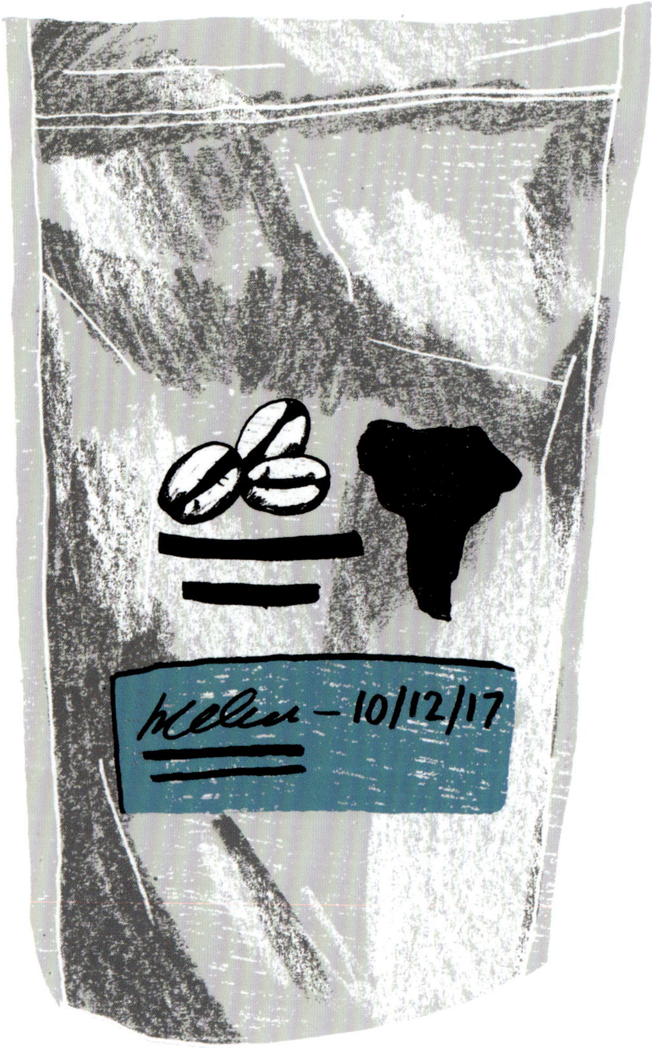
10/12/17

SEE ALSO
Brix *p38*
Extraction *p86*

Refractometer | TESTING

Refractometers are used in a number of industries and work on the principle of light refraction – it is all in the name. You take a sample of a liquid and the apparatus shoots light through it, measuring how the solids suspended in the liquid push the light around. The concept is then to work back from here and figure out how many solids are in the liquid based on how much the light is refracted. The same apparatus is used in wine and fruit to measure ripeness and figure out sugar concentration, but in coffee it is used to measure the amount of coffee solids that have ended up in the beverage. The results must be considered in context, though they do have the potential to provide insights into the coffee-making process.

SEE ALSO
Green *p109*
One-way valve *p164*
Oxidation *p167*

Resting | FRESHNESS

The concept of freshness in coffee is easy. When a coffee is harvested, it is at its most fresh. Freshness from roast is at its height when the coffee is pulled out of the roaster's cooling tray. Freshly ground coffee is coffee that was ground immediately before being brewed. This idea of freshness has become intrinsically linked to ideas of quality. So fresh is best …? Not quite. "Fresh is best" is an easy narrative and one that is broadly true. Coffee harvested 18 months ago does not score as well as coffee harvested last week. Coffee roasted yesterday tastes better than coffee roasted a year ago, and so on. However, the best results lie somewhere in between, and, for the most part, very fresh coffee is not optimal. Coffees can have a "green" quality just after being harvested; they are often a touch astringent and lack sweetness and structured acidity. Coffee that has just been roasted needs to lose the CO_2 and will often "open up" several days after roast. In fact, depending on the coffee and the roasting style, this flavour peak can be much longer after roast, around three to six weeks in some cases. The roaster will be able to advise on when they think their coffee is at its best.

Reverse osmosis | FILTRATION

This type of filtration is often a slightly more complex and expensive process than that provided by cartridge filters (ion exchange cartridges). In reverse osmosis, water is forced at high pressure against a membrane and you end up with an almost mineral-less solution on one side and a highly concentrated solution of minerals on the other. Most people use the "empty" side and add a bit of the concentrate back in. In soft water areas it is not unheard of to reverse this so as to increase the mineral content. In very hard water areas reverse osmosis is the only way to push mineral content down, unless you distil your water. Reverse osmosis systems can be quite wasteful, in some cases creating 50 per cent waste water, but many systems have greatly improved upon this. From a coffee point of view, the key thing to realize is that, like cartridge-based filtration, the system can only manipulate the water that you started with. Re-mineralization systems do exist and are increasingly being explored. These will allow more control over actual water composition.

Ripe | HARVESTING

It is widely held that perfectly ripe cherries contain the best coffee. There are, however,

SEE ALSO
Buffer *p38*
Cartridge filter *p48*
Water *p236*

SEE ALSO
Brazil *p35*
Brix *p38*
Refractometer *p189*

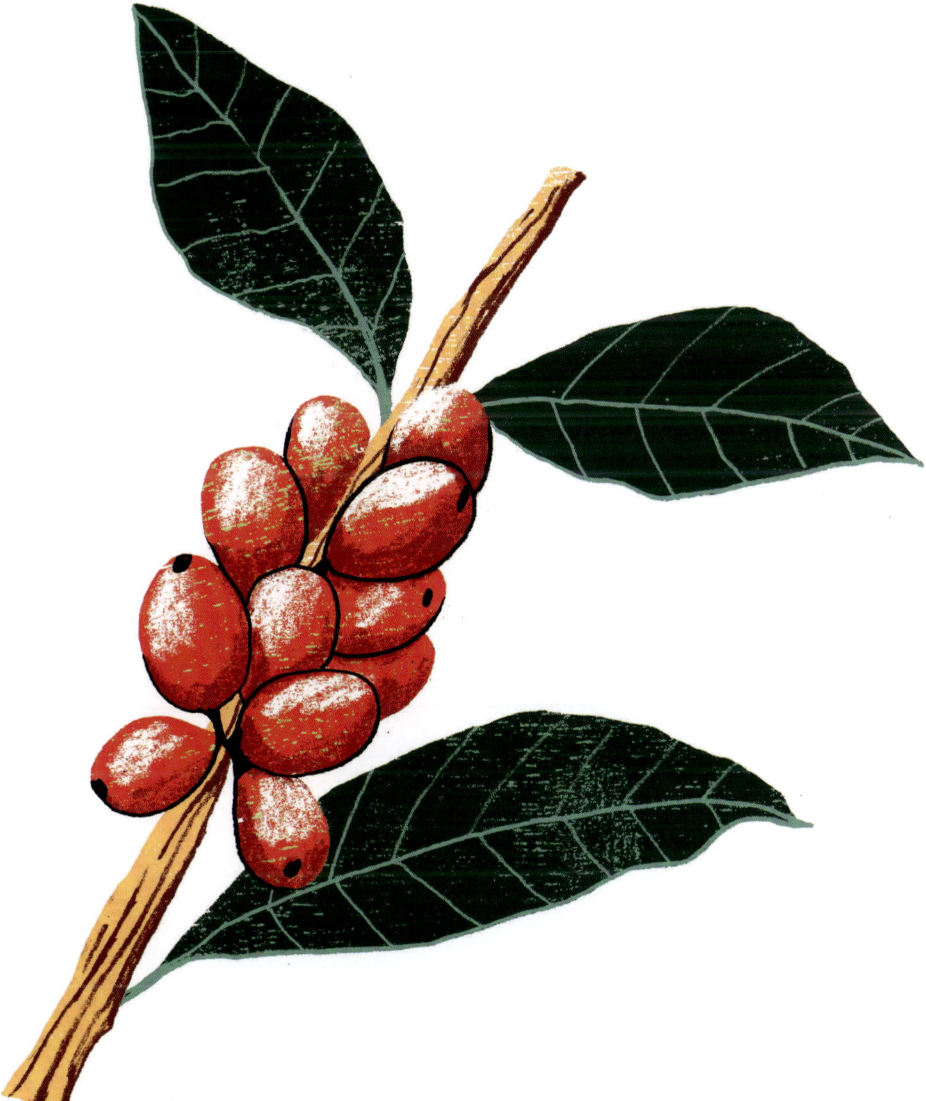

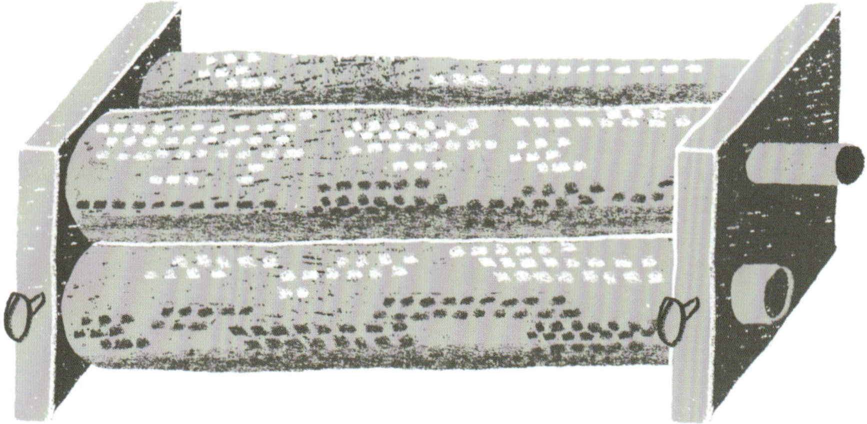

times in coffee production when "over-ripe" cherries will be chosen for the specific flavour profile they can bring. Perhaps the most pertinent question is: exactly what constitutes a ripe coffee cherry? It is most frequently the coffee cherry's appearance that is used as a guide to ripeness. For most varieties this will be when the coffee is at its most vibrant red before it starts to go purple and brown, which are indicators of over-ripeness. So while we can all agree that ripe cherries produce the best results in the cup, the exact shade of red can often vary from variety to variety, and nowadays it is more common for farmers to measure the sugar content of the cherry to help discern optimal picking times. Handpicking has its benefits here, but modern technology can also achieve excellent results by sorting the cherries after they have been harvested. In countries like Brazil a big tractor will strip the coffee plants and then all manner of gizmos are used to sort ripe from unripe – such as pressure sorters that measure how hard the cherries are.

Robusta

See "Species".

Roller grinder | GRINDING

The most common way to grind coffee that you will see in shops and homes around the world is burr grinding. However, there are multiple ways to grind coffee. Blade grinders are the least desirable; they hack at the coffee and create a very uneven spread of sizes. Roller grinders are popular with commercial coffee companies. Imagine two rolling pins with spiked surfaces that sit atop one another. The coffee passes

SEE ALSO
Flat burr *p93*

between them and gets ground down in the process. Roller grinders can have several series of rollers and are capable of producing very evenly ground coffee as well as grinds that are more spherically shaped.

Rwanda | ORIGIN

Rwanda is a country that can produce exceptional cup qualities, abundant with flavours of berry fruits and florals, winey acidity, and complexity. Rwanda is a relative newcomer to the speciality scene; the country's coffee-producing past was largely commercial and limited in scale. Add to this the turmoil of the mid-1990s, meaning that it was not until mid-2000s that the first washing station was built. Since then, Rwanda has become the first and only African country to host a Cup of Excellence and the coffees from this origin have started to get the recognition they deserve.

SEE ALSO
Cup of Excellence *p64*
Defects *p67*

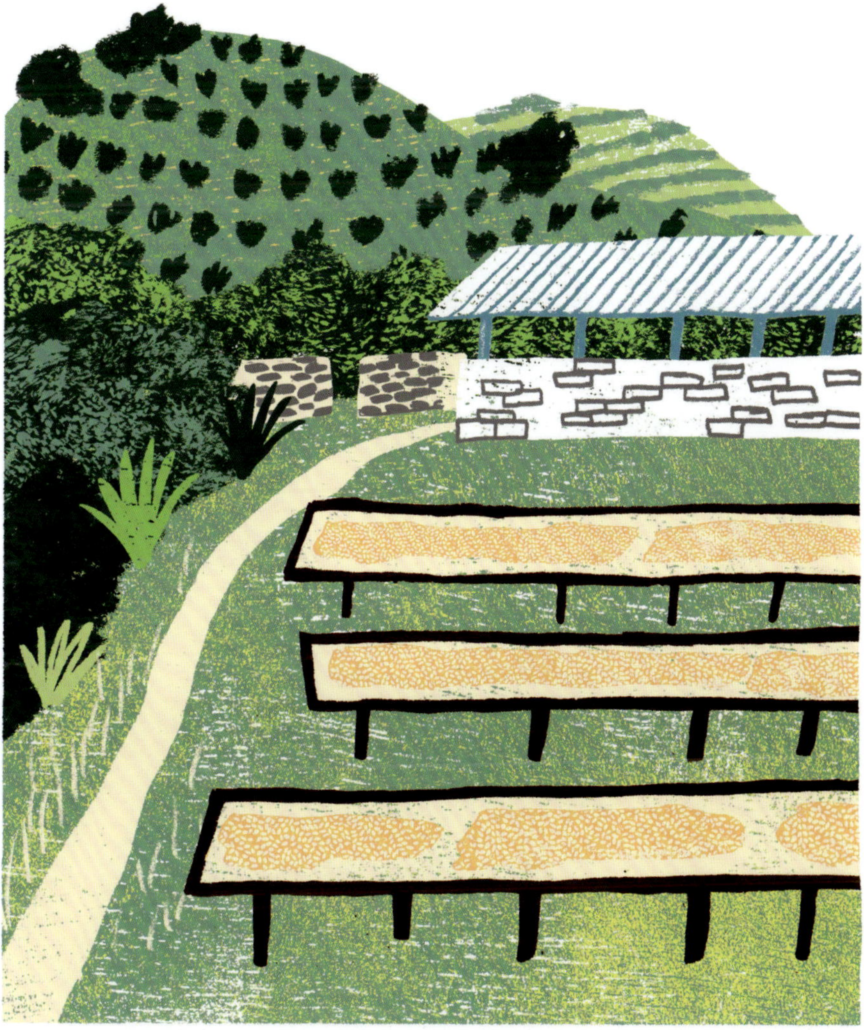

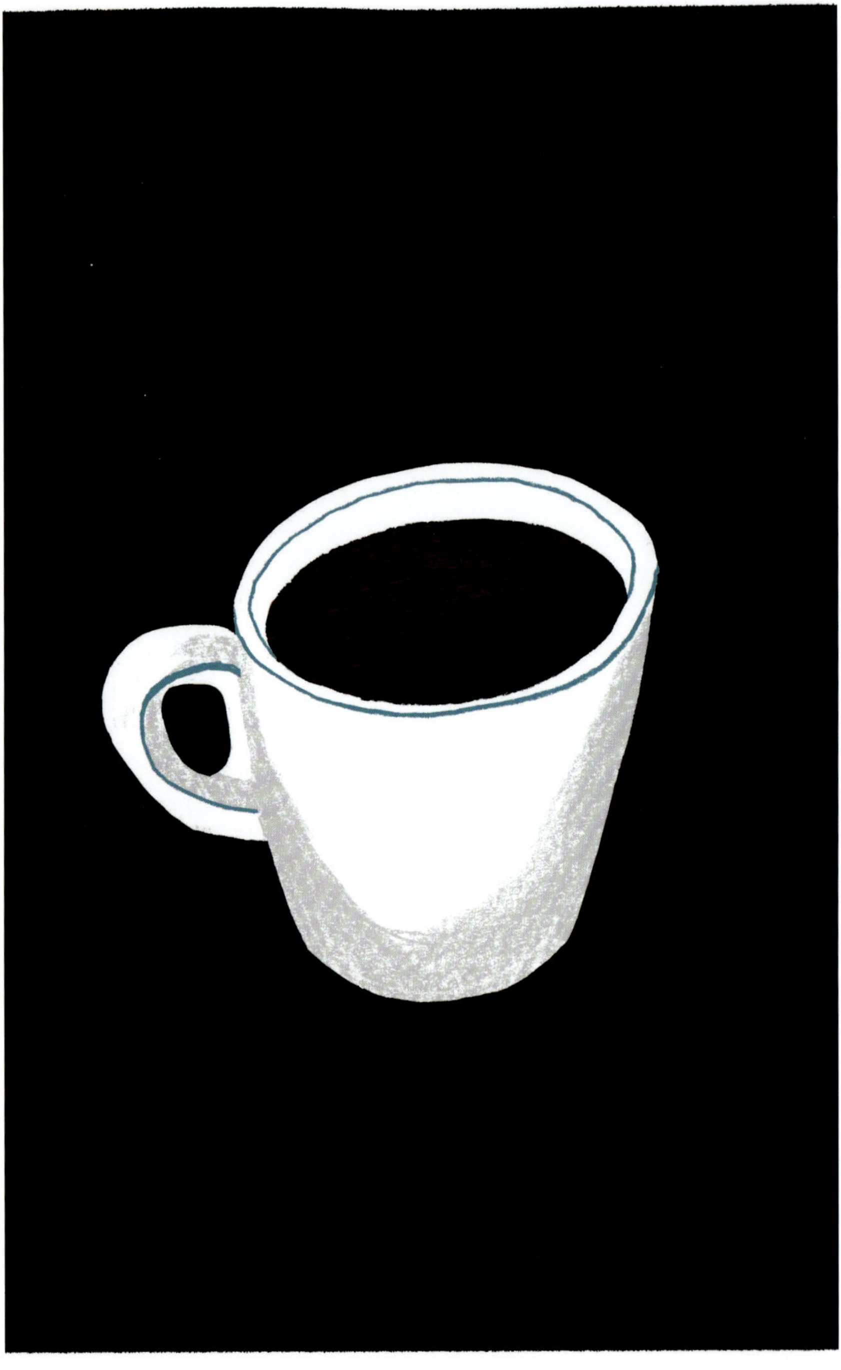

S

Sensory science | TASTING

My first real introduction to the world of sensory science was through the work of the Oxford University professor of experimental psychology Charles Spence. Essentially, Spence studies how everything other than the actual food and drink affects your experience and perception of them. This includes all kinds of details, such as the weight of the cutlery, the plate shape, the colour of a cup, or the ambient sound. Coffee, for instance, is perceived as being almost twice as intense when served in a white cup compared to a black one. Interestingly, the coffee in the white cup is also perceived as less sweet. It is fascinating how complex our eating and drinking experiences are. Was the best cup of coffee you ever had simply the best, or was it the coming together of a great coffee with the right setting, the right colours, the right *everything* for you? This is why it is so important when tasting and scoring coffee to create a repeatable, clean, quiet, and unbiased environment. There is, of course, no such thing as an absolutely unbiased environment, so consistency is key.

Signature drinks | COMPETITIONS

The term "signature drink" is, in the world of coffee, exclusive to the World Barista

SEE ALSO
Barista *p23*
Espresso *p79*
World Barista
    Championship *p239*

Championship. Since the competition's inception in 2000 the signature drink has been a staple of the round of drinks required of the competitor, alongside espresso and a steamed-milk beverage. The brief is pretty loose, really, and amounts to some kind of espresso-based "cocktail". Alcohol is, however, not allowed (there is a separate competition for this, called Coffee in Good Spirits – often shortened to CIGS). One of the main goals of a signature drink is not to drown out the character of the coffee but instead complement it to create a unique drink that celebrates its ingredients – especially, of course, the coffee. This is hard. Many a barista competitor will have toiled night after night exploring undrinkable combinations until they crack the code. The signature drink is often the most theatrical element of a barista's competition routine.

Silver skin | GROWING; ROASTING

At the centre of the coffee cherry sit two coffee seeds side by side. These two little seeds are encased in a light, semi-transparent layer known as a silver skin. Next is a layer of parchment/husk and the pulp or flesh of the cherry. The silver skin is the only part of the original setup left attached to the seeds when green coffee has been processed and exported. Natural-processed coffee tends to have more silver skin, and washed coffee less. During the roasting process this silver skin easily removes itself from the bean and becomes chaff. Propelled by the roaster's airflow, the chaff is pulled into a collector somewhere in the roaster. One needs to be careful to clean out and dispose of chaff in the equipment. When we roast, a pretty little chaff "snow shower" falls down from a chimney out the back of our roastery.

SEE ALSO
Green *p109*

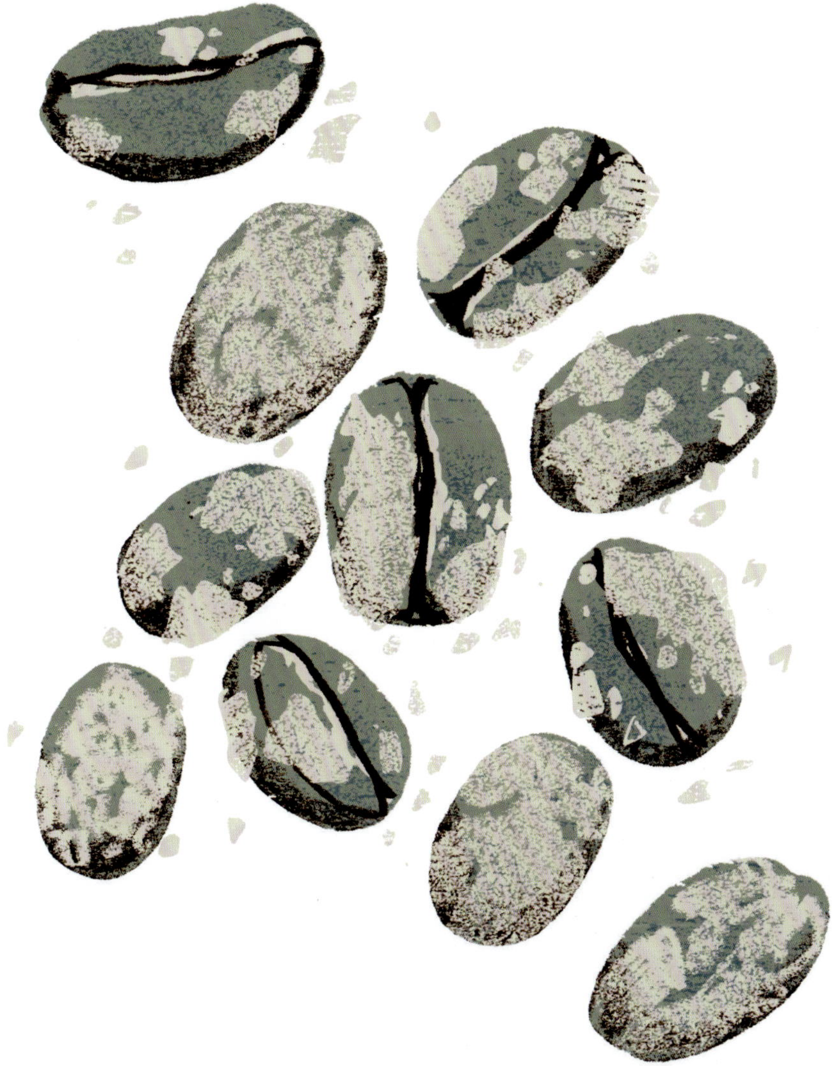

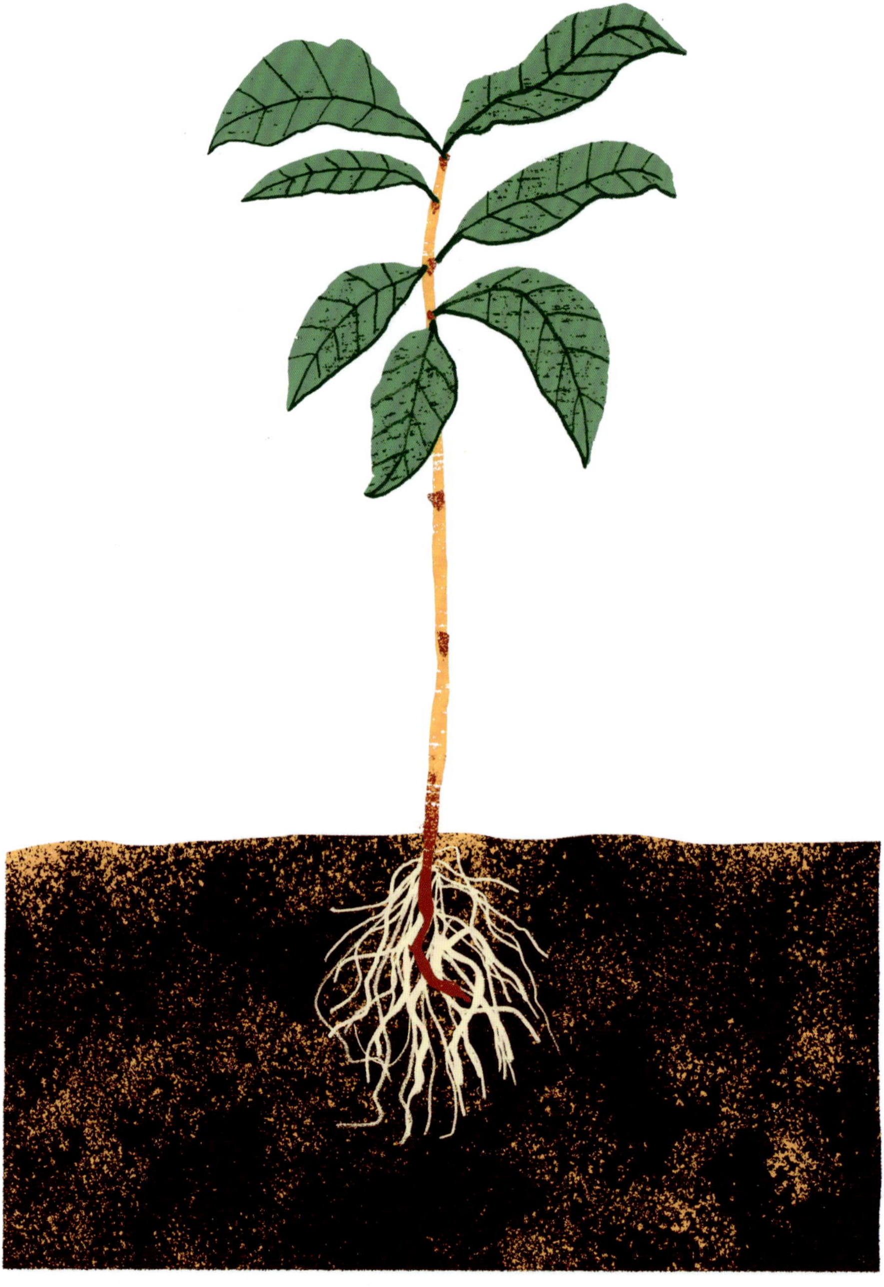

Single origin

See "Origin".

Slow brew | COFFEE CULTURE

You may have come across the term "slow bar". This simply refers to a filter coffee bar, but a little more can be inferred from the name. Typically, a slow bar sells single-serve, manually brewed filters. At its heart is the making of quality coffee and it is a reaction to the fast-food ethos – both in terms of service and preparation – that has come to characterize so many coffee shops. The slow bar is all about taking time to embrace the ritual of crafting a cup of coffee, to watch it being made, to engage with the barista, or simply sit and take a moment. Evidently, coffee-shop economics are more typically built on speedier service, and some stores will offer a slow bar as part of its offer and, quite rightly, charge more for the experience.

SEE ALSO
Barista *p23*

Soil | GROWING

The coffee plant, like any other crop, draws its nutrients from the soil. This, in turn, affects the way the plant grows and the coffee it produces. The pH number (measuring acidity and alkalinity) and phosphorus, nitrogen, and potassium levels are key markers for farmers to understand the management of their crop. Fertilizers need to be considered in conjunction with soil composition. Like sunlight, temperature, altitude, variety, and processing, soil composition is just another aspect of the *terroir* and greatly influences the flavour profile of the coffee. Measuring and managing soil in conjunction with these factors will contribute greatly to realizing exceptional cup quality.

SEE ALSO
Agronomy *p15*
Altitude *p16*
Terroir *p214*

SEE ALSO
Q Grader *p183*
Radiation *p185*

South Korea | COFFEE CULTURE

South Koreans, it would seem, are mad for speciality coffee, and it is a phenomenon that is only getting bigger. There are, for example, more Q Graders in South Korea than anywhere else in the world by a long shot. Often, around the world, the roasting process is a separate, larger operation and these companies then sell their coffee wholesale to cafés, restaurants, and so on. In Korea, however, shops that roast their own coffee are extremely popular and this phenomenon has led to impressive small in-shop pieces of roasting equipment. The South Korean-made Stronghold, for instance, is a clever electrical roaster that uses infrared radiation along with heated air to roast the coffee.

SEE ALSO
Altitude *p16*
Arabica *p18*
Variety *p228*

Species | ROBUSTA AND ARABICA

There are many *Coffea* (coffee) species that occur naturally in the wild and all are indigenous to the east coast of Africa. Madagascar has the highest number of coffee species, as recorded by Aaron Davis, Head of Coffee Research at the Royal Botanic Gardens, Kew. Amazingly, more than half the world's coffee species was not documented until Davis and his team decided to venture out, find, and catalogue them all in the late 1990s. The two species that make up nearly all the coffee grown for consumption are *C. robusta* and *C. arabica*. Robusta is seen as the inferior of the two. It grows at much lower altitudes, typically between sea level and 300m (1,000ft). It is highly disease resistant and typically produces twice the yield per tree than Arabica. It has been estimated that Robusta makes up 30 per cent of the coffee grown in the world, although this figure is contested. Not all

커피

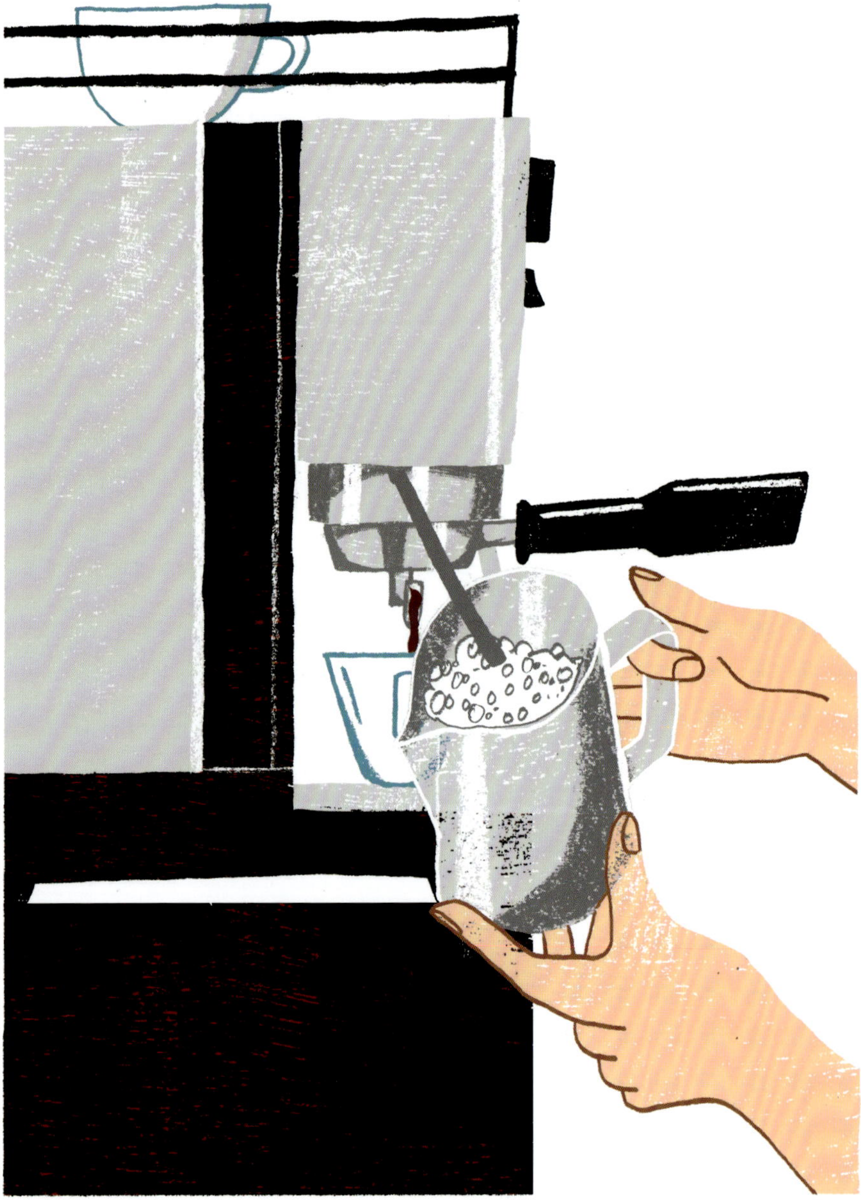

Arabica is of a top quality and it is possible to have a Robusta that outperforms an Arabica. Robusta, however, cannot compete with the best Arabica crops. You will often see Robusta blended with Arabica and, although there are many varieties, you can surmise that a Robusta will produce a more bitter, heavier cup with less "brightness" and fewer fruit notes. A good Robusta will display chocolate and hazelnut notes.

Spittoon | TASTING

It is not a stretch to claim that coffee's central purpose for most drinkers is as a vehicle for the consumption of caffeine. It is thus somewhat ironic that this aspect of coffee can be a burden for the coffee professional, especially if they are in any kind of quality control role in which tasting lots and lots of coffee is the order of the day. This means that in most coffee-tasting roles it is customary to slurp, hold the coffee in the mouth, assess it, and then spit it out. Any kind of vessel can be used as a spittoon, but of course items specifically made for the purpose are the best. A well-crafted spittoon is a rather lovely thing, even if what goes into it is not. Spitting also helps avoid palette fatigue. A good palette cleanser is a plain cracker, which soaks up the liquid and oils from the mouth.

Steaming | MILK FROTHING

The modern coffee shop phenomenon that has conquered the globe is in many countries driven as much by steamed milk as it is by espresso. Australian coffee culture, for instance, has elevated milk steaming to a refined culinary art. Believe me, for the beginner approaching the steaming of milk for the first time, it is alarming

SEE ALSO
Cupping *p64*

SEE ALSO
Espresso *p79*
Latte art *p139*
Sensory science *p197*

how difficult it can be. High-powered steam is the first thing you need; often home enthusiasts blame themselves for bad results when it is their low-powered machine that is really scuppering their abilities. Placement of the steam wand tip just below the surface of the cold milk and just off centre is the place to start. The idea is to then get the milk "tumbling" and swirling as you lower the jug to add air and therefore foam to the milk. The key is to add the air in short bursts – the swirling should stop the milk settling. All this needs to be done before the milk gets too hot. Once you get past 60°C (140°F), the quality of flavour and the foam start to fade away. Steaming milk well is the prerequisite to performing latte art.

Strength | DRINKING

There are a few terms in coffee that have the potential to elicit confusion. "Strength" is one of those. The primary misunderstanding is around the reaction between caffeine and flavour. The caffeine one in particular is a minefield. Stating exactly how much caffeine the coffee contains and how much of that is likely to end up in the drink is nearly impossible. Another confusion, from a more technical point of view, is the relation of strength to extraction. Obviously, if you use more coffee, you have the potential of a drink with more caffeine, but size creates an illusion. An espresso can be very intense and strong, but the serving size means it probably does not contain as much caffeine as a big mug of much weaker-tasting filter coffee. It is essentially just a volume game. In regard to the strength guides found on more commercial coffee packaging, there are also problems. There is no recognized standard for these.

SEE ALSO
Caffeine *p41*
Espresso *p79*

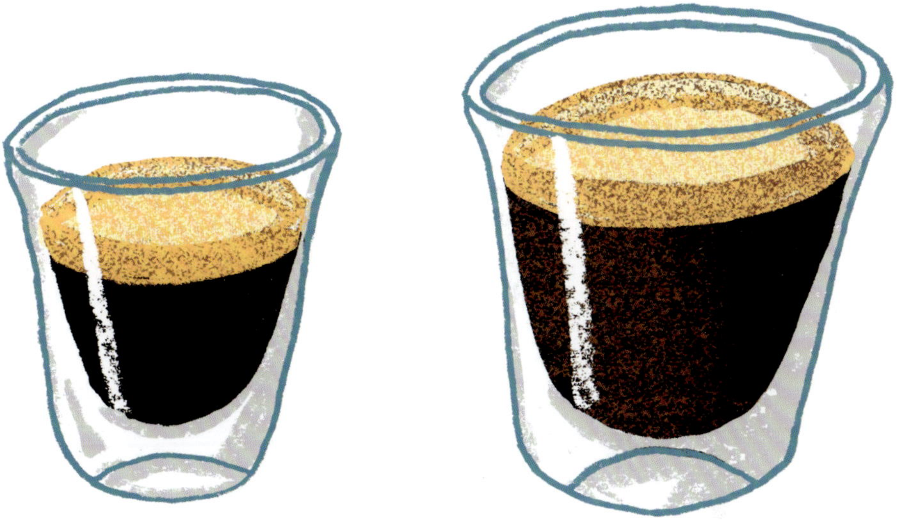

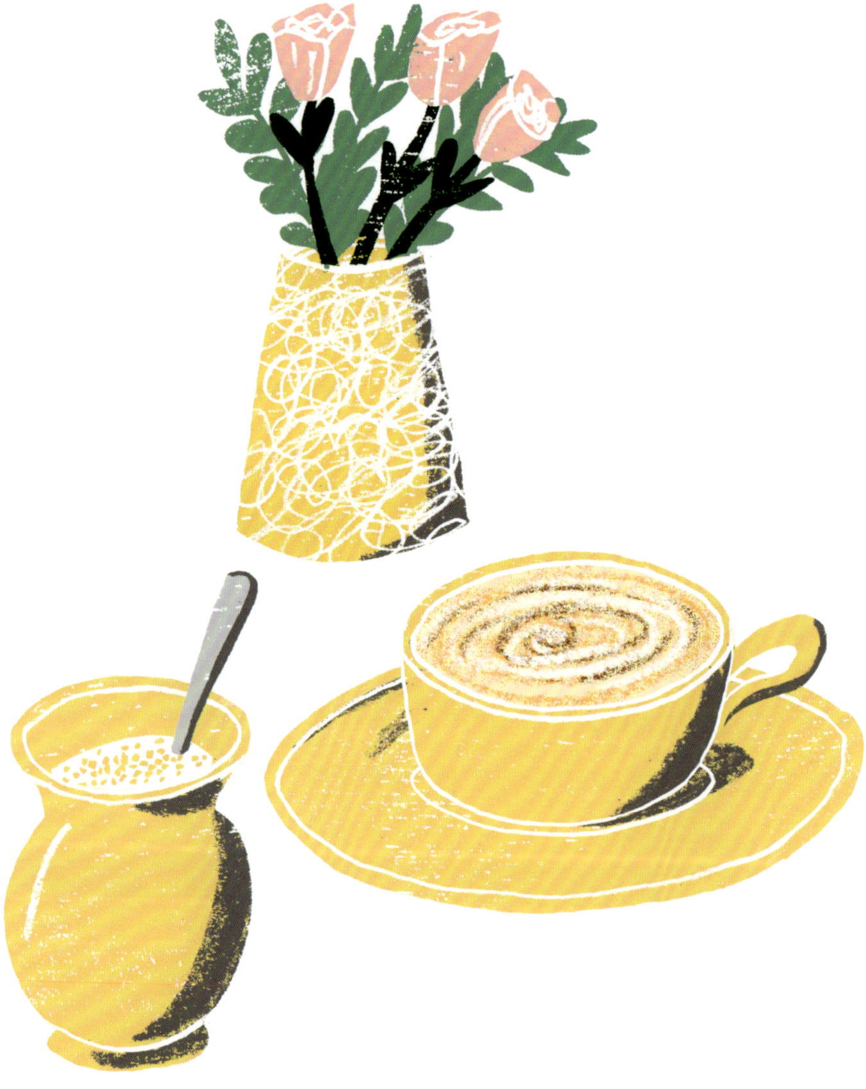

The companies behind the product use these made-up strength guides with various intents. The goal may be to describe the darkness of roast or to refer to the fact that Robusta has been used and the resulting coffee has a higher caffeine content. Lastly, the reference could be to the origin of coffee itself and the strength of flavour of that bean.

Sudan Rume | VARIETY

Sudan Rume has actually been behind the scenes in the coffee industry for some time now, as it is quite often crossed with other varieties to add quality and disease resistance. However, due to its low yields, the variety itself has not seen high levels of production. In 2015 Saša Šestić put the variety firmly on the map when (combined with some carbonic maceration) he used it to win the World Barista Championship. There has never been a time when cup quality is valued as highly as it is now, which makes the lower yield of a variety like this seem less unappealing. The variety originates from Sudan's Bome Plateau and consistently delivers a lot of aromatics and stone-fruit acidity and sweetness. Many farmers are experimenting with the variety in the Americas and achieving exciting results, and a popular F1 hybrid named Centoamerica has appeared in El Salvador.

SEE ALSO
Carbonic maceration *p47*
El Salvador *p77*
Variety *p228*
World Barista
  Championship *p239*
Yield *p245*

Sugar | SWEETENER

"Coffee should be black as hell, strong as death, and as sweet as love", so goes the Turkish proverb. For many people, the addition of sugar to coffee is a defining aspect of their relationship with the beverage. Coffee has the potential to have its own natural sweetness, but more often than

SEE ALSO
Acidity *p13*
Caffeine *p41*
Espresso *p79*

SEE ALSO
Gustatory *p113*
Olfactory *p163*

not coffee is bitter and the addition of sugar adds balance. Sugar, like caffeine, is addictive and often a cup of coffee serves the dual purpose of delivering both caffeine and sugar, and an individual's preference for how they want to "build" their coffee drink can be a touchy subject. Things get tricky in that coffee's flavour can be very complex and its meeting with sugar is not always predictable or pleasant. As we make our way into the realms of higher-scoring coffee, acidity becomes more prominent and complex and the bitterness diminishes, and the addition of sugar becomes not only less necessary but can actually unbalance the drink. Much like a glass of wine, a carefully prepared cup of speciality coffee is a finished drink. The coffee was chosen, roasted, and brewed without sugar content as part of the equation. On the other hand, in the more traditional world of Italian espresso, the opposite is true and the coffee was chosen and roasted specifically to achieve balance when sugar is added.

Super taster test | TASTING

Discussing taste and flavour is difficult: we have to traverse the landscape of preference and opinion as well as the pitfalls of language – we do not all necessarily interpret the same word in the same way, or link it to the same flavour experience. Do we both mean the same thing when we say "smooth" or "winey", for example? Already on loose ground, we have to add to this the fact that, across the population, we all vary quite dramatically in our taste setup, so to speak, and can have wildly different experiences of the same foodstuff. This is where the super taster test can help us. The super taster test is somewhat misleadingly named. This test is a little strip of white paper that you hold on your tongue with a closed mouth for several seconds. You may taste nothing, just paper, or you may react violently, pull a face of disgust, wash your mouth out with water, and spend the following few hours trying to rid yourself of the sensation. The difference is not down to the paper, but to your sensitivity to the chemical compound on the paper – propylthiouracil. Your sensitivity here is directly related to the amount of taste buds on your tongue, and the population ranges from extremely sensitive to almost non-sensitive. This directly correlates to our sensitivity to bitterness. It is important to note that the super taster test does not measure the abilities of our nose, which is vital in tasting. There are, naturally, wide variations in individuals' "noses" across the population. So is taste genetic? Well, no, although there are genetic differences. Tasting ability, as in discerning character in all types of food from coffee to cheese, is very much an experience-based skill. One needs to assess and taste a lot of coffee to be good at discerning the differences, thereby building a "taste library". Also, it has been shown that sensitivity to things like sugar can be learned and will change over time. So there you have it: tasting is a minefield.

SEE ALSO
Cup of Excellence *p64*
Fairtrade *p89*
Leaf rust *p140*

Sustainability | GROWING; TRADING

Sustainability is a catch-all term and there are many aspects of the seed-to-cup journey that we can consider with sustainability in mind. Ultimate sustainability needs to be both economical and environmental. For example, growing something in a more environmentally friendly way but, in doing so, losing the ability to make a living from it is not sustainable, and vice versa. From an economic point of view, the speciality movement, Cup of Excellence scheme, and so forth have been working hard on rewarding farmers with more financial incentive for pursuing higher cup quality. The Fairtrade certification has focused more on making commodity coffee a more sustainable crop. It is a genuine concern in a plethora of producing countries that failure to make coffee growing economically sustainable has resulted in, and will continue to result in, coffee crops being abandoned for other crops. Agriculturally, we have other sustainability concerns. Leaf rust can devastate crops and feeds into the reason why harvesting coffee can be financially unrewarding. Climate change causes the same problems by altering growing conditions and nurturing disease. Rising labour costs in developing countries also threaten production. In these cases, technology has the potential to help. This complex array of issues is often shared by all producing countries, though sometimes the challenges are unique to a country, which has different organizations and structures in place. All in all, though, concerns about sustainability continue to require every bit of our attention.

Syphon

See "Vacuum pot".

T

SEE ALSO
Espresso *p79*
Evenness *p84*
Extraction *p86*
Nutate *p161*

Tamping | ESPRESSO

Tamping is the act of compressing ground coffee down into the basket with the use of a tamper – effectively a flat circular metal disc with a handle. This technique is part of preparing espresso. What exactly does tamping do? The goal is to get the pressurized water to pass through the bed of coffee evenly, picking up the flavour from all the grounds. If you take a look at the water exiting the machine, it is like a shower, featuring several streams of water. We do not want the water to carry on through the coffee like this. By tamping the coffee we create a barrier, causing the water to pool on top of the coffee like a disc, and then, when there is no longer anywhere for it to go, the water passes through all the coffee. A common misconception is that tamping can dramatically impact extraction. It certainly affects the evenness of extraction by changing how the coffee is packed, but if, for example, your grind is very coarse and you cannot get enough flavour out of the coffee, tamping hard will not compensate for this.

SEE ALSO
Freezing *p98*
Terroir *p214*

Temperature | HOT AND COLD

The impact of temperature can be seen and tasted at varying points throughout the seed-to-cup journey. At the farm, or *terroir*, level, changes in temperature will change the growing conditions of the coffee plant and can be critical during the drying part of the processing of the coffee, too. Temperature affects the storage of coffee and its lifespan. Roasting is pretty much all about applying varying amounts of temperature in different ways. Most of us experience the impact of temperature during the brewing of coffee – the temperature of the water we use to make the coffee affects the flavour. You have probably heard that one should not use boiling water to brew with, because this will "burn" the coffee. Good advice, although potentially misleading. When brewing we are dissolving, not cooking, coffee, and as such the temperature of the water alters which compounds, and therein which flavours, are released by the coffee. If the coffee has been burnt, this will have happened during the roasting process.

Terroir | GROWING

SEE ALSO
Agronomy *p15*
Altitude *p16*
Climate change *p56*
Soil *p201*
Variety *p228*

Terroir is a French term most often applied to wine, and derived from the French word *"terre"*, meaning "land". It refers to the many environmental factors that constitute a crop's growing conditions and may be used to encompass other diverse elements that influence the crop at its source, including human influences. *Terroir* is effectively the story of a particular lot of any crop. I think the term is particularly pertinent in coffee and is a great example of a word from which many things can be inferred. A great confluence of different elements at origin all hugely impact and shape a coffee's flavour before it goes off to be roasted and brewed. In this case, *terroir* would include the variety of coffee grown, the soil, the climate,

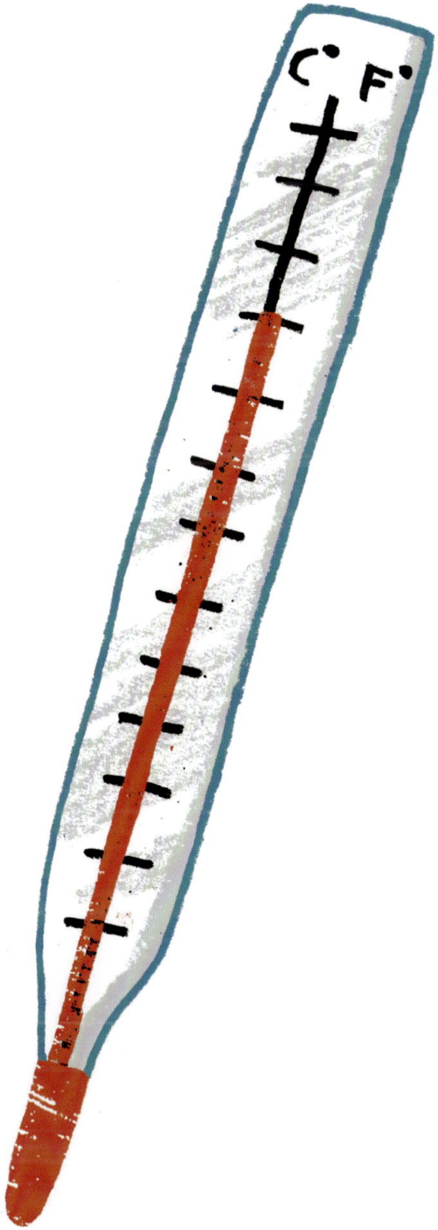
C° F°

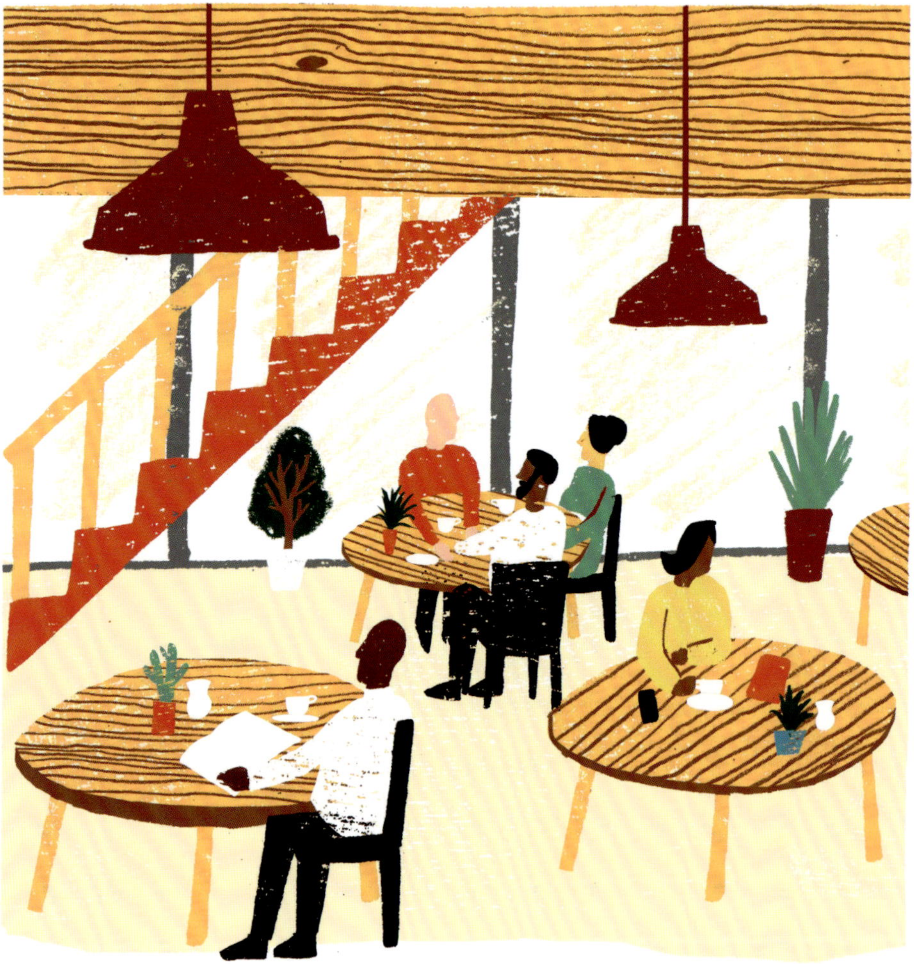

the picking, and the processing. Each element has its own inner world of complexity, but none of them is acting independently.

SEE ALSO
Green *p109*

Thermodynamics | SCIENCE

My work with a chemist on a couple of coffee projects is the reason for this entry appearing in this dictionary. I think it is fair to say that an absurd amount of what happens in coffee is down to thermodynamics. One example of thermodynamics in action is the nature of how physical changes in temperature can result in so-called "phase changes". But thermodynamics is more broadly the "movement of energy", and it includes every physical process in the universe. Human beings enact a lot of phase changes by either applying heat or cooling things down. There are many examples in coffee. Freezing green coffee is using thermodynamics to elongate the life of coffee. Roasting is thermodynamics in action and in a pretty complex way, with compounds breaking down and creating lots of flavoursome by-products. Then there is brewing, where we utilize heat to alter extraction. Pretty cool really.

Third place | COFFEE CULTURE

Home is the "first place", and work the "second". The "third place" has been written about by a number of authors, most influentially the American urban sociologist Ray Oldenburg in his book *The Great Good Place* (1989). Oldenburg argues that third places are important for civil society, democracy, and a sense of place. A third place should be a levelling space (where role or status in society does not matter) in which conversation is the main activity, and is easy to access by regulars and newcomers alike. Coffee shops can be very effective third places. Other examples are gyms, parks, and pubs. It is tempting to categorize the "coffee shop" as a singular, monolithic thing. Coffee-driven spaces, however, are extremely diverse and there are many different interpretations. I think many coffee shops offer a natural third space, while others blend into the second space (the workplace); a few are more product-oriented or culinary in the experiences they offer.

Third wave | COFFEE CULTURE

The concept of the "third wave" in coffee culture is a slightly contentious one – trying to sum up a complex phenomenon with a catch-all phrase is usually doomed to failure. The term "third wave" was coined by industry expert Trish Rothgeb and has been widely explored by others. The term is US-centric, but the main ideas behind the concept, which describe a changing approach to coffee, can be applied to cultures around the world. The "first wave" was the commercialization of coffee, mainly defined by mass-market instant coffee. The "second wave" was the emergence of the coffee shops that now dominate the high street, such as Starbucks. This phenomenon occurred in the 1960s in the United States and represented the adoption of the Italian espresso-based drinks culture that drove these businesses. The "third wave" refers to the higher culinary appreciation of coffee and all that this entails: a focus on subtleties of flavour, provenance, and process. There is often talk of what the "fourth wave" is or will be. In all honesty, I think all future movements within speciality coffee will be more specific explorations within the parameters of the third

SEE ALSO
Espresso *p79*
Independent coffee shops *p124*
Origin *p166*

T

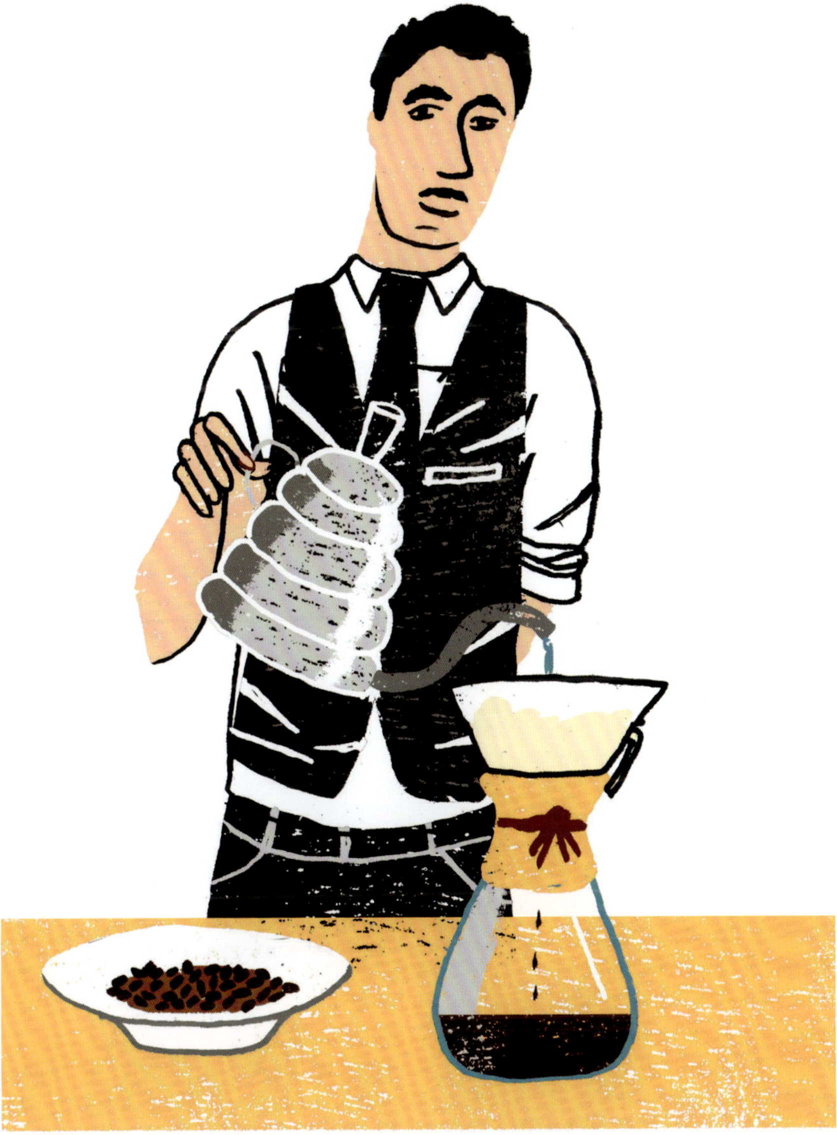

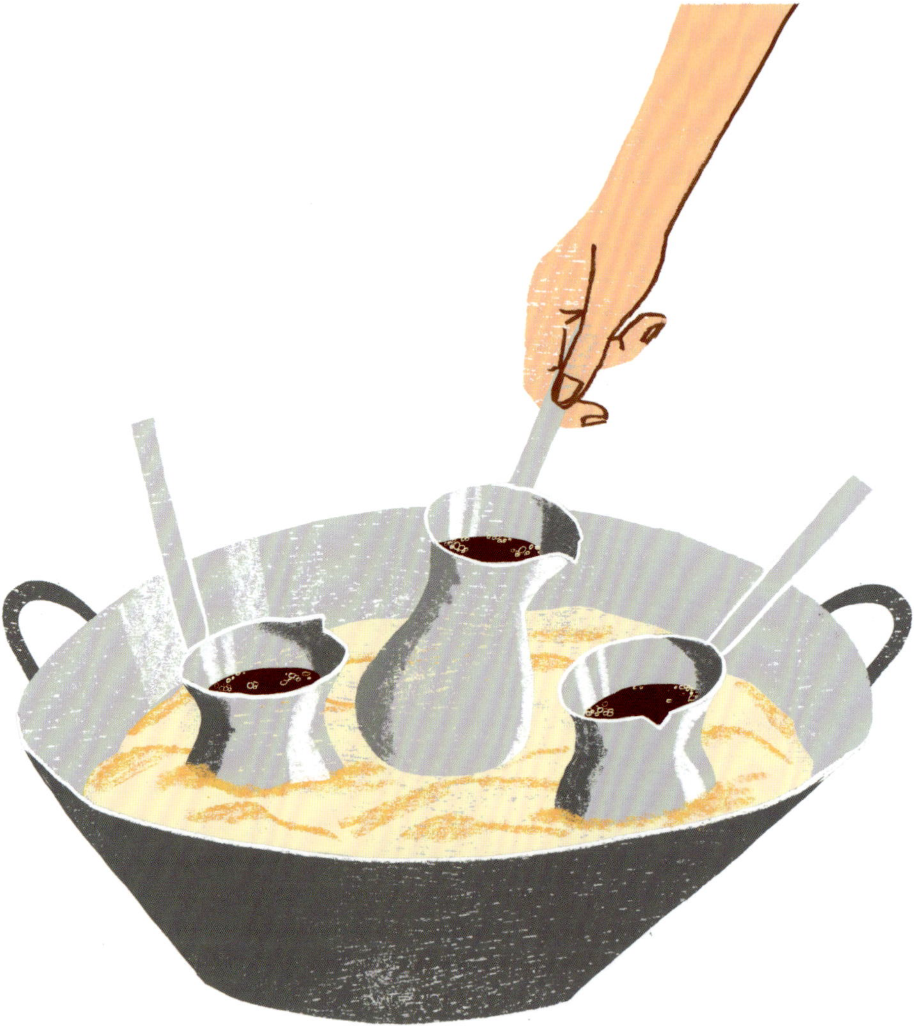

wave. The problem with using any of these definitions too literally is that the third wave now acts as a label for the whole of the independent coffee shop movement. However, large numbers of independent coffee shops focus on "fresh" or artisanal concepts, but are not truly exploring the culinary appreciation of coffee.

Turkish coffee | BREWING; COFFEE CULTURE

Sometimes termed "ibrik coffee", Turkish coffee refers to a typical style of coffee preparation that originates from that country. This is a method that uses a finer grind than any other, with the coffee pounded to achieve a powder-like result. There are many variations to the exact recipe used, but the main principle is to simmer the coffee in water using a *cezve* (a coffee pot; known in the West as an ibrik), often with sugar added, but not always. The coffee may be brought to a simmer more than once, depending on what is customary. The coffee is then poured from a height to achieve a foamy surface and the fine grounds allowed to settle to the bottom of the cup. This is one of the few coffee preparation methods that utilizes no filter. It is not a common method for preparing speciality coffee, but that is not to say it could not be done. With correct understanding and control of temperature, the method is capable of producing extremely good extractions and full-bodied complex flavour profiles.

Typica | VARIETY

The grandfather of modern coffee varieties, Typica was the variety shipped around the world by the Dutch as coffee production began to take hold in the seventeenth century. Modern

SEE ALSO
Clean *p56*

mutations and genetically selected varieties stem from Typica. Many of these developed varieties produce a higher yield than Typica, but you will still find the variety among crops all over the world yielding a top-notch cup quality. The variety tends to produce round, clean, sweet cups of coffee.

SEE ALSO
Gustatory *p113*
Olfactory *p163*

Umami | TASTING

Umami is one of the five basic tastes, along with sweet, sour, salt, and bitter. These tastes are the domain of the mouth (gustatory system) as opposed to the nose (olfactory system). The word has Japanese origins, courtesy of the chemist Kikunae Ikeda (1864–1936), and directly translates as "delicious taste". Umami has its own specific taste receptors, which has led scientists to label umami a distinct taste. Umami can be described as a pleasant savoury taste with a long aftertaste. It is, however, unpleasant when isolated or when tasted in too high concentration, without enough salt to balance. Umami has been shown to improve the taste of low-sodium foods such as soup, and many food producers have played with adding umami in the form of glutamate (which is the source of umami flavour) to improve their products. This savoury note is not an element we expect to see a lot of in a good coffee. When it is too strong, umami is generally experienced as meaty or brothy, but a small amount can add complexity and richness.

SEE ALSO
Boston Tea Party *p32*
Third place *p217*
Third wave *p218*

United States of America | COFFEE CULTURE

The United States is, by volume, the largest consumer of coffee in the world (Finland is the largest consumer per capita). Coffee offerings and experiences range across the full spectrum from a quick, easy, and cheap refill diner coffee through to speciality quality-driven coffee meccas. It is therefore hard to pigeonhole the country's coffee culture into a little dictionary post. Perhaps it is best to speak of a bunch of individual coffee cultures that all link together across the country. Seattle is the home of Starbucks and the coffee shop model that has spread across the world and had such a wide influence. The concepts of the third wave and the third place were both formulated here. And there is certainly no doubt that since the fateful days of the Boston Tea Party coffee has become integral to the culture of the country.

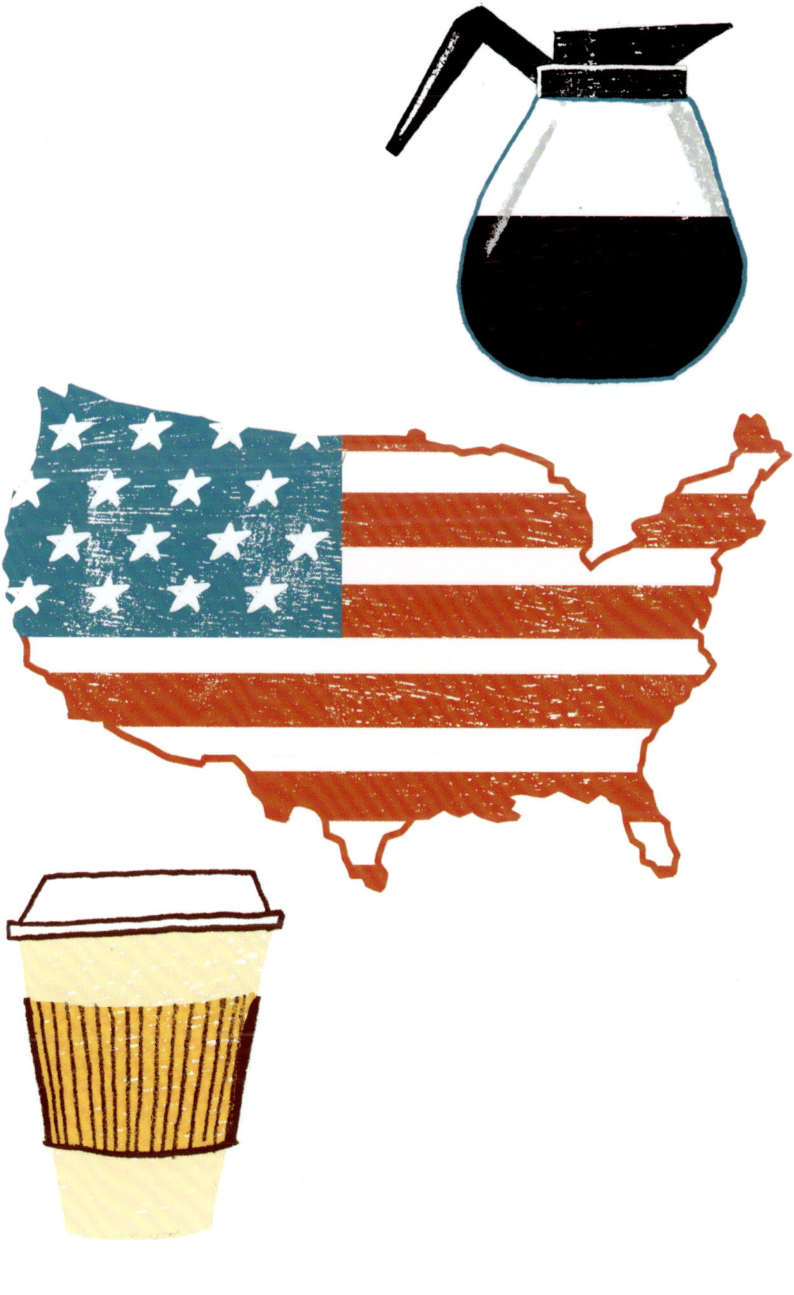

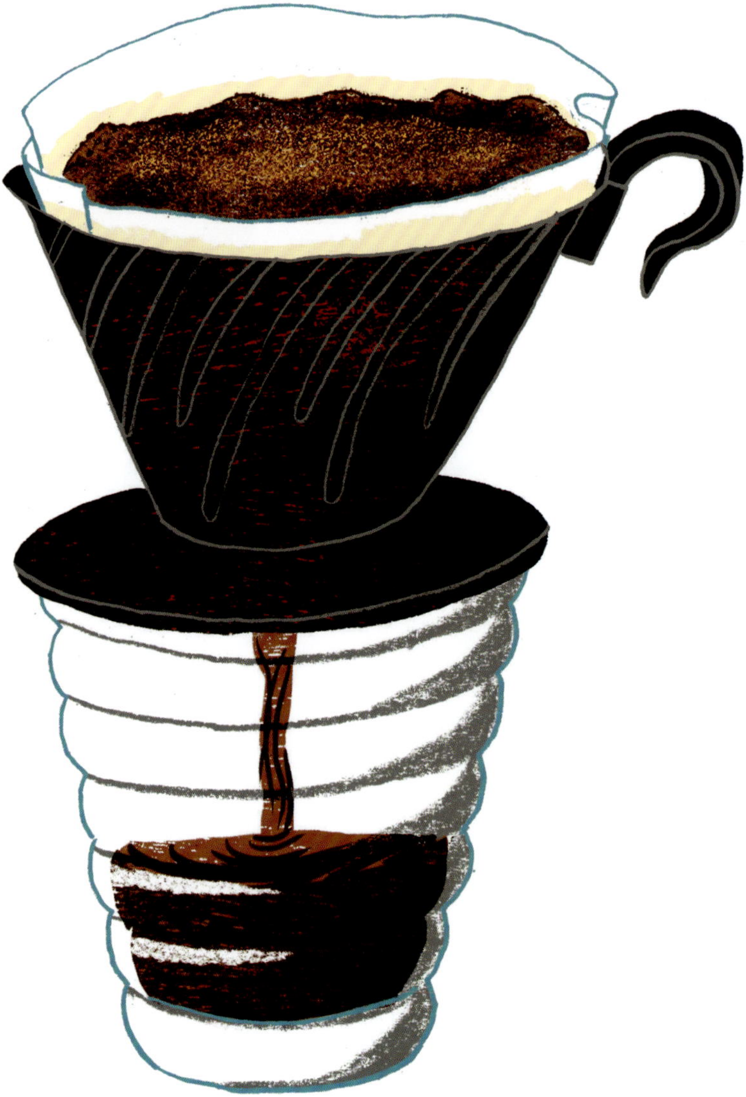

SEE ALSO
Chemex™ *p55*
Full immersion *p103*
Vacuum pot *p227*

V60 | BREWING

The brewing products of the Japanese company Hario are evidently very successful. Like the Syphon vacuum pot, the V60 pour-over has come to be the best known of its type. Most V60-type devices are essentially just a cone of some kind with a hole at the bottom. A paper filter sits inside and the device sits atop a vessel or cup. Ground coffee is placed in the filter and water poured atop the coffee, which then makes its way through the coffee and the paper filter. The method is quite simple and very manual, but technique, especially how the water is applied, is key. The V60 has unique swirling ridges, though what really makes the difference are the V60 papers, as they taste nicer than other papers.

SEE ALSO
Extraction *p86*
Pressure *p179*

Vacuum pot | BREWING

The vacuum pot – "vac pot" for short – is most commonly encountered under the trade name Syphon. The Syphon is actually a specific design of the vacuum pot made by the Japanese company Hario, but, like Hoover in the UK and Ireland, it has come to represent the device itself. There is no more dramatic brewing method for filter coffee. The most common comparisons heard are those of a school science experiment and, more recently, something off the hit TV show *Breaking Bad*.

Visually, the vac pot consists of two glass bulbs, one sitting atop the other, with a heat source beneath. Water is placed in the bottom bulb, and, depending on the design, there is either a paper, cloth, or glass filter between the two chambers. As heat is applied, the water heats up and pressure is created in the bottom chamber, forcing the water up to the top chamber at a critical point. Coffee is then added to the top chamber and is steeped for as long as the user desires. When the heat source is taken away a vacuum is created, sucking the brew into the bottom chamber, while the grounds remain up top. This method has a reverse temperature curve, meaning that the heat of the brew rises throughout; this is due to the insulating effect of the coffee on the water. This has the downside that vacuum-pot-brewed coffee can often over-extract when brewed for too long. Used well, however, the method can produce delightful coffee, all while providing a mesmerizing theatrical show.

Variety | GROWING

Variety is the spice of life and coffee has it in abundance. The term "variety" in coffee refers to subspecies of the two main coffee species that we grow to make coffee from – *Coffea robusta* and *Coffea arabica*. There is a vast number of subspecies of Arabica, each of which has its own flavour tendencies. There is a distinction to be made between varieties that are naturally occurring subspecies of Arabica and cultivars that have been developed by agricultural or horticultural means. In reality, nearly all coffee varieties grown are cultivars, though the two terms get used interchangeably. It remains fascinating to taste the same variety of coffee plant grown in two very different countries.

SEE ALSO
Bourbon *p35*
Castillo *p51*
Geisha *p105*
Origin *p166*
Pacamara *p169*
Sudan Rume *p209*
Typica *p221*

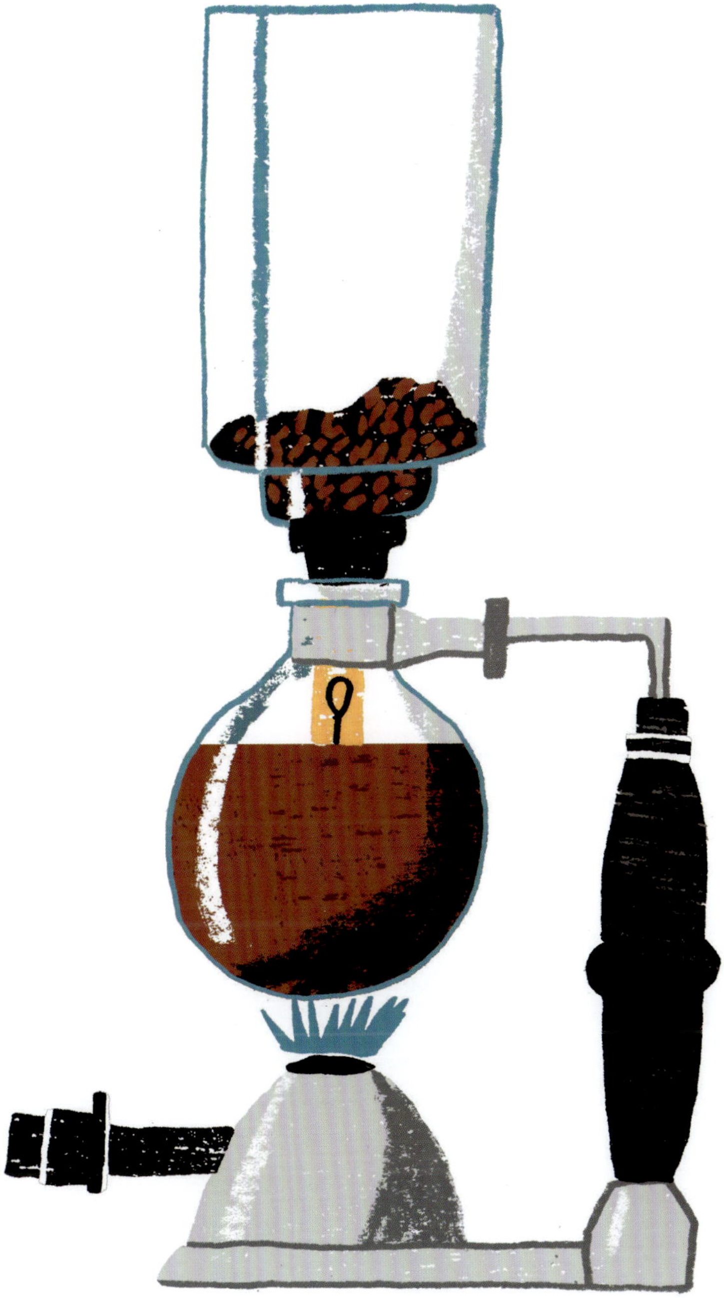

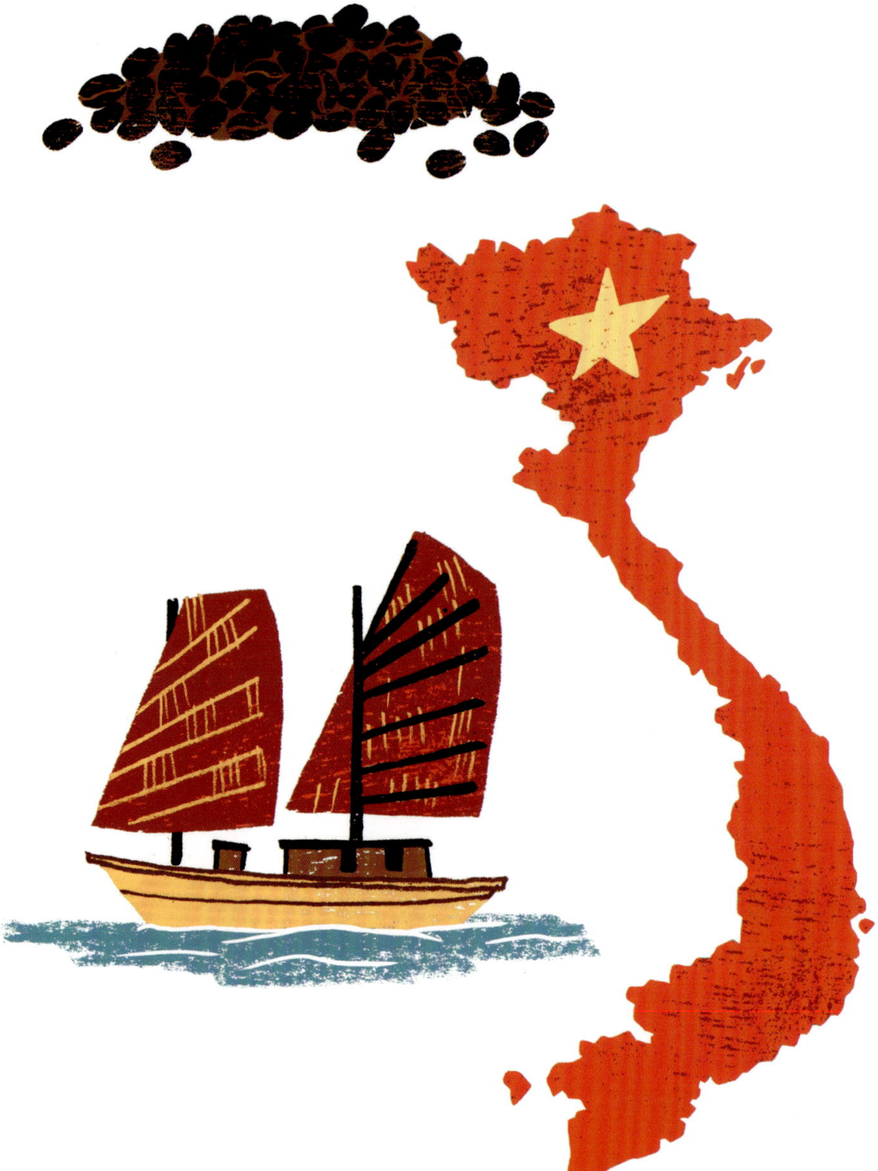

This once again highlights how many factors impact on a cup of coffee's flavour.

Vietnam | ORIGIN

Vietnam is a massive coffee producer, second only to Brazil as the largest coffee producer in the world. Almost all of the production in Vietnam is comprised of the Robusta species. Catimor – an Arabica hybrid – is also grown, and there are increasing amounts of Arabica being planted to explore higher-quality yields. Like Brazil, production in Vietnam has a big impact on coffee prices worldwide. As a visitor to the country, I found the most unique aspect of the country's coffee to be the way it is prepared and consumed. Coffee is made using a small single-serve metal pour-over called a *phin* that steeps the coffee and then filters down into the cup. It is customary for condensed milk to be added to the coffee, which is then usually served over ice. The resulting coffee is often a very sweet, rich, and strong brew.

SEE ALSO
Brazil *p35*
C market *p41*
Species *p202*

Volatiles | TASTING

The flavour of coffee is made up of a collection of volatile and non-volatile compounds. A lot of aromas are volatile, which essentially means that they are more likely to pack up and leave. Volatiles are released by the roasted coffee, a process that is accelerated when you grind coffee and get that intense aroma, which is still more dramatic if the coffee is ground hot. The addition of hot water releases even more volatiles. These aromatics, along with oxidation, are a huge part of why freshness in coffee plays such a pivotal role. A lot of clever research and packaging design are about capturing and keeping these volatiles from escaping.

SEE ALSO
Freezing *p98*
Le Nez du Café® *p140*

SEE ALSO
Espresso *p79*

Volumetrics | BREWING

A volumetric machine is one that has the ability to dispense a set amount of water when making coffee. This is a function of most semi-automatic espresso machines. The mechanism does not work by time but by volume, which is counted by a little paddle-like device that sits in the machine. Water being dispensed has to pass this paddle, and so setting a volumetric means that you are setting a number of turns of the paddle. This system can be very accurate, but this will not necessarily correspond to a consistent length of espresso shot. You are setting the water before it passes though the coffee, so the amount of water that the coffee will hold has to be taken into consideration. If the ground dose is either not weighed or is of an inconsistent grind, then volumetrics will not give you a consistent shot length. Gravimetrics is a newer term used to describe machines that have scales built into the drip tray and can therefore weigh the shot for you. Both systems can aid the production of consistent espresso if handled well.

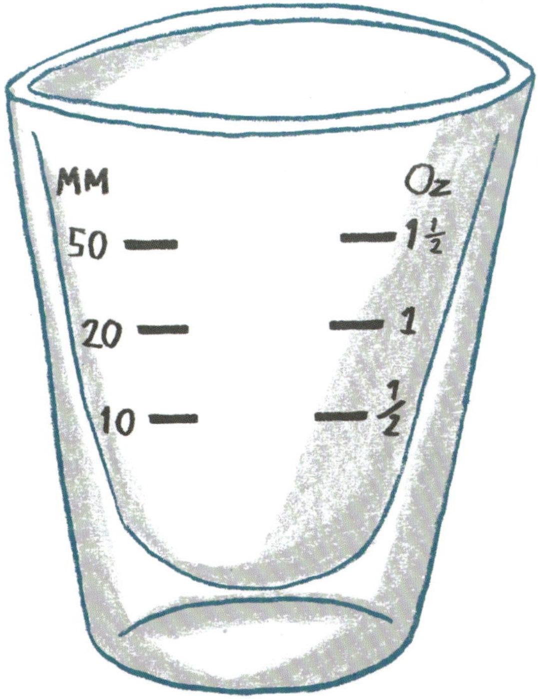
MM
Oz
50
1 1/2
20
1
10
1/2

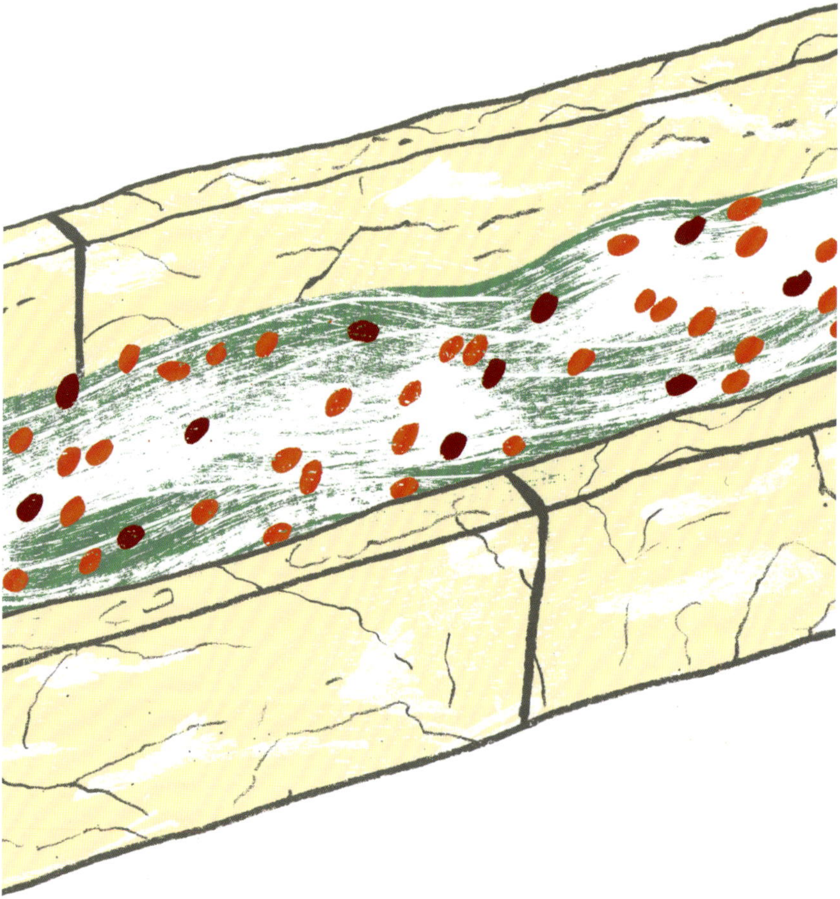

SEE ALSO
Defects *p67*
Fermentation *p90*
Mechanical drying *p145*
Mucilage *p151*
Natural process *p156*
Raised beds *p186*

Washed process | HARVESTING

In the world of speciality coffee, the washed method dominates. So named due to the large amount of water used, the process, like all others, varies widely. Broadly, though, the method comprises the following stages. First, the freshly harvested cherries are de-pulped, with the cherries passing through a cog-like rolling mechanism that pulls the skin and most of the flesh off the bean. At this point, the beans are still covered in a layer of mucilage. The coffee is then fermented in a trough of water to remove the remaining mucilage. During this stage, "bad" beans float to the top and are removed. Finally, the coffee beans are dried. This can be achieved in a number of ways, such as sun drying or mechanical drying. The regulated fermentation and drying can give a producer more control over quality and defects compared to the natural process. Washed coffee often presents a more prominent and defined acidity. Changes in the fermentation have a big impact on the coffee. Kenyan coffees undergo a second fermentation, which is thought to be part of the reason they tend to have such vibrant fruit and complex acidity. The tiniest alterations in processing can have startling results and are still being explored.

SEE ALSO
Buffer *p38*
Extraction *p86*

Water | BREWING

Water is the quiet and elusive partner of coffee. You cannot make coffee without it, and unfortunately subtle differences in water composition drastically alter the favour of a coffee. In recent years there has been a renewed focus on the importance of water, as the whole community seeks to understand more and more about coffee. It has long been understood that water quality matters, but now we are looking to see exactly how it affects flavour. A key notion to take on board is that good-tasting water does not necessarily make good-tasting coffee. The bicarbonate content that makes a branded bottled water a very smooth water to drink is responsible for removing acidity and sweetness in coffee. The key is to think about water as a solvent and to consider how it does that job. The three most important elements as far as flavour in coffee is concerned are calcium, magnesium, and bicarbonate. All coffee is actually roasted to suit a given water – that is, whichever water is used to taste and quality-control the roast/coffee. This means different roasts and coffees are likely to be suited to different waters. If you are really into the geekery, you can buy minerals and "manufacture" your own water. Playing with bottled waters is also popular, while better coffee-centric filtration systems are likely to emerge in the near future. The other aspect of water is its impact on equipment. Scale build-up is a common problem in medium to hard water areas, and this wreaks havoc on the tiny parts in espresso machines. Less common but also problematic is the potential for acidic waters to corrode metals. All in all, water is a mighty big part of the coffee equation, but one that is surprisingly easy to forget about.

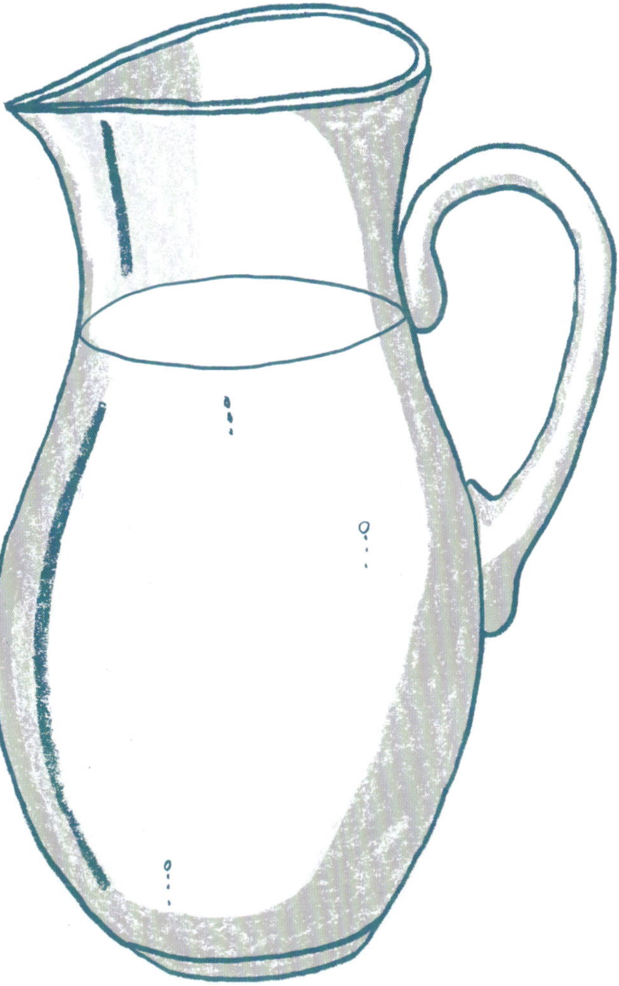

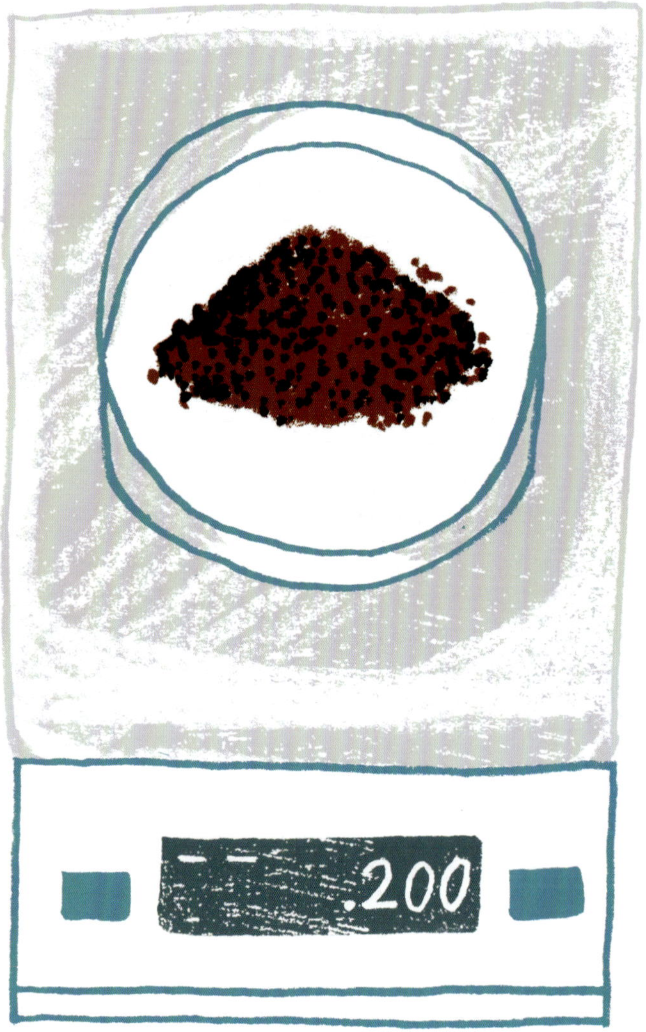
.200

SEE ALSO
Espresso *p79*
Volumetrics *p232*

Weighing scales | BREWING

A set of scales has become commonplace in the world of speciality brewing. It is hard now to believe that, just a few years ago, weighing exact quantities/ratios seemed a drastic practice and was therefore uncommon. Saying that, it has long been practised in filter-coffee brewing, most likely due just to its relative ease there compared with espresso. A useful comparison is baking. The precise ratios of ingredients used have a big impact on the success of baked goods. This is also true of coffee. Measuring by eye is simply not good enough. Two different grinds will take up different amounts of space, and blooming coffee can obscure water volumes. Having a decent set of scales that is both quick to read and measures to two decimal places makes a big difference. Interestingly, the speciality movement initially distanced itself from volumetrics as it was seen as "button pushing". Then we moved over to scales and weighed doses and shots, and eventually realized that those pre-set buttons could actually be very useful.

SEE ALSO
Barista *p23*
Espresso *p79*
Signature drinks *p197*

World Barista Championship | COMPETITIONS

The first World Barista Championship took place in the year 2000 in Monte Carlo. Since then it has gone from strength to strength and become an integral part of the speciality coffee community. When I first got into barista competitions, the concept seemed obscure and odd to many people. However, as the role of the barista and the complexity of coffee have become more widely recognized, this reaction has definitely changed, and for the better. The competition is mainly an espresso-focused competition and takes place on a stage with a soundtrack, a group of judges, and one competitor per "performance". The event has proved an impressive platform to showcase various elements of not only the barista role but all of the coffee world, with the top routines becoming the talking point of the community – pushing things forward and channelling innovation and exposure. Up until the time of writing, the format of the competition has been relatively fixed: 15 minutes in which the barista must produce 12 espresso-based drinks – 4 espressos, 4 steamed-milk drinks, and 4 signature drinks. However, the competition is undergoing an evolution and looks set to change to reflect the constant developments occurring in the world of coffee.

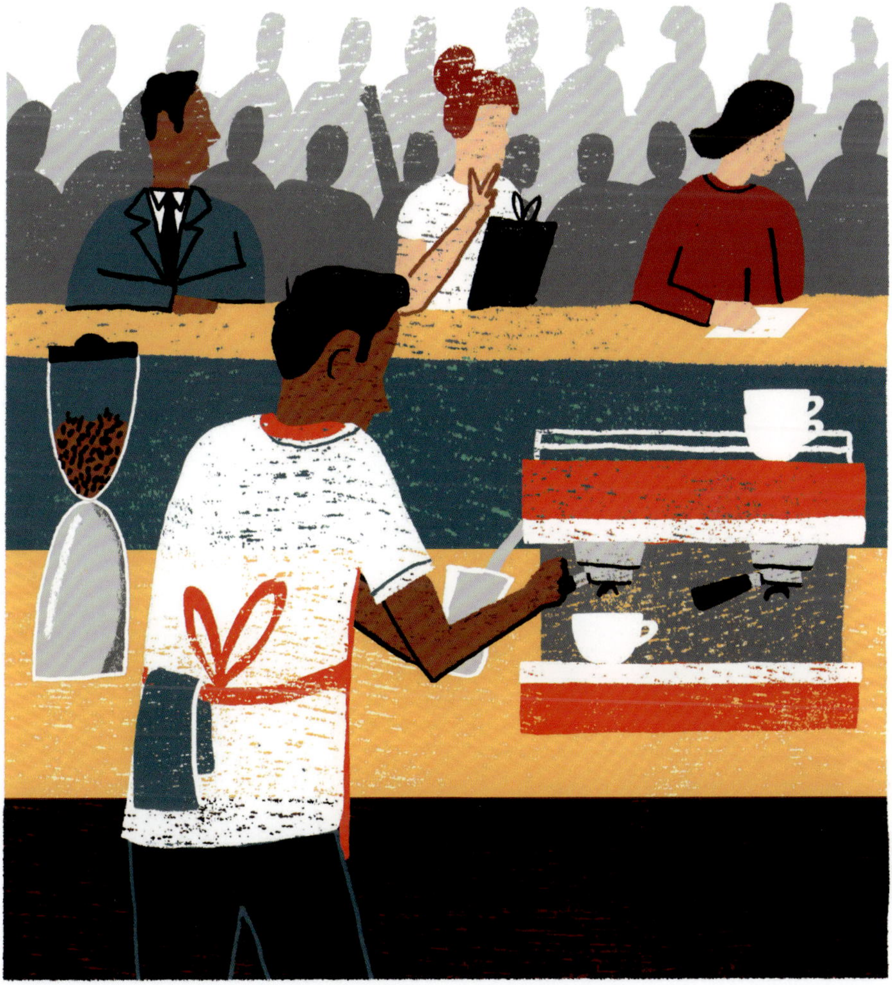

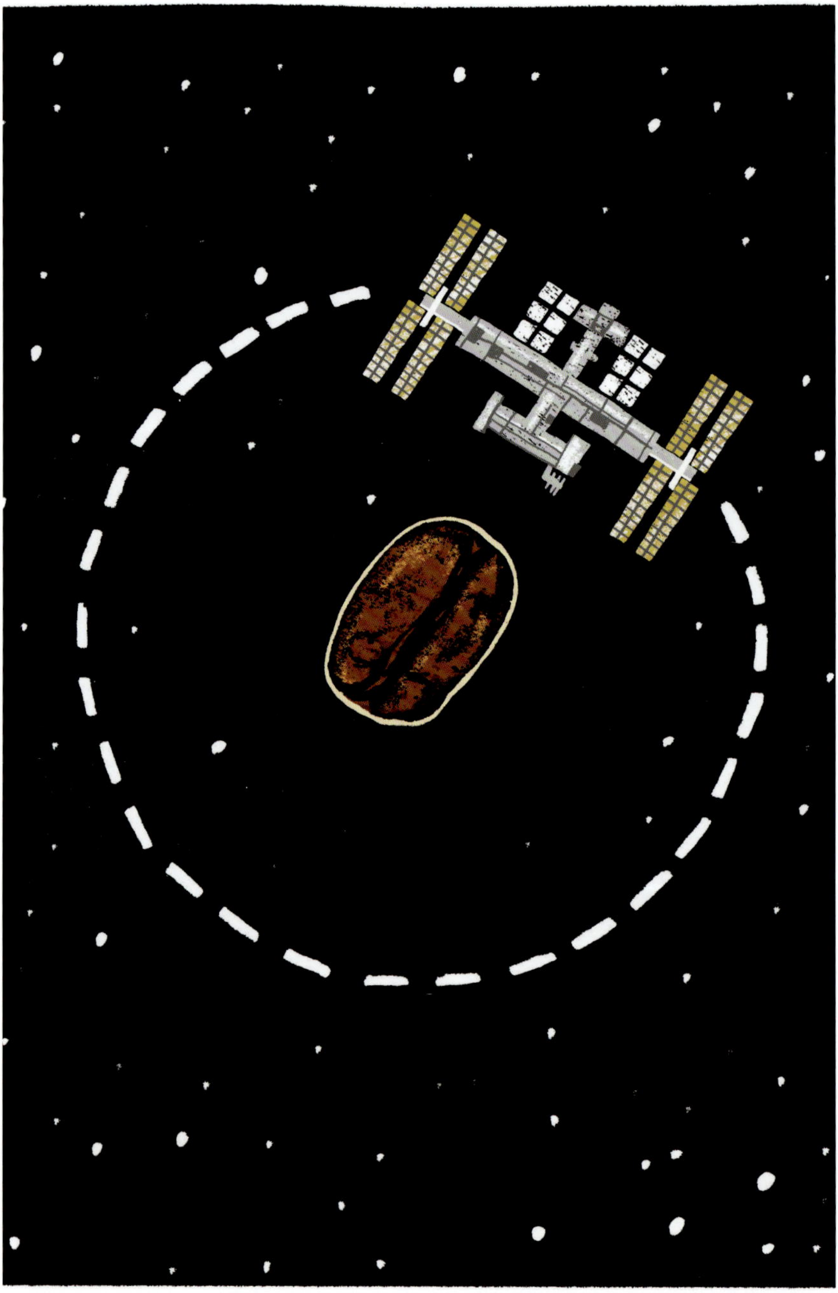

SEE ALSO
Aeropress™ *p13*

Coffee X | SPACE COFFEE

Coffee X is a design project led by the Rhode Island School of Design that is seeking to create the perfect brewing device to make a tasty cup of coffee on the International Space Station. The design is based on the Aeropress™ and looks to solve space and function hurdles in a zero-gravity environment, using a water pouch and contained components. Well-known Italian coffee company Lavazza has produced its own aerospace-engineered coffee-brewing system utilizing coffee-capsule technology, reinforced water tubes, and a straw-fed drinking vessel. Sitting up in space looking out over the world enjoying a freshly brewed cup of coffee must be quite something.

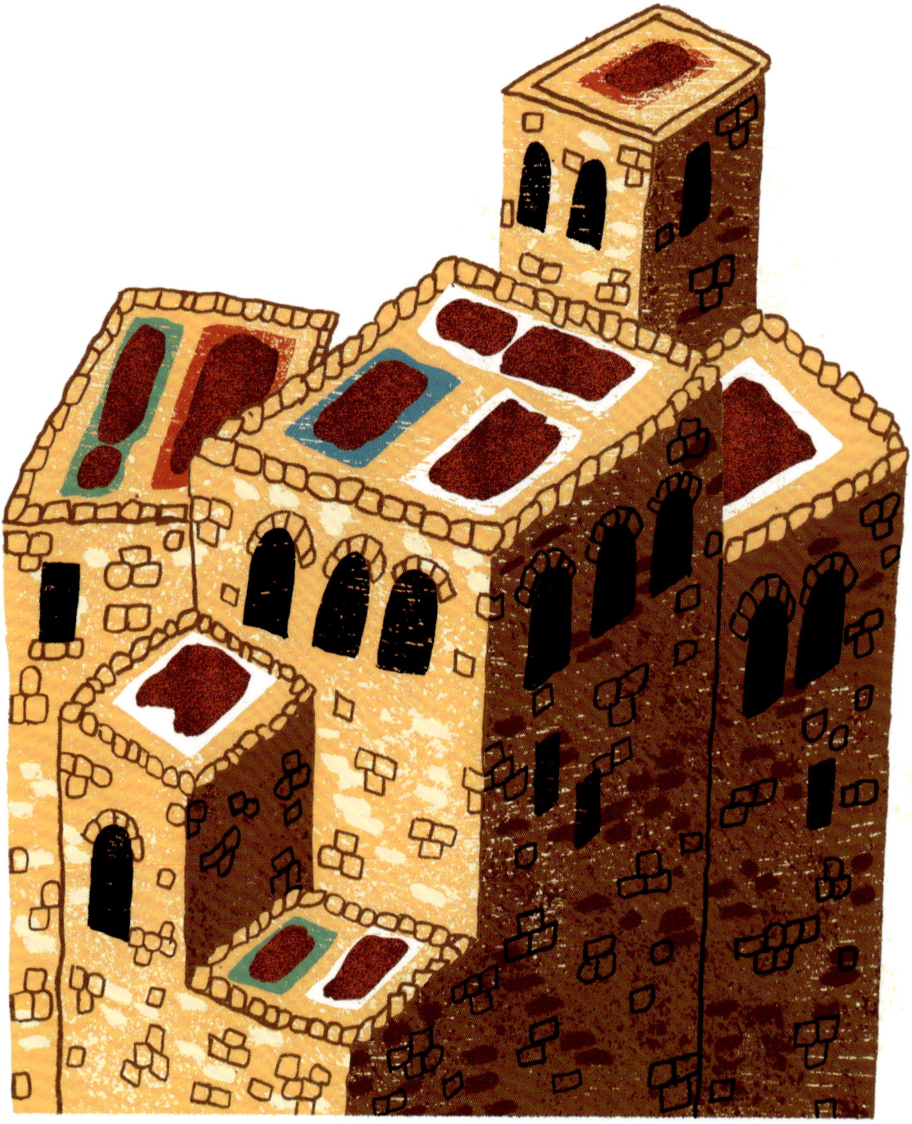

Y

SEE ALSO
Ethiopia *p80*

Yemen | ORIGIN

Nowadays it is very tricky to get hold of a coffee grown in Yemen. It was, however, the first place where coffee was propagated outside Ethiopia, with producers making the most of its importance as a trade link between East and West, especially via the port of Mocha. Mocha is the name under which much Yemeni coffee has been sold, as well as Ethiopian coffee for that matter, which resembles Yemeni in terms of the wild and fruity flavours created by natural processing. Yemen's chronic lack of water means that all its coffee is dried using the natural process, typically on the rooftops of buildings. Great Yemeni coffee can have incredibly distinctive flavours – lots of deep, dried fruit and winey acidity. However, it is very, very hard to get much traceability out of Yemen, and the coffee is in high demand. Pair this with ongoing political unrest and the country's arid climate, which makes only a few per cent of the land suitable for growing crops, and you can see why finding good Yemeni coffee is a real task.

SEE ALSO
Brew ratio *p36*

Yield | TERMINOLOGY

To yield something is to produce or generate a quantity of that something via a process. This is a useful term in coffee as it simplifies a whole lot of language that can be troublesome. For example, when discussing the weight of coffee, do we mean the weight of ground coffee or the weight of the drink? Or, even more abstrusely, we might even be referring to the weight of coffee that ends up dissolved in the drink. We use "yield" to refer to the resulting cup of coffee. A typical brew recipe will contain two weights: the dose and the yield. The yield refers to the weight of the beverage produced, inclusive of water and dissolved coffee.

SEE ALSO
Bourbon *p35*
Democratic Republic of Congo *p68*
World Barista Championship *p239*

Zambia | ORIGIN

Situated in southern Africa, Zambia borders multiple coffee-producing countries, such as Malawi, Tanzania, and the Democratic Republic of Congo. Zambia is one of several African countries with heaps of potential and promise that is yet to be fully explored. Fifty per cent of the country's coffee is of the Bourbon variety and can produce exceptional cup profiles. Catimor, which yields a lower-quality cup but is more disease resistant, is also being planted. The Zambian coffee industry is relatively young, with coffee only being introduced during the 1950s, and is characterized by large estates and good technology. Lower cup quality can be attributed to typical barriers, such as transportation in a landlocked country, lack of resources for washed processing, and disadvantageous trade relationships. There are organizations working to improve quality, and Zambia regularly enters a competitor at the World Barista Championship. Great Zambian coffees tend to exhibit wonderful layers of sweet fruit with floral qualities.

Index

Page numbers in **bold** refer to main entries

A

Abbay, Semeon 86
acidity 13, 38–9, 176, 201, 210
Adler, Alan 13
Aeropress™ **13–15**, 104, 179, 243
ageing 163, 164, 167, 172
agitate 15
agronomy **15–16**
Agtron scale 16
altitude **16–18**
Anderson, Sarah 83
Arabica **18–21**, 43, 56, 80, 83, 202–5, 228
aroma: blossom 31
 cupping 64
 dry aroma 75
 Le Nez du Café® 140
 volatiles 231
art, latte **139–40**
Australia 146, 205

B

bags 164–5
barista 23, 146, 197–8, 239–40
basket **23–4**, 179
 grooming **110–13**
 tamping 213
bean to cup 24
beans: density table 71
 drying 156–9, 171–2, 186, 235
 first crack 93
 green 109
 mucilage 151
 peaberry 175
 quaker **183–4**
 silver skin 198
 washed process 235
 see also grinding; roasting
Bialetti, Alfonso 149
blending **27–8**, 166
bloom 28
blossom 31
body **31–2**

Bolivia 32
Borém, Flavio 156
Boston Tea Party **32–5**, 224
Bourbon **35**, 169
Brazil **35–6**
brewing: Aeropress™ **13–15**, 104, 179, 243
 agitate 15
 bean to cup **24**
 brew ratio 36
 capsules **44–7**
 Chemex™ **55**
 Coffee X **243**
 cold brew **59–60**
 espresso **79–80**
 extraction **86–7**
 flow rate **97–8**
 French press **101–3**
 full immersion **103–4**
 gear 105
 heat exchanger **117–18**
 moka pot **149–51**, 179
 multi boiler **151–2**
 naked shot **155–6**
 pressure 179
 slow brew 201
 temperature 214
 thermodynamics 217
 Turkish coffee 221
 V60 227
 vacuum pot **227–8**
Brix 38
buffer **38–9**
burr grinders 93–4, 193

C

C market **41**, 89
cafetières 101–3
caffeine **41–3**, 67, 205, 206, 209, 210
cappuccino **43–4**, 94
capsules **44–7**
carbon dioxide 28, 67, 164, 179, 190
carbonic maceration **47–8**
cartridge filter 48

cascara 48–51
Castillo 51–2
Caturra 52
channelling 52–5
Chemex™ 55
cherry 118–20, 126, 151, 156, 175, 186, 190–3, 198, 235
China 55–6
"civet coffee" 136
clean 56
climate change 56–9, 212
coffee houses 84, 142–4
coffee shops 60–3, 79, 84, **124**, 218, 221, 224
Coffee X 243
cold brew 59–60
Colombia 60
compounds 75–6
Congo, Democratic Republic of 68–71
Constantinople 60–3
Costa Rica 63
crema 24, **63–4**, 79, 179
cultivars *see* variety
Cup of Excellence 64, 159, 194, 212
cupping 64–5

D

Davis, Aaron 202
De Ponti, Luigi 149
decaf 43, **67**
defects 67–8
Democratic Republic of Congo 68–71
density table 71
development 71–2
dose 72, 161, 232, 246
drum roaster 72–5
dry aroma 75
dry distillates 75–6
drying: mechanical 145–6
 natural process 156–9
 parabolic 171–2
 raised beds 186
 temperature 214

E

Ecuador 77
El Salvador 77–9
espresso 79–80
 basket 23–4
 caffeine 43
 crema 63–4
 flat white 94
 flow rate 98
 God shot 106–9
 Italy 131
 lever machine 142
 multi boiler 151–2
 naked shot 155–6
 portafilter 176–9
 pressure 179
 strength 206
 tamping 213
 volumetrics 232
Ethiopia 80–3
Eugenioides 83
Europe 84
evenness 84–6
extraction 86–7

F

Fairtrade 89, 175, 212
fermentation 47, **90**, 235
fika **90**, 161
filters: cartridge 48
 Chemex™ 55
 full immersion 103–4
 portafilter 176–9
 reverse osmosis 190
 V60 227
 vacuum pot 227–8
Finland 159–61, 223–4
first crack 93
flat burr 93–4
flat white 94
flavour notes 97
flow rate 97–8
flowers 31
foam 43–4, 63–4, 79, 206
Freese, Kalle 129

freezing 98–101, 217
French press 28, **101–3**, 104
fresh crop **103**, 173
freshness 189
full immersion 103–4
futures market 41

G

Gaggia, Giovanni Achille 142
gear **105**
Geisha **105–6**, 169–71
God shot 106–9
gravimetrics 232
green **109**, 145
 freezing 98–101
 storage 172
grinding 109–10
 flat burr 93–4
 flow rate 98
 roller grinder 193–4
grooming 110–13
growing coffee: agronomy 15–16
 altitude 16–18
 blossom 31
 climate change 56–9
 harvesting **103**, 193
 leaf rust 140–2
 soil **201**, 214
 sustainability 211–12
 temperature 213–14
 terroir **214–17**
Guatemala 113
gustatory 113–14, 163, 223

H

harvesting **103**, 193
Hawaii 117
heat exchanger 117–18
Honduras 118
honey process 63, **118–20**
Howell, George 64

I

"ibrik coffee" 221
Ikeda, Kikunae 223
importing **123–4**
independent coffee shops **124**, 221
India **124–6**
Indonesia **126–9**
instant coffee **129**
International Coffee Organization (ICO) **130**
invention **130**
Italy **131**

J

Jamaican Blue Mountain **133**
Japan **133**

K

Kaldi **135**
Kenya **135–6**
Kopi Luwak **136**

L

latte **94**
latte art **139–40**
Le Nez du Café® **31, 140**
leaf rust 59, 113, **140–2**, 212
lever machine **142**
Lloyd's of London **142–4**

M

machines **130**
 basket **23–4**
 bean to cup **24**
 heat exchanger **117–18**
 lever machine **142**
 multi boiler **151–2**
 portafilter **176–9**
 volumetrics **232**
Madagascar **202**
Maillard reaction **145**
Marisande, Camilio 47, 83
mechanical drying **145–6**
Melbourne **146**
Mexico **146–9**
milk: cappuccino 43–4
 flat white **94**
 latte art 139–40
 steaming **205–6**
Mocha **245**
moka pot **149–51**, 179
mucilage 118–20, 126, **151**, 235
multi boiler **151–2**

N

naked shot **155–6**
natural process **156–9**
Nestlé 44–7
Le Nez du Café® **31, 140**
Nicaragua **159**
nitro cold brew 60
Nordic **159–61**
nutate **161**

O

Old Brown Java **163**
Oldenburg, Ray 217
olfactory **163–4**
Oliver table 71
one-way valve **164–6**
origin **166**
osmosis, reverse **190**
oxidation **167**

P

Pacamara **169**
packaging 164–5, 231
Panama **169–71**
paper 55, 227
Papua New Guinea **171**
parabolic **171–2**
past crop **172**
peaberry 136, **175**
Perger, Matt 161
Peru **175–6**
pH values 13, 38–9, 201
phosphoric acid **176**
plunger **101–3**
portafilter 155, **176–9**
pour-over **103–4**
pressure **179**
producing **180**

Q

Q Grader **183**, 202
quaker **183–4**

R

radiation **185**
raised beds **186**
Rao, Scott 186
rate of rise **186**
refractometer 38, 86, **189**
resting **189–90**
reverse osmosis **190**
Rhode Island School of Design 243
ripe **190–3**
roasting: Agtron scale 16
 blending **27–8**
 development **71–2**
 drum roaster **72–5**
 first crack 93
 Maillard reaction **145**
 radiation **185**
 rate of rise **186**
 resting **189–90**
 silver skin 198
 in South Korea 202
 temperature 214
 thermodynamics 217
 and water 236
Robusta 21, 43, 83, **202–5**, 228
roller grinder **193–4**
Rothgeb, Trish 218
Rwanda **194**

S

scales, weighing **239**
sensory science **197**
Saša Šestić 47, 83, 113, 209
Sheridan, Michael 52
signature drinks **197–8**
silver skin **198**
single origin 166
slow brew **201**
smell, sense of 163–4
soil **201**, 214
South Korea **202**
species **202–5**
  Arabica **18–21**, 83, **202–5**
  Eugenioides 83
  see also variety
Spence, Charles 139, 197
Spindler, Susie 64
spittoon **205**
steaming 142, **205–6**
"stockfleth" 110
storage 98–9, 164–6, 167, 172, 214
Strand, David 129
strength **206–9**
Sudan Rume 83, **209**
sugar **209–10**
  Brix 38
super taster test **210–11**
sustainability **211–12**
Sweden 90, 161
Syphon 227

T

tamping 161, 213
tasting: body **31–2**
  clean 56
  cupping **64–5**
  flavour notes 97
  gustatory 113–14, 163, 223
  olfactory **163–4**
  sensory science **197**
  spittoon **205**
  super taster test **210–11**
  umami 223
  volatiles **231**
tea **32–5**
temperature **213–14**
terroir 47, 201, 213, **214–17**
thermodynamics **217**
third place **217–18**
third wave 84, 89, 124, 166, **218–21**, 224
Tøllefsen, Odd-Steinar 86
Turkish coffee **221**
Typica **221–2**

U

umami **223**
United States of America **223–4**

V

V60 227
vacuum pot **227–8**
valve, one-way **164–6**
variety **228–31**
  Bourbon 35, 169
  Castillo **51–2**
  Geisha **105–6**, 169–71
  Pacamara 169
  Sudan Rume 83, **209**
  Typica **221–2**
  see also species
Vietnam 231
vintages 101
volatiles **231**
volumetrics 232

W

washed process **235**
water **236**
  buffer **38–9**
  channelling **52–5**
  flow rate **97–8**
  full immersion **103–4**
  multi boiler **151–2**
  natural process **156–9**
  pressure 179
  reverse osmosis 190
  tamping 213
  vacuum pot 228
  volumetrics 232
  washed process **235**
Watts, Geoff 83
weighing scales **239**
Wendelboe, Tim 161
World Barista Championship **239–40**, 247

Y

Yemen **245**
yield **245–6**

Z

Zambia **247**

Acknowledgements

I would like to thank: my wife, Lesley – she is the most incredible, supportive, and intuitive person I have ever met; my parents, Geoffrey and Valerie, for teaching me many things and always encouraging me to pursue my own interests; my brothers, James and Leo; all of my family; Travis Riley, for editing this book and for bouncing many a concept around; Samuel Goldsmith, for nagging at me to write; Christopher H. Hendon, a collaborative partner I have valued working with immeasurably on all things scientific; Norman Mazel, for a top entry suggestion; Mike Gamwell, Bethany Alexander, Saša Šestić, Sang Ho Park, Hidenori Izaki, Matteo Pavoni, Ben, Olli, Doug, Charlie Cumming – the most amazing colleagues and staff without whom we could not make any of our coffee adventures a reality; our customers – people from all walks of life who have wanted to take part in our journey; Joe Cottington, Natalie Bradley, Jonathan Christie, Dasha Miller and everyone at Octopus Publishing, as well as Tom Jay for his illustrations; finally, everyone in the global coffee community for their energy, passion, generosity, hard work, teachings, and engagement – it is an amazing thing to be part of.

First published in Great Britain in 2017
by Mitchell Beazley, an imprint of
Octopus Publishing Group Ltd, Carmelite House,
50 Victoria Embankment, London EC4Y 0DZ
www.octopusbooks.co.uk
www.octopusbooksusa.com

An Hachette UK Company
www.hachette.co.uk

The authorized representative in the EEA is Hachette Ireland,
8 Castlecourt Centre, Dublin 15, D15 XTP3, Ireland
(email: info@hbgi.ie)

This edition published in 2025

Text copyright © Maxwell Colonna-Dashwood 2017
Illustrations copyright © Tom Jay 2017
Design and layout copyright © Octopus Publishing Group 2017

Distributed in the US by Hachette Book Group
1290 Avenue of the Americas, 4th and 5th Floors
New York, NY 10104

Distributed in Canada by Canadian Manda Group
664 Annette St., Toronto, Ontario, Canada M6S 2C8

All rights reserved. No part of this work may be reproduced or utilized in any form or by any means, electronic or mechanical, including photocopying, recording or by any information storage and retrieval system, without the prior written permission of the publisher.

Maxwell Colonna-Dashwood asserts the moral right to be identified as the author of this work.

ISBN 978-1-84091-929-5

Printed and bound in China

10 9 8 7 6 5 4 3 2 1

Commissioning Editor: Joe Cottington
Creative Director: Jonathan Christie
Illustrator: Tom Jay
Editor: Natalie Bradley
Copy Editor: Robert Anderson
Production Controller: Dasha Miller

MIX
Paper | Supporting responsible forestry
FSC www.fsc.org FSC® C008047

About the Author

Maxwell Colonna-Dashwood is a champion barista, who has won the UK Barista Championship three times and has gone on to reach each final in the resulting World Barista Championship. He is co-owner of an award-winning independent coffee company including roastery and coffee shop.

Having travelled the world studying the science and art of coffee, Maxwell co-authored his first book, *Water for Coffee* (2015), with Dr Christopher H. Hendon of the Massachusetts Institute of Technology (MIT), an exploration of the chemical interactions between water and coffee and how they can be manipulated to create a higher-quality cup.

Maxwell is excited by the possibilities of collaborating with experts in other disciplines – from chemistry to psychology – and exploring the details in coffee both to deepen his understanding of this amazing drink and to pursue exceptional flavour and quality. *The Coffee Dictionary* is a distillation of the knowledge that he has accumulated and is his first book for the general reader.